Yale Historical Publications
David Horne, Editor

History of Art: 11
George A. Kubler, Editor

R*ailway termini and hotels are to the nineteenth century what monasteries and cathedrals were to the thirteenth century. They are truly the only real representative building we possess. . . . Our metropolitan termini have been leaders of the art spirit of our time.*

Building News, 1875

THE RAILROAD STATION

AN ARCHITECTURAL HISTORY

BY CARROLL L. V. MEEKS

New Haven

Yale University Press

1956

To my three graces:

C S M

V A M

L C M

PREFACE

This book is primarily a study of the architecture of the Western world since 1800, as revealed by a single type of building—the passenger railroad station; but because this type is especially representative of the new problems of design posed by the Industrial Revolution, it is hoped that an analysis of it may reveal the possibility for a re-evaluation of 19th-century architecture as a single style dominated and unified by the aesthetic doctrine of picturesque eclecticism.

There was no functional precedent for the depot; every solution had to be invented. The wonder is not that the stations were sometimes awkward and inconvenient but that they were in many respects efficient and audaciously successful. The station was an essential part of the new system of transportation; it reflected the impact of the technology and mobility of the masses. It played its part in the opening up of the frontier; it is associated with conurbation, the spread of suburbs, the development of resorts. There are enough examples, furthermore, to provide a cross-sectional view of architecture since 1830. More than 80,000 stand in the United States alone. It is a matter of regret that it has not been possible to ascertain or verify every pertinent fact, even after prolonged endeavor. It is hoped that informed readers will share their knowledge with the author.

The material for this study has been drawn from both Europe and America because the story cannot otherwise be told completely; for fully half a century America lagged behind Europe in railroad building. The great steps in solving the new problems functionally and architecturally were taken on the Continent and in all essential respects taken before the end of the century.

An attempt has been made to follow chronologically the several aspects of the railroad station: as architecture (serving new functions), as engineering (construction of huge roofs in new materials), and as works of art (expressing taste). The emphasis here is less on stylistic sources than on significant creative elements. The role of the railroad station in the planning of cities has not been treated in these pages. My brief paper on this subject, "Depots in the City Plan," appeared in the *Journal of the American Institute of Planners, 14,* No. 2 (1948), 4–14.

To the research which went into the making of this book, all the individuals who have contributed time, material, and advice cannot be enumerated, and to single some out for individual mention is not intended to minimize the contributions of others—such as those of the many friends who brought their favorite stations to my attention. I am particularly appreciative of Dean Bannister's urging me toward my goal; of C. L. Winey's assistance with the bibliography and the loan and gift of many precious items; of the kindnesses received from Kenneth John Conant and Sidney Withington. I am grateful to my colleagues at Yale who, like my wife, have suffered and cooperated cheerfully; to librarians at Harvard and Yale and in Boston, New York, and Washington, and to public relations officers and chief engineers of many railroads on both sides of the Atlantic, for their patient attention to my inquiries. To the trustees of the John Simon Guggenheim Foundation who awarded me a fellowship, my warm thanks. I am particularly indebted for gracious cooperation to those excellent librarians Lydia Wentworth, Ruth Cook, and Katherine McNamara.

For permission to incorporate material which has previously appeared in their pages I wish to express my gratitude to the editors of the *Journal of the Society of Architectural Historians,* the *Architectural Review,* the *Magazine of Art,* the *Architectural Forum,* and the *Art Bulletin.*

Over the years many hours of patient labor have been contributed by students and others in maintaining the collection and files which are the foundation stones of this edifice: Brent Friedlander, E. G. Ekman, J. E. Gillan, George Houk, H. L. Laycock, Robert Mitchell, W. A. Huber, T. A. Feyk, Stephen Ocko, Paul Lockhart, John Ross, Philip Lozinski, John Jacobus, Marian Card Donnelly, Natalie B. Mattison, M. W. Stuhldreher, Thomas N. Maytham, Peter Bohan, George M. Butcher, Jr., R. A. Norton, J. L. Martin, Theodore Sizer, Harley J. McKee, Ugoccione di Sorbello, and David M. K. McKibbon. The cornice is composed of the drawings of Jack Rose.

To Henry-Russell Hitchcock, Nikolaus Pevsner, John Coolidge, George Heard Hamilton, Christopher Tunnard, Talbot Hamlin, and George Kubler goes my gratitude for their faithful and discriminating counsel. It was Everett V. Meeks who encouraged and stimulated my interest in architecture. To Henri Focillon I owe the direction of my work as an architectural historian. It was he who first turned my attention toward the 19th century as one ripe for re-evaluation, and he who roused my interest in engineers' glass cages.

C. L. V. M.

New Haven, Connecticut

April 1956

CONTENTS

LIST OF ILLUSTRATIONS

1. THE NINETEENTH

CENTURY STYLE:

PICTURESQUE ECLECTICISM

The architecture of the 19th century, including the last years of the 18th century and the early years of the 20th, has generally been considered as a series of independent revivals lacking common denominators, coherence, or unity. This conventional view was perhaps the only possible one at first, since it was far easier to recognize the familiar details lifted from the past than to probe beneath them for the underlying originality.

Many students agree, however, that the period was in other respects unified; Jules Romains truly says that the years from 1815 to 1914 form a cultural unit characterized by intellectual emancipation, a flowering of the creative spirit, and a vastly enhanced significance of life for each individual.[1] The unity is shown, as Jacques Barzun has remarked, by the ordinary man's habit of condemning it "in one lump." [2] T. E. Hulme was convinced that 1914, in fact, marked the end of an era and that a new classic period, a new age, was approaching.[3]

The architecture of the period also forms a unit. Three methods will be used to demonstrate this proposition: a definition of the new aesthetic—the picturesque; an appraisal and demonstration of the creative and positive side to the then current concept of eclecticism; and a definition of style according to three phases, which for the 19th century may be called early, middle, and late picturesque eclecticism. The first phase ended about 1860, the second

1. *The Seventh of October* (New York, 1946), pp. 217 ff.

2. *Romanticism and the Modern Ego* (Boston, Little, Brown, 1943), p. 161.

3. *Speculations* (London, 1924), pp. 54–7.

about 1890, and the last about 1914. Though each of these methods is distinct, each tends to reinforce the other.

Two themes are fundamental to this study: the aesthetic of the picturesque and the possibilities inherent in metal construction. To these we might apply Whitehead's conception of the life cycle of an idea. He himself applied it to Gothic architecture: at the beginning of the four-century Gothic period, aspects of this new idea were being discovered and developed and successive elements of novelty introduced and explored, until in the 15th century there seemed nothing more to do. The idea comes to a full stop; there is a complete break followed by a return to older classical ideas. Whitehead follows this pertinent observation with another: new material, as well as a new way of looking at an idea, may give it a happy turn.[4] In the period we are considering here, the new aesthetic and technical concepts born in the late 18th century produced the novel architectural attitudes and inventions of the 19th century.[5]

Because the number of buildings erected in the years under consideration far exceeds those of any preceding era, and since wars and rebuilding have not yet reduced their number to a manageable handful, some device had to be adopted in this book to limit the examples. It is necessary to assume, as the scientist does, that what is true of a carefully selected sample will be true for the whole. The examples chosen had to serve a similar function, of course; otherwise different uses and different traditions, which limited the architect's freedom of expression, would invalidate conclusions drawn from the sample. For instance, the study of a group of buildings containing both churches and theaters would prove less than that of a group made up exclusively of churches, in which the pressures of liturgy and conservatism would bear with nearly equal force on all. In a preliminary examination a series confined to legislative buildings was used.[6] In this book the railroad station is the functional type to be examined.

The Picturesque Aesthetic

In order to identify the unifying factors in 19th-century architecture, it is essential first of all to define and trace the persistence of the picturesque aesthetic. Christopher Hussey, who hinted at this device in his pioneering

4. Lucien Price, recorder, *Dialogues of Alfred North Whitehead* (Boston, 1954), pp. 256, 257.

5. See below, Chaps. 2, 3, for discussion of metal construction.

6. See my "Picturesque Eclecticism," *Art Bulletin, 32* (1950), 226–35.

work,[7] felt that the picturesque was the special mode of vision of the whole century, though he applied it to architecture only for the period ending about 1845, preliminary to a "romantic" phase. He held that the picturesque was not in itself a style but rather a method of combining and using styles. These observations mark the first penetration beneath the superficial notions of revivalism. The second person to advance the conception was James Mac-Quedy, who noted that "early Victorian buildings have enough in common to outweigh all their differences. As a group, they are in reaction against the constraint of academicism." [8] To this we would add that the early modern architecture of the 20th century was in turn a reaction from the studied irregularity of the picturesque with its exuberance of outline. Nikolaus Pevsner has supported such an interpretation.[9] He prefers the label "picturesque" to "poetic" or "humanist" and uses the same terms for its characteristics that were used by Sir Uvedale Price, the first formulator of the doctrine, whose books became its testament.[10] Pevsner, however, does not insist, as I do, that the picturesque was the predominant aesthetic of the whole century.

Table 1. Phases of the Picturesque Eclectic Style

Phase	Time	Type of Eclecticism	Form	Preferred medium	Chapter of this Study
Early picturesque eclecticism	1790–1860	symbolic	rising	tinted drawings	2, 3
Middle " "	1860–90	synthetic	crest of verticality	lithography	4
Late " "	1890–1914	creative	subsidence	photography	5, 6

Others have suggested that there was a second current of taste, the vernacular. It is my contention that this was not an independent stream, that the picturesque point of view dominated all strata of taste and was so universal as to constitute a broadly inclusive system analogous to those formulated by Wölfflin and Fokker for the Renaissance and baroque styles.

The theories which were to crystallize in the picturesque doctrine were developing throughout the late 18th century. Edmund Burke separated the more emotional qualities of astonishment and terror—constituents of the

7. *The Picturesque,* London, 1927.

8. *Architectural Review, 79* (1941), 81.

9. "The Picturesque in Architecture," *Journal of The Royal Institute of British Architects,* ser. 3, *55* (Dec. 1947), 55–8.

10. *An Essay on the Picturesque,* London, 1794–98; *Essays on the Picturesque,* London, 1810; and *On the Picturesque,* Edinburgh, 1842.

"sublime"—from the calmer qualities of the "beautiful." [11] He attributed both to the physiology of vision. William Gilpin went still further in the destruction of older concepts in isolating the category of "Picturesque Beauty." [12] Robert Adam and Sir Joshua Reynolds followed his lead in singling out qualities that contributed to the picturesque in architecture as well as in landscape. The basis of taste was shifting from reason to sensibility. Picturesqueness came to be regarded as the principal source of beauty. Sir Uvedale Price codified these discoveries in his books and from them English-speaking critics throughout the 19th century derived their critical vocabulary.

The unique feature of the new theory was its consistent emphasis on visual qualities. In the industrial era the quality of the visual impression made upon the beholder by the exterior of the building was of primary importance, corresponding in significance to the modern theory which gives primacy to functionalism. There is abundant testimony to this effect: in 1841 A. W. N. Pugin wrote: "in these times all that does not catch the eye is neglected"; [13] in 1869 the *Builder* said that "attention was being wholly directed to broad effects of light and shade and balance of form"; [14] in 1872 Sir Charles Eastlake held that the test of a good building was, "is it offensive to the eye?" [15] Since Wölfflin, visual systems of analysis have proved to be a fruitful method of criticism, particularly appropriate when applied to a period which stressed appearance. It is not irrelevant to point out that Wölfflin was himself a product of that period.

Observing the qualities which aroused the enthusiasm of the critics of the day (the illustrious roster includes Pugin, Ruskin, Wyatt, Barry, Fergusson, Kerr, and Statham) we find that five principal ones emerge. Comparing them with Wölfflin's five "classic" and five "baroque," we can see that our picturesque ones are closer to his baroque ones (Table 2, opposite).

Wölfflin's first pair of qualities, "linear" and "painterly," correspond to the picturesque quality of *variety*. The most conspicuous manifestation of this quality is the obvious striving for a varied silhouette: "the grandeur, richness and variety" of the summit.[16] Chimneys, towers, and gables sprouted from the elaborate roofs of palaces and prisons. Variety could of course be achieved

11. *A Philosophical Inquiry into the Origin of Our Ideas of the Sublime and the Beautiful*, London, 1757.

12. Hussey, pp. 110–18.

13. *The True Principles of Pointed or Christian Architecture* (London, 1841), p. 45.

14. *Builder, 27* (1869), 61 ff.

15. *A History of the Gothic Revival* (London, 1872), p. 333.

16. Price, *On the Picturesque,* p. 349.

in other ways—by surface treatment and particularly through asymmetry. The repetition of identical motives, associated with the classical styles, was deliberately avoided. There are implications of lavishness. Baldness was considered by Wyatt a serious fault. An effect of richness, which we tend to condemn as vulgar and showy and which Veblen called "conspicuous consumption," was preferable to looking pinched or meager, in fact, was consciously sought for. It was one of the ways to impart what Lewis Mumford calls "the sense of spaciousness and aristocratic ease, the extra needed to sustain the spirit." [17]

The second picturesque quality, *movement,* corresponds in a general way to Wölfflin's "plane" and "recession." Movement was found to be an outstanding merit of Vanbrugh's work by Robert Adam in 1778, by Reynolds in 1786, by Price, and still later by Wyatt and Soane. Movement, says Adam, is concerned with "the rising and falling, advancing and receding, with the convexity and concavity, and other forms of the great parts. . . ." [18] Movement relates the masses and elements to naturalistic landscape and is most easily discerned when the building is viewed from a distance. As C. J. Richardson observed in 1870, "The architect usually considers that if his building looks well when seen by moonlight, or through the medium of a foggy or dull atmosphere, it is picturesque, and he is satisfied." [19] "Massiveness" is an 18th-century synonym for this. It is not, as Price says, mere heaviness but is "the accompaniment, and, as it were, the attendance of the inferior parts in their different gradations" to the principal building.[20] In 1883 an enthusiastic account of the new station for the Michigan Central Railroad in Detroit

Table 2. Characteristics of Four Styles *

Classic	Baroque	Picturesque Eclecticism	Modern
linear	painterly	variety	planarity
plane	recession	movement	space-time
closed	open	irregularity	transparency
multiplicity	unity	intricacy	interpenetration
clearness	unclearness	roughness	simplicity

* The first two columns are Wölfflin's.

17. "Monumentalism, Symbolism and Style," *Architectural Review, 105* (1949), 180.

18. *Works, 1* (1773), Intro., quoted in Hussey, p. 189.

19. *Picturesque Designs in Architecture* (London, 1870), p. 3.

20. *On the Picturesque,* p. 331.

shows in detail, in similar language, how the agreeable effects of movement were achieved by the late Victorian architect (Fig. 133).

> The main motive . . . is the leading up of all its parts from both directions to the main tower. This tower will be 157 feet in height to the ridge, and will be a conspicuous and imposing object from every point of view. From this culminating point the masses of the building will diminish in height towards the ends, although the recession is prevented from becoming monotonous by the hold and emphatic projection of the gable mass at the base of which will be the main entrances, and by the lesser projection that will relieve the Woodbridge Street front.[21]

The third quality, *irregularity,* is related to Wölfflin's "openness" and is in opposition to his "closed" form. To achieve irregularity, the designers preferred spontaneity and accident to calculation. Pugin, like Frank Lloyd Wright, thought that irregularity should express the functional parts. Others were less particular about the means, provided the effect was attained. Sir Joshua Reynolds had advised irregularity to give the building "something of scenery" [22] and associated it with accident. Price mentions "sudden breaks and variations of form." [23] Asymmetry is one of the means most frequently resorted to. The correspondence between parts should be not too obvious in order to avoid the monotony of classical buildings. In 1870 C. J. Richardson echoes this: "an exact correspondence of parts is often disguised by an appearance of splendid confusion and irregularity." [24] Pugin had paved the way by his attack on the standards of the Regency: "a long unbroken mass of building without light and shade is monotonous and unsightly." [25] The advocates of the new aesthetic were positive in their point of view and were not just carelessly slipping away from academic rules.

The fourth picturesque quality is *intricacy,* which is related to Wölfflin's "multiplicity" and "unity." Intricacy signifies that the relationships of the parts are complex, not to be discerned immediately. The beholder must make an effort to decipher the relationships; his interest will be increased by the temporary perplexity. Price's admonition to the picturesque designer was

---

21. Quoted in Walter Berg, *Buildings and Structures of American Railroads* (New York, 1904, preface dated 1892), p. 395.

22. *Fifteen Discourses Delivered in the Royal Academy* (London, John Dent and Sons, and New York, E. P. Dutton, Everyman's Library, 1906), p. 224.

23. *On the Picturesque,* p. 364.

24. *Picturesque Designs in Architecture,* p. 9.

25. *True Principles,* p. 3.

that nothing will "compensate the absence of every obstacle to curiosity, and every hope of novelty." [26] It was felt that intricacy increased the aesthetic intensity of the observer's experience. Striking examples of the application of this principle to station design are most numerous in the High Victorian period but may also be seen in such stations as the one formerly on Broad Street, Philadelphia (Fig. 126).

The fifth picturesque quality, *roughness,* is related to Wölfflin's "clearness" and "unclearness." Roughness involves emphatic stone joints, quarry-faced ashlar, and roofs of coarse tile or stone; it is directly opposed to the smooth surfaces, carefully finished joints, and precise clarity of classic practice. If extended to its limit, roughness becomes decay and ruin, thus including in the natural effect the products of neglect and erosion that tend to obscure further the original articulation. H. H. Richardson's masonry and shingle work have this quality, for which Ruskin's term was "savageness." Today "ruggedness" still arouses admiration, according to a recent comment in the *Architectural Forum.*[27]

It is apparent, then, that the five picturesque qualities are closer to Wölfflin's baroque categories than to his classic ones. This intimacy is not accidental; the picturesque code was based to some extent on admiration for Vanbrugh's work, which was both baroque and picturesque.

To explain why these five qualities are stressed it is necessary to review some of the alternatives. Price used many other terms, such as "piquant," "irritation," "anachronism," and "surprise," which have lost their original force and seem less cogent now than the ones we have listed. A group of five terms was proposed by F. P. Chambers [28] seventeen years after Wölfflin. He set five qualities of romantic art opposite five of classicism, as follows: "redundance," "frailty," "bizzarria," "irregularity," and "roughness" versus "austerity," "finish," "solidity," "grace," and "regularity." Two of these, "roughness" and "irregularity," coincide with Price's. "Variety" seems to have been more in use than "bizzarria." "Intricacy" is more positive to modern ears than "redundance." Chambers contrasts "frailty" with "solidity." Neither term is essentially a visual one—some think that the architects of the 19th century built rather *too* solidly—hence I prefer Price's terms to Chambers'.

One would expect to be assisted in this matter by Ruskin, the most eloquent and prolific critic of the day, but he dealt less with visual effects than with moral qualities; thus his seven lamps of architecture—sacrifice, truth, power, beauty, life, memory, and obedience—are not comparable to those of Price,

26. *On the Picturesque,* p. 337.

27. *Architectural Forum, 90* (1949), 83.

28. *The History of Taste* (New York, 1932), p. 216.

Chambers, or Wölfflin. As Wyatt delightedly pointed out, like Vitruvius' heptad they are equally valid for the buildings of all periods but useless for distinguishing the unique qualities of any one period, be it medieval or Victorian. In *The Stones of Venice,* Ruskin lists six attributes of Gothic architecture which prove more suggestive: [29] (1) redundance, also used by Chambers and to which I prefer "intricacy"; (2) rigidity, which is a general quality of all architecture, like Sir Henry Wotton's "firmness"; (3–5) savageness, naturalism, and grotesqueness, all of which seem to be covered by "roughness"; and (6) changefulness, which is possibly analogous to "movement." In the sixth Ruskin fails to emphasize, as Price did, the prime importance of the plasticity of the whole composition, which was to be seen not as separate planimetric façades but as many interlocking, three-dimensional parts.

Ruskin, after all, was more interested in ornament than structure. His crusade for honesty in the use of materials added polychromy in the form of constructive coloration to the tools at the architect's disposal. This became a popular method of increasing variety. Examples include the Oxford Museum and Waterhouse's Manchester Assizes, followed in this country by buildings by Peter B. Wight and stations by Ware and Van Brunt. What had begun as a desire for truthful expression of material led to an exhibitionistic display of varied materials, contrasting voussoirs, and patterned slate roofs.

Since both Pevsner and Hussey have limited the role of the picturesque to the first half of the century, it is important to show that its dominance can be traced much later also. In 1905 the *Builder* in its obituary to Alfred Waterhouse, acknowledged to be one of the outstanding British architects of the century, described Waterhouse's picturesque manner of design as "his characteristic breaking up of outlines and surfaces by clever and unexpected maneuvers in wall plane and sky line . . . his talent for leading up to and making the most of the salient angle in plan." [30] His hotel, added to the Lime Street Station in Liverpool (nearing completion in 1869), exemplifies his advice to students of architecture in 1889 "to take care lest a design prove to be anything but a pleasure to the eye" and not to neglect "the outline seen against the sky." [31] It is not surprising that an architect of Pugin's generation should be faithful to picturesque concepts to the end of his long life, but later generations were hardly less faithful. What had begun as an aristocratic taste penetrated the whole society. By midcentury the bourgeoisie, who were exercising more and more powerful roles as patrons in both public and

29. *The Stones of Venice* (3 vols. London, 1853), *2,* 154.

30. *Builder, 89* (1905), 221.

31. "Architects," in E. H. Pitcairn, *The Unwritten Laws and Ideals of Active Careers* (London, 1889), p. 343.

private commissions, had become thoroughly indoctrinated. Never as subtle an aesthetic as the Renaissance or the academic had been, the picturesque in its brash, obvious way was bound to remain popular with the new, comparatively unsophisticated, powerful classes of the industrial age.

We have quoted from Richardson's *Picturesque Designs in Architecture,* published in 1870. H. H. Statham (1839–1924), the architect and editor, writing in 1898 used terms like those of the 1850's and 1870's: "a striking and impressive structure . . . massed into blocks . . . picturesqueness and contrast." [32] More surprisingly, American architecture at the Chicago Fair of 1893 was judged by the same critical canons. The official British judge in architecture, William Emerson, reported approvingly that the Machinery, Fisheries, and most of the State Buildings were "most picturesque" but criticized Van Brunt's Electricity Palace because "the towers are feeble in outline." [33] Only two years earlier Robert Kerr had said of America that "graceful and picturesque edifices . . . are to be found everywhere." [34]

It might be readily admitted that America could still be indulging in picturesqueness because it was, as usual, somewhat behind the change of taste in Europe. Hence it seems worth while to adduce yet one more overseas quotation. W. Hamilton Beattie won the competition held in 1895 for the North British Station Hotel in Edinburgh.[35] He said that he wanted a freer and more picturesque treatment than Adam's Register House nearby, that he had carefully considered the roofs and skyline, and thought he had succeeded in achieving picturesque variety. Indeed he had: the riot above the cornice is scarcely less than that at Chambord. The English, after a century of adherence to the picturesque, had not tired of it. Nor had it died out on the continent; it appeared in such representative late buildings as the city halls of Copenhagen (1892–1903) and Stockholm (1912–23).

The strength of the 19th-century faith in the picturesque is indicated by the ability of its architects to find it almost anywhere. Similarly impelled by our faith in functionalism, we stress the structural logic and the orderly, rational aspects of Gothic. To Sir George Gilbert Scott and his contemporaries, Gothic was primarily irregular and varied. J. L. Petit deplored the "reduction to symmetry" of Canterbury by modern restoration. He found St. Paul's "highly picturesque," with variety of outline well carried out.[36] The Parthenon, Roman

32. *Modern Architecture* (New York, 1898), pp. 6–7.

33. *Journal of the Royal Institute of British Architects,* ser. 3, *1* (1894), 65 ff.

34. Interpolation by Robert Kerr in James Fergusson, *History of the Modern Styles of Architecture* (3d ed. 2 vols. rev. by Robert Kerr, London, 1891), *2,* 351.

35. *American Architect, 50* (Oct. 12, 1895), 22–3.

36. In the *Building News, 10* (1863), 448.

ruins, and the Acropolis complex were sometimes cited to prove that classic could be as picturesque as Gothic. Such concentration on the picturesque is no more exaggerated than our ideal of simplicity, which has made us see richness in any other period as a defect.

The legacy of the picturesque is still with us. Our admiration for the work of Sullivan and Wright is partly due to the persistence in their work of the qualities of movement, variety, and intricacy. Wright indeed has been curiously misunderstood by those who admire in his work characteristics which they also find in the international style. This is a failure to distinguish between radically different aesthetic philosophies. It helps in our understanding of Wright to think of him as a successor to Alfred Waterhouse; their careers overlapped for thirty-five years, and in both there is the freedom from the straightjacket of a single vocabulary, an interest in new materials used decoratively, an avoidance of the bald, and a devoted attention to richness. In contrast with the architects of the international style, both men avoid flooding interior illumination and bright reflective surfaces. Both favor chiaroscuro effects. Interior light in Wright is usually screened, filtered, and low in intensity, as it was in 19th-century buildings.

It is now necessary to consider what other approaches have been made toward the critical integration of the architecture of the last century. The term "romantic" has sometimes been applied to the culture of the century but without a coherent application to the architecture. Even Jacques Barzun has denied that there was an expression of romanticism in architecture comparable in force and power to its literary manifestations.[37] Perhaps this is so, although some of the stations named in these pages may be thought to come very close. He characterizes romantic art as being possessed of the following six qualities, which are related to the five we have selected as typical of the picturesque: drama, strife, contrast, color, richness, and variety.[38] Barzun's opinion is shared by Alfred Neumeyer,[39] who names sculpture as a second art in which romanticism failed to find a stylistic expression of its own. Hussey sees late 19th-century architecture as a pastiche.[40] Agnes Gilchrist limited the architecture of romanticism to the Greek and Gothic revivals; more tellingly, she observed that a desire for something different can be satisfied by a change in form whether or not it is original.[41] Geoffrey Scott was prejudiced against

37. *Romanticism and the Modern Ego*, p. 98.

38. *Ibid.*, pp. 98 ff.

39. "Romanticism," *Encyclopedia of the Arts*, p. 866.

40. *The Picturesque*, pp. 4–5.

41. *Romanticism and the Gothic Revival* (New York, 1938), p. 5.

picturesque and romantic types of architecture because of their unrestrained fantasy and lack of academic logic.[42] He did, however, notice the picturesque elements in baroque architecture of which Vanbrugh's buildings provided 18th-century critics with examples to illustrate the picturesque doctrine.

We can perhaps avoid some of these difficulties and prejudices by abandoning the term "romantic," which has become so expanded that it cannot be used as the name of a particular style of architecture. "Picturesque" is a term of the period and is therefore both appropriate and descriptive for the architecture of romanticism.

Another possible alternative name for the aesthetic peculiar to the century is "scenic." Like "picturesque" it was in common use at the beginning of the century and has since been justifiably applied to the magniloquent compositions of John Nash; but it has the disadvantage of being more appropriate to groups of buildings set in a landscape than to a public building in the heart of a city. "Scenic" is more concerned with over-all effect than with such specific qualities as variety, intricacy, and ruggedness.

Creative Eclecticism

The stylistic unity of the period under consideration is strongly implied by its unswerving adherence to the picturesque doctrine, but its unabashed eclecticism may appear to be in conflict with such a conclusion. The architectural detail is quite obviously borrowed and diversified. It encompassed ancient Greek, medieval, and Renaissance styles. It went still further afield; on occasion it even tried on exotic costumes from the East. Can so much borrowing result in a unified original style? A resolution of this apparent conflict is provided by a better understanding of what eclecticism meant to its 19th-century advocates. The development and refinement of the concept took place in three stages (Table 1, p. 3). As the 18th century waned and academicism lost its hold, eclecticism was at first primarily governed by symbolic association. Later on it became synthetic. This phase prepared the way for its third and most creative phase at the end of the century.

The earliest phase, symbolic eclecticism, was limited to the engrafting and commingling of buildings of different styles in one area such as a garden, square, or street, but not in one building. The aim was to stimulate romantic moods by the observer's associations with each style of alien and, it was thought, superior cultures. This type of eclecticism is highly artificial and self-conscious. The stylistically varied buildings of a group are built con-

42. *The Architecture of Humanism* (New York, 1928), pp. 85 ff.

temporaneously; the resulting diversity and piquant contrasts recall such famous groups as that around the Piazza San Marco in Venice, although there the combination of Byzantine, Gothic, and Renaissance styles was not simultaneous but sequential.

Among the early applications of symbolic eclecticism are the grounds at Stowe, Hagley, and Kew Gardens. The latter were laid out in the 1750's by Sir William Chambers; there in one place, visible one from another and all built at the same time, are buildings based on the Moorish, Chinese, and Byzantine styles, while nearby there are Greek and Roman edifices too. On the continent Gondoin's *Place* of 1780 in Paris, made up of a church, a medical school, and a prison, was not harmonized in the baroque manner; instead each building stood out independently, expressing through its form the character of its use. The Italian Pietro Selvatico contended in the 1840's that churches should be built in Early Christian or Gothic style, cemeteries in Byzantine or Gothic, cafés in the Arabian, and dwellings in one of the Renaissance styles. An application of similar principles occurred in England in John Foulston's city square at Devonport. He built the city hall and Memorial Column in Greek, the public library in Egyptian, the church in Gothic, and the Mount Zion Chapel in "Hindoo." [43]

The practitioners of symbolic eclecticism did not agree on the meaning of their symbols. In the following period—that of the familiar classic and Gothic revivals—there was less confusion.[44] Although architects turned from one mode to another as Jefferson and Napoleon did, there was less deliberate juxtaposing of them—a single style might pervade a whole group of buildings: Gothic in Cambridge, Greek in Edinburgh, Renaissance in Munich. As in the preceding phase, each building drew upon only one stylistic source, and in later stages this limitation was relaxed; but as the revivals gained strength their advocates became more and more authoritarian and the freedom indulged in by the early symbolic eclecticists was no longer tolerated. Gothicists like

43. Foulston's choice of what he called the "Hindoo" style for the synagogue is a very early example of the symbolic association of the Eastern styles with Jewish religious buildings; see discussion in Rachel Wischnitzer, *Synagogue Architecture in the United States* (Philadelphia, 1955), pp. 6–7. Symbolic eclecticism is being practiced even today. A distinguished New Haven architect has recently built two churches simultaneously on the same block: for a Congregational parish he used the Colonial style and for the Christian Science parish, one of the modern styles.

44. Everard Upjohn has written that the germ of eclecticism lay in the revivals: Upjohn, Paul S. Wingert, and Jane G. Mahler, *History of World Art* (New York, Oxford University Press, 1949), pp. 358 ff. As I have shown, the germ had been planted before the period of the major revivals in the work of the symbolic eclecticists in the early 18th century.

Pugin asserted that Gothic and Gothic alone was the only possible style. The classicists were equally dogmatic. Armed with abundant weapons from the rapidly accumulating treasuries of the archaeologists, both camps tightened the controls. As a result, a higher standard of archaeological accuracy became mandatory; the experts challenged the authenticity of every detail, and woe to the architect if moldings were half an hour too late!

Creative spirits could not long be held in thrall by such scholarly fetters, and eclecticism moved into a new phase.[45] In this second major phase—the synthetic—elements from several styles were combined in a single building. Sir Joshua Reynolds had attacked this type of eclecticism in painting, saying that "to mingle the Dutch with the Italian school is to join contrarities which destroy the efficacy of each other";[46] but less than a century later, exactly the opposite position was advocated by Wyatt Papworth, editor of the most authoritative architectural publication of the day. He wrote that "nothing narrows the mind and cramps the invention more than blind admiration and the pursuit of one style to the condemnation of every other" and defined the new type of eclecticism as "the engrafting and commingling of the characteristic features of two or more styles as occasion may require."[47] Such a definition was becoming the majority view. One of its supporters was Sir George Gilbert Scott, who was opposed to the type of eclecticism we have called the synthetic and to the stricter revivals it engendered: "In the sense of expressing the liberty of the same architect choosing for each building just what style he may fancy,—now one, and now another,—it [eclecticism] is manifestly vicious and no good would be likely to come of it. . . . In the sense, however, of borrowing from all we know of art, elements wherewith to enrich, amplify, and render more perfect that style which we have laid down as our nucleus and ground-work, eclecticism is a principle of the highest value, and one to which all styles of art but the very earliest have been indebted for their perfection."[48]

The synthetic type of eclecticism was indeed very old; it was practiced by the artists of Hellenistic Greece and it was taught in the 16th century by Lomazzo and Zuccaro. Scott, as we have seen, regarded it as the natural process by which each age leaned upon its predecessor and so advanced. Such a point

45. Michelangelo had predicted the fate of such plodding revivalists when he said that he who follows in the footsteps of another never overtakes him.

46. Letter to the *Idler,* No. 79, Saturday, October 20, 1759.

47. *The Dictionary of Architecture,* Architectural Publication Society (8 vols. London, 1853?–92), *2,* 11.

48. Sir George Gilbert Scott, *Remarks on Secular and Domestic Architecture* (2d ed. London, 1858), p. 265 n. (1st ed. 1857)

of view is unacceptable to many creative artists today who prefer to emphasize originality and disclaim precedent, but even today many of the greatest artists and architects frankly admit their indebtedness to the past. A hundred years ago the idea of continuity was hardly challenged: architects and artists were taught to build upon the work of their predecessors. According to Viollet-le-Duc, probably the greatest teacher of his generation, the architect's education must proceed in two stages: first he must learn to analyze the masterpieces of the past; then he must make his own synthesis.[49] The method of synthesis underlay such 19th-century styles as the Victorian Gothic, the Second Empire, the Queen Anne, and the Richardsonian Romanesque. For instance, the principal motive of the Victorian Gothic style was the pointed arch, but its details were derived from French, German, Italian, and English sources.

Emancipation from archaeological accuracy and stylistic purity was the authorization for an increased degree of originality. It was also preparatory for the third phase of eclecticism, which was distinguished from its predecessors by the fact that after the 1860's more and more emphasis was placed on the desire to be original and the wish to be creative. We find these ambitions expressed in many places and in varying degrees. Sir Matthew Digby Wyatt told the undergraduates at Cambridge "not to tread on the very dangerous and almost untenable grounds of *entire innovation*." [50] In 1885 an American was advising prospective church builders: "Don't expect the architect to invent either a new order of architecture or any new variety of Gothic. Within the wide limits embraced by the name Gothic there is ample scope for the genius of an architect." [51]

Both admonitions imply an increasing degree of permissible latitude. There is considerable evidence that the later eclectics were synthesizing in order to be original. Viollet-le-Duc complained, "We have seen designs made up of the most fantastic mixture of styles, fashions, epochs and means, yet betraying not the slightest symptom of originality." [52] His own design for a monument in Algiers is a highly original example of synthetic eclecticism, though perhaps vulnerable to Van Brunt's comment that too many aim merely to astonish.[53]

While the revivalists and eclectics all turned toward the past for forms, the creative eclectic added the will to create something new. Some of the less

49. Summarized in John Summerson, *Heavenly Mansions* (New York, Charles Scribner's Sons, 1949?), p. 141.

50. *Fine Art* (London, 1870), p. 81.

51. Francis J. Parker, *Church Building* (Boston, 1885), pp. 25–6.

52. *Discourses on Architecture* (2 vols. Boston, 1875–81), *I*, 474.

53. Henry Van Brunt, *Greek Lines and Other Essays* (Boston and New York, 1893), pp. 214, 225.

archaeologically minded revivalists had wanted to be creative. The idea that only a style which had not previously been carried to its full development could be taken up again and be carried forward was shared by William Goodyear, writing in 1893, who agreed that this principle explained the success of Richardsonian Romanesque.[54] Van Brunt, one of the architects of the Worcester Station (Fig. 124), had it in mind when he wrote in explanation of the failure of the revivals in England and the success of American developments that in the United States "our eclectic and cosmopolitan" use of precedent was infinitely more promising. True progress, he thought, is possible by a liberal system of experiment with precedent.[55]

Sir Matthew Digby Wyatt, echoing Viollet-le-Duc, advised that the student should "stock his mind with the choicest forms, proportions and elements from the past from which he may derive the materials for a recombination in an attempt at originality." [56] James Fergusson advocated the use of the Italian, or as he called it "the Common Sense," style because, "never having attained completeness . . . [it] not only admits of, but insists on, progress. It courts borrowing principles and forms . . . pillars or pinnacles, . . . towers, and spires, or domes . . . it owns no master but true taste . . . and it courts originality." [57] This is a rationale of eclecticism which may strike us as naive, although it is a franker acceptance of the realities of the situation than our attitude. The same tolerance was shown at the end of the century. Louis H. Gibson counseled that after meeting the physical requirements, structures should then be decorated "with the best motives which the world's architecture has to offer us. If we can do this in an original spirit, it is well, but originality is not essential." [58] Others, like Petit, saw that the desired picturesque had to be invented: "Selecting Gothic is not enough to secure picturesqueness . . . many modern Gothic structures are not as picturesque as a railway shed . . . we are more likely to attain picturesqueness by working according to the spirit of our age than by transferring ourselves to an extinct one." [59]

Some writers of the period were sharp enough to sense the original element in the newer buildings. E. M. Barry, architect for the Cannon Street Station

---

54. William H. Goodyear in his *A History of Art* (New York, 1888 and later eds.) shows a commendable critical vigor. He is very conscious of the original elements in late 19th-century architecture.

55. *Greek Lines and Other Essays,* p. 220.

56. *Fine Art,* p. 102.

57. *History of the Modern Styles of Architecture, 2,* 115 f.

58. *Beautiful Houses* (New York, 1895), p. 30.

59. J. L. Petit, in the *Building News, 10* (1863), 448.

Hotel (Fig. 107), observed that "so-called revivals are often difficult to distinguish from practical innovations." [60]

An anonymous author in the *Quarterly Review,* warning the critics against the very trap into which they were to fall, remarked tellingly that "for the most part the public is able to appreciate the merit of all the various styles of architecture, and to judge them not by reference to some type from which they have deviated, or to some model of which they have fallen short, but, as in fairness they should be judged, by their agreement or disagreement with the more durable laws of taste." [61] His laws may not have been durable, but they did include picturesqueness and eclecticism. To distinguish between the eclectic and creative components, he named some examples: " 'Elizabethan or Jacobean, revived Gothic,' 'Georgian Gothic' and 'Wyatville castellated.' "

Dean Stanley replied to the criticism that the architecture of the 1870's was too imitative by saying, "the very eagerness of reproduction is itself an original inspiration and there is in it also a peculiar grace." [62] It is this "peculiar grace" which is the manifestation of the creative element.

At the end of the century, when the vocabulary had shifted, the use of Renaissance forms was no greater bar to originality. Renaissance architects had borrowed from the past but their palaces were creative designs.

No age has so determinedly striven to be original as our own. Where the last century expressed originality only with caution, it is now often felt that each building must aspire to the unrealizable ideal of originality in structure, plan, form, and decoration.

The dangers of the eclectic system were apparent to all. What rules could its proponents follow? Modern writers seem to think that they had none and wanted none. Upjohn has said that the eclectics were guided only by associations (symbolic eclecticism), national prejudice, training, and whim, and seems to imply that for the eclectic "form follows fancy." Sullivan's partner, Adler, said of the revivalists that "form follows historic precedent." [63] Talbot Hamlin has suggested that one of the ideals was ostentation.[64] The results sometimes seem to confirm these criticisms; but highly significant guiding principles did in fact exist.

60. Quoted in G. Gilbert Scott, ed., *Personal and Professional Recollections by the Late Sir George Gilbert Scott, R.A.* (London, 1879), appendix, p. 384.

61. "Landscape Gardening," *Quarterly Review, 98* (Dec. 1855), 206.

62. "Funeral Sermon, on the Death of Sir Gilbert Scott," in Scott, ed., *Recollections,* p. 390.

63. Dankmar Adler, "Function and Environment," reprinted in Lewis Mumford, *Roots of Contemporary American Architecture* (New York, Reinhold, 1952), p. 244.

64. *Architecture through the Ages* (New York, G. P. Putnam's Sons, 1940), pp. 597–8.

Our failure to recognize the widespread acceptance of these rules and our assumption that they were not understood by the majority can be explained by our own recent history. We have lately passed through the period of the Art Nouveau, which, although it was original, seemed to lack rules. More recently still came modern architecture, in which the freedom from rule was a conspicuous characteristic. It was admired because of this very freedom. Today, the novelty of the cult of originality having diminished in intensity, a new respect for discipline is arising. Thus we are in a mood more receptive to the idea of rules and are better conditioned to see them in other periods.

The following set of rules or standards for judgment were expressed by the 19th-century writers Scott, Wyatt, Semper, Viollet-le-Duc and his translator Van Brunt, and Goodyear, and are here rephrased and combined for convenience.

A creative eclectic building should be judged, first, by whether it adheres to the constructive principle involved; second, by whether the exterior is an expression of the interior in either an ideal or a literal sense; third, by whether the forms have been employed with freedom and independence rather than with literal exactness; fourth, by whether the reminiscences have been wisely coordinated and placed in perfect agreement with each other; fifth, by whether it serves the conditions and uses the materials dictated by the age; sixth, by whether the result is simple and comprehensible. These are principles which, seventy years later, do not seem alien.

Mounting self-confidence characterized the final third of the last century. The philosophy of creative eclecticism brought the realization that the rules of the academies are not absolute, that the conception of ideal beauty is not fixed forever but is subject to revision by each generation. In this favorable climate architects could claim freedom and rebel against dogma. In depot design H. H. Richardson's numerous stations (Figs. 136, 137) and A. Dervaux's Gare de l'Ouest at Rouen (1913–28) are creatively eclectic, resembling nothing in the historic past (Fig. 191). The last decades of the period are full of good work, much of it still unrecognized, some of it lifted out of context and hailed as "exceptional" or "early modern," and some of it showing that the muses did not invariably preside over the drafting boards. Creative eclecticism led to a gradual sloughing-off of the residue of past forms of any kind and the creation of wholly new ones to fill the vacuum. Modern architecture clearly obeys the late 19th-century rules concerning expression of structure and material and the suitability of form to function. In 1897 Eugène Grasset indicated that the process was a deliberate one, observable at the time.[65]

65. Quoted in H. F. Lenning, *The Art Nouveau* (The Hague, 1951), p. 53.

This relation of creative eclecticism to the earlier phase of eclecticism may be summed up in two pairs of examples. Henry Austin's railroad station in New Haven (Fig. 36) combines eclectic detail and original massing: far-flung horizontal extension; flaring eaves; low, hipped roofs; and a floating detached superstructure—anticipating similar features in Sullivan's New Orleans Station of 1892. The latter (Fig. 33) has been purged of most of the derivative stylistic features. Similarly Viollet-le-Duc, in his design of the 1860's for a "Masonry Building," is under a heavy burden of eclecticism while striving to express the possibilities of metal in compression in his disturbing struts.[66] Yet only a few years later, in Frankfurt am Main, the way was found to express tapering steel supports entirely freed of traditional eclectic overlays (Fig. 148).

Eclecticism is the second of the three lines of inquiry being followed in the search for unifying factors. There remains the analysis of the period prior to 1914 in terms of its three developmental phases.

Phases of the Picturesque Eclectic Style

The division of any style into subordinate parts is a familiar critical device that does not require detailed explanation. For the style of the 19th century, however, the novelty of the application requires amplified treatment (see Table 1, p. 3).

A few previous attempts at such treatment have been made. In 1942 John Coolidge stated that Victorian architecture was based upon "a changing repertory of revivals, a changing conception of the role that historical styles should play in contemporary design, and a changing feeling for mass, space, shape, color, and texture";[67] it is the direction of this changing feeling that we will analyze. A little later Buford L. Pickens made a detailed examination of the Victorian architecture of Detroit and found three phases: pre-Victorian, characterized by the subordination of the parts to the whole; Victorian, impressionistic effect of the aggregation of parts; and post-Victorian, emphasis shifting back to continuity of surface and effects of mass and solidity.[68] Both writers were finding a pattern of development in a hitherto misinterpreted period. The sculptural core beneath the stylistic bric-a-brac was isolated and found to change from phase to phase. Neither of these systems is as compre-

66. *Discourses on Architecture, 2,* pl. 21.

67. *Mill and Mansion* (New York, Columbia University Press, 1942), p. 49.

68. "Treasure Hunting in Detroit," *Architectural Review, 96* (1944), 169–76.

hensive as the one I propose in the following pages; my system, on the other hand, is not as detailed as that of Henri Focillon, which embraced four phases: experimental, classic, refined or mannerist, and baroque.[69] Some of his observations are, however, incorporated. If the railroad station, and by extension all the architecture of the century, can be shown to pass through a cycle of related phases, it follows that the period had a distinct style of its own. It is understood that while a style of art will alter its themes and emphasis from one phase to another, such change is not necessarily progress in the evolutionary sense.[70]

A typical configuration is established during each phase, reflecting "men's formal imaginative demands which vary so unaccountably from age to age," as Sir Kenneth Clark put it.[71] The simplest demonstration of this axiom is to observe the silhouettes. The silhouettes of a series of railroad stations, chronologically arranged, are shown in Fig. 40. In the first one the form is overwhelmingly horizontal; a gradual increase in vertical elements follows until they become dominant; subsequently there is a return to horizontality. The sequence of the silhouettes is like a great wave which begins early in the century and sweeps up to a crest, subsiding toward the beginning of the 20th century. The analogy of the wave is helpful in following the changing relations between horizontality and verticality during the 19th century. Observation of the silhouette can be extended to include the entire mass. This emphasizes the over-all composition and subordinates distracting stylistic detail. Similarities of form become more pronounced and minor differences of vocabulary are minimized.

In its first phase a style develops special types of plan along with a fresh vocabulary of forms and simple, flat, linear effects. The early phase of the picturesque eclectic style begins in the late 18th century when England began to exercise a dominant role in taste, of which the first manifestation was the impact on the continent of her landscape gardening. The style parallels England's rise as a world power and ends in the early 20th century just as her ascendancy in other fields was waning. The pre-eminent influence in architecture throughout the century was England's too. Germans like Schinkel and Persius traveled there and were stimulated to new creativity. Semper, another innovator, took refuge in England before going to Switzerland and Vienna. During the reign of Victoria, relations between her country and

69. *Art d'occident,* Paris, 1938; and *The Life of Forms in Art,* New Haven, 1942.

70. Peter Fingesten, "The Theory of Evolution in the History of Art," *College Art Journal, 13* (1954), 302 ff.

71. *The Gothic Revival* (New York, Charles Scribner's Sons, 1929), p. 11 (1st ed. London, 1928).

France were close. The ideas of the picturesque had become current during the reign of George III and were accompanied by some experimentation with broken outlines and vertical accents, but on the whole, academic formulas prevailed. Most buildings were defined by flat planes, and their horizontal stratification was terminated by an emphatic cornice.

Meanwhile the "architecture of revolution," well analyzed by Emil Kaufmann,[72] was forming. The pure geometrical block haunted the imaginations of Boullée in France, Gandy in England, and Gilly in Germany. The works of Soane, Ledoux, and Latrobe—less radical than their projects—are equally severe. The cube, sphere, and cylinder became more tyrannical than even Palladio had been. Detail was subordinated to stark mass. In the following decades such absolutism was gradually modulated. A colonnade was applied to the front of the basic prism. Following Peyre, low Pantheon-like domes pushed their way above the flat roofs. Plasticity returned: pavilions advanced further and porticoes projected more boldly. Verticals were reintroduced in the form of tower-pavilions, exemplified in Soane's Dulwich Gallery (1811–14) and Schinkel's Königswache (1816–18). Movement and irregularity attacked purity of outline and simplicity of geometry. Sir John Soane's heaped-up, hollowed-out "Tivoli Corner" (Bank of England, 1804–07) received praise as the best instance in town of the picturesque.[73] John Nash strove to give life and movement to his vast terraces around Regent's Park and to Regent Street; he was so preoccupied with visual effects that his designs might have been painted for a panorama.

It was at this point that the railroad station appeared. By this time the tendencies of the first phase of the style could be clearly observed. The pure geometric confines of the "architecture of revolution" were definitely ruptured. Small stations such as Crown Street, Liverpool, were less affected, but at Lime Street Station I, Liverpool (Fig. 42), the lesson of Nash's terraces was clearly shown. The extensive screen is held together by a uniform order and cornice but it is interrupted four times by arched portals crowned by attics. The envelope has been slit, the silhouette has been broken, and the long mass has been transformed into a rhythmic series of nine subparts. The Doric screen at Euston (Fig. 17) has still more elements and greater differences in heights. It is anticlassic by comparison with the Athenian propylaea. The

72. "Three Revolutionary Architects," *Transactions of the American Philosophical Society, 42*, Pt. 3, Philadelphia, 1952, and *Architecture in the Age of Reason*, Cambridge, 1955.

73. Comment by "Candidus" in *Civil Enginer and Architect's Journal, 4* (London, 1841), 121. Hussey also praised Soane as "the greatest exponent of picturesque architecture in the Greek medium": quoted in F. Saxl and R. Wittkower, *British Art and the Mediterranean* (London, 1948), p. 75.

huge gateway, smaller guard houses, and narrow terminal blocks are strung like beads along the transparent grill. Each element has a pronounced third dimension. At the more economical Derby Trijunct Station (Fig. 19), Francis Thompson was limited to minor differences in height and projection. The head building of Temple Meads Station, although Gothic in detail, is symmetrical and horizontal and builds up to an axial climax. But the horizontality is modified by buttresses and turrets, the expression of a dawning desire for verticality shared by the architects of stations at Hanover, Chester (Fig. 63), and Leipzig.

We can see related modifications in such famous classical revival buildings as the National Gallery and University College in London. A characteristic form at this time is that of interlocking blocks, as seen in the Church of Notre Dame de Lorette, Paris (1823–36) and the Glyptothek in Munich (1816–30). In this type of composition the long, low main block is pinned down by a taller, thinner one which rises in front of it and clamps over it.

During the late 1840's and the 1850's, horizontality and verticality seem to be in equilibrium. The commonest expression of this point on the rising wave occurs in the buildings of the Italian villa or "railroad" style. Many of these combine low masses with one or more towers. Examples include London Bridge Station (Fig. 21), Chester Station (Fig. 63), King's Cross, London (Fig. 57), and later ones such as the second Gare du Nord in Paris (Fig. 61) and the Hauptbahnhof in Zurich (Fig. 62). A great impulse toward this type of composition was given by the Houses of Parliament, which were slowly rising through the 1840's: horizontal blocks were combined with numerous vertical accents, and—more daringly—vertical masses (the two great towers and one minor tower) were placed asymmetrically. Subsequently such compositions are to be found everywhere in small as well as large buildings.

By the time the middle phase of a style is reached, usually the break with the preceding style has been accomplished and techniques, idioms, and aesthetic goals have been crystallized. The new style is victorious, and the emphasis is on refining and developing its own standards. Sometimes there are also tendencies toward personal expression, as when in the middle phase of the Renaissance, Giulio Romano invented a highly personal manner. There may be a tendency toward refinement of structure. In the middle phase of the Gothic style the architect of the Sainte Chapelle dematerialized the medieval structural system by thinning and lightening it even though structural truth had to be sacrificed and true stability ensured by an invisible iron armament. In the middle phase of picturesque eclecticism the silhouettes achieved a maximum degree of agitation (Fig. 40). St. Pancras Station in London is one of the climactic monuments. There is a bolder use of asymmetry and verticality and the principle of frontality is rejected. The academic way of viewing a building was to consider it as made up of one or more plane façades to be seen from an axis perpendicular to it. Now buildings were designed to be seen in the round, from many points of view, in each of which the masses are composed differently; hence the fondness of corner lots and elevated, free-standing sites approached by winding drives.

Verticality could most easily be obtained by the lavish addition of towers. As it became more and more sought after, horizontal lines were suppressed. Even if some slight expression of the stratification of the interior persisted, it could be minimized by applying tower-like pavilions, by pinching thin windows between buttress-like elements, or by continuing wall motives through the cornice line in dormers like the lucarnes of the Francis I style. Asymmetry became almost mandatory. Even in urban situations, some architects succeeded in varying the treatment to the right and left of the axis, as in the superlative Manchester City Hall or, more positively, by the irregular placing of unlike towers, as in the Foreign Office (1868–73) and St. Pancras Station (Fig. 109). The impulse to obscure regularity is prevalent again today in our ubiquitous canted and curved interior partitions.

The anticlassical state of mind induced several types of imbalance: an indulgence in superincumbent overhangs, towers with upper stages swelling out like tree tops above narrow trunks, exaggerated effects of attenuation, ceilings which tend to crush the supporting walls, and well- and tunnel-like spaces. The emphatic consequences are in sharp contradiction to the age-old satisfaction with unequivocal stability. They make their appeal to the nonbiological needs for a mild sense of physical danger, novelty, and curiosity.[74]

The first type was derived from the juts and overhangs common in the secular architecture of the Middle Ages, rare in their monumental buildings. The mid-19th century, which turned every tendency into a mania, went much further. For a while architects delighted in arranging features which would hang perilously over the supports. In domestic architecture this can be seen in the elaborately contrived series of details which project more and more boldly with each superposed feature, sometimes in bow windows, sometimes gables, not infrequently at the corner of the building. An early instance of this trend can be seen in the design for the station at St-Germain-en-Laye (Fig. 67), in which a belfry clings like a bat beneath the eaves of the central gable. The Harrisburg, Pennsylvania, station of the 1850's (Fig. 74) increases the relief of the detail on each ascending story in a related drive for top-heaviness. The hotel of the Cannon Street Station in London (Fig. 107) expands above the main cornice, and Waterhouse exhibited the same tendency

74. Account of a speech by Donald Hebb in the *New York Times* (Jan. 4, 1955), p. 6.

in his hotel in Liverpool (Fig. 108). The height of the mania came during the Queen Anne period, exemplified in Boyington's Chicago station (Fig. 132). Richardson made use of the same effect to a lesser degree at his New London station, in which the second floor overhangs the first. Traces of imbalance lingered on as late as Dervaux's Rouen station in our century (Fig. 191). This indulgence in what may be called toppling effects is just one of several ways in which the middle phase went to aesthetic extremes.

The proportions of masses and spaces as well as detail became subject to a kind of attenuation. The conventional ratios of width to height were revised toward slenderness. This is most notable in windows, which not only achieved pointed heads but took on the other dimensions of the lance as well. Where a classical architect would have had one window, two or three slender ones now give the desired proportions.

Well-like interior spaces became acceptable. An early example of these exaggerated upended spaces can be seen in Sir John Soane's Museum, London, 1812. Others include the stair-halls of the Manchester and Philadelphia City Halls, the domed halls of the state capitols of Connecticut and Rhode Island, and features of the Brussels Palais de Justice. A variant spatial effect was achieved by hollowing out a multistory block and surrounding the inner court with galleries. These courts evolved in the direction of emphasized length and height. Compare the court of Bunning's Coal Exchange (London, 1847–49) with those in the New Haven City Hall (1861) or Memorial Hall at Cambridge (1871–74). Similar courts were contrived in libraries and department stores, and in the 1880's they were introduced into office buildings. In domestic architecture a parallel trend can be traced in Queen Anne houses and Seaside Cottages. The striking effect was often intensified by the juxtaposition of several halls of different shapes and proportions, only partially screened off from one another and permitting diagonal and oblique vistas of entrancing intricacy. Compared with the Middle Ages, the complexity is greater and the illumination more sharply contrasted; compared with the baroque, more elements are used and the relationships seem more accidental. The city hall of Bradford, Yorkshire, has a masterly flow of space diagonally and vertically, now in curved and now in straight currents, nearly concentric and differentiated by varied enclosures and illumination. Both inventions, the well and the multiple galleries, are combined in the foyer of the Paris Opera.

Horizontal spaces were exaggerated also. Corridors aspired to be tunnels, suggestive of the ones in which the railway bored its way through more difficult terrain. Again, proportion was significant: these galleries were made very long for their height and width. The tunnel was an inevitable shape for a train-shed, but it was not confined to them. It appeared in the corridors of

23

monumental buildings. Sometimes the controlling idea was the open railway cut, not the tunnel; in that case the top-lighted gallery was compressively high and narrow, as in the Manchester Assizes.

Externally, the most conspicuous part of a building became its silhouette. Whatever one may think of such buildings as St. Pancras Station and the old Trocadero, their outlines glimpsed against the sky had the power of commanding attention. Never before or since has there been such a universal desire to crown a building so triumphantly. Expense seemed to be inconsequential; the roofs must be steep and broken up. They bristled with turrets, gables, pinnacles, cresting, or whatever devices would ensure the greatest amount of intricacy and irregularity. Burges was a master at this, second only to Waterhouse. On this side of the Atlantic we had such experts as Leopold Eidlitz (1823–1908), Richard Morris Hunt (1827–95), Henry Van Brunt, and the younger Upjohn.

The aesthetic goals we have been analyzing were carried to extremes in the middle phase, so that a reaction was inevitable. In the late and final phase of any style there is often a striving to surpass the work of the preceding phase by increasing the scale or multiplying the number of major elements. Sometimes virtuoso structural feats are indulged in. This is what occurred to the late Gothic in the 15th century, to the Renaissance in the 17th century, and once again to the buildings of the late Victorian age. The extreme perpendicularity of the middle phase was rejected, the movement of the masses was restricted, symmetry crept back, and the number of minor parts was reduced. The controlling cornice did reassert its traditional power, but only to a weakened degree. The jagged outline was restrained and the stupendous roofs were lowered. But the changes were only relative; the delights of the immediate past could not be renounced at once. The main mass became more horizontal. It was held down by a weighty entablature, but the skyline above was still studied. Stumpy blocks replaced the spikes and bristles. Bubbly domes took the place of soaring towers, as in the Berlin Reichstag (1874 ff.) and the Library of Congress. Richardson's late works show the same subsidence and so does the Chicago Fair of 1893, which was perhaps classical but hardly classic. In American stations verticality continued to be fashionable through the 1880's, as in Frank Furness' additions of 1892–93 to the Broad Street Station in Philadelphia (Fig. 126). The transition from the 19th-century wave to the beginning of a new one in the 20th century is witnessed by such stations as that in Washington, D.C. (Fig. 163). Its geometry is not perfectly pure; classical detail obscures it. The architects of the international style had only to strip away the columns and arches to reveal the stark abstraction of the underlying form.

Thus the last phase of picturesque eclecticism prepared the ground for the emergence of the international style, widely recognized as an original style belonging to the 20th century.

Two further observations remain. At the height of any phase of a style the main stream will frequently be flanked on one side by a dwindling eddy from the previous style phase and on the other by an accelerating current of the avant garde. We can see this in the late 1840's where the Gare de l'Est (Fig. 50) represents the mature station and the Gare d'Austerlitz, with its strung-out look, is *retardataire*. Elsewhere towers and blocks combine to give a broken, avant garde silhouette, sometimes even daring to be asymmetrical, as in Turner's London Bridge Station (Fig. 21). Second, the concept of the several phases of a style can be applied to the development of the work of individuals. Michelangelo is the best known instance, but it is applicable to more recent men—H. H. Richardson, for instance, and in our own day, Le Corbusier, whose early cubistic buildings are in marked contrast with his recent ones, like the Unité d'Habitation at Marseilles.

During the long life of picturesque eclecticism, each of its changing moods found an appropriate medium through which to depict its accomplishments. The stucco-covered blocks of the first phase, often color-washed, were appropriately recorded in tinted drawings. During the middle phase only lithography could do justice to the architect's intention. When the jagged outlines and brilliant color of the buildings of that phase had yielded to the massive masonry characteristic of the late phase, it was the camera which recorded its grandeur (see Table 1, p. 3).

Throughout the 19th century the principles of picturesque eclecticism controlled the architect's arrangement of masses and silhouettes, while the changing concepts of eclecticism suggested the shapes of his arches, roofs, and towers. The following chapters, analyzing the history of the railroad station, will present the phases of the picturesque and of eclecticism accompanying one another like the members of a ballet. Sometimes one steps faster or leaps higher than the other, but all dance to the same music—all take part in the unfolding of a single tale.

2. FUNCTIONAL

PIONEERING

(1830-1845)

The Iron Horse Arrives

The railroad station was a century old in 1930. Created as the solution to a new architectural problem, it had by then passed through experimental and mature phases and more recently a period of gigantism. The American depot for the first third of its life feebly imitated European stations, vainly struggling to equal them. It was not until the 1870's, when enough large cities existed relatively close to one another (as in Europe from early times), that comparable stations began to rise in the United States.

In common with so many 19th-century inventions, the creation of the first modern railroad happened independently in two places at once: in England with the opening of the Liverpool and Manchester Railway, and in the United States with the opening of the Baltimore and Ohio Railroad. In 1830 four elements, already in existence, were combined to create them. The first of these elements, specialized track, was the most ancient, going back to Assyrian military trackways and more recently to the iron tracks used in 16th-century mines. The second element, the conveyance of freight, can be traced to the early 18th century; the third, the conveyance of passengers, to 1807 in the five-mile-long Swansea and Mumbles line with its horse-drawn car. The fourth element, mechanical traction, was derived from a whole series of experimental vehicles.[1] When these four elements were combined into one system, the way was open for the rapid development of the modern railway network and its accompanying 100,000 passenger stations.

1. Charles Lee, *The Evolution of Railways,* 2d ed. London, 1943.

The first British station, at Crown Street, Liverpool (Fig. 1), is no longer in existence. Baltimore has the honor of preserving the first American depot, the Mount Clare Station of 1830 (Fig. 2). It was hardly more than a box office for the excursion to Relay, which was the first business of the line. There was no train-shed, not even a porch (the cars themselves were unroofed, since passengers were accustomed to riding on the outside of stage coaches). It was built of brick, polygonal in shape to fit the site, late Georgian in style. Wholly unpretentious, it was the ancestor of the colossal terminals of today. What were its ancestors? Neither of the two preceding modes of transportation —the canal and the century-old turnpike system—had developed special buildings for the use of passengers. Inns were used, as they had been for millennia, as departure points, as relay stations, and as terminals and restaurants. Each stage coach had been regarded as an independent unit, even though it might be owned by a large company, be run on an exact schedule, and be a link in a complex transport system. The only special building developed during the coaching era was the tollhouse. That at Bewdley, built by Thomas Telford in 1801, remains in all its abstract, robust geometry (Fig. 3); in both form and function it resembles the Mount Clare Station, of which it may be considered a parent. The contrast between the two, in elegance of material and dignity of form, typifies the relationship between the architecture of transportation in the two regions for the following half century.

From the tollhouse, too, the most characteristic feature of the 19th-century station may have evolved: the vast train-shed filled with smoke, steam, and the cheerful noise of a dozen bustling engines. An early tollhouse on the Cumberland National Highway extended its roof across the road like a porte-cochere so that the coach might stand under its cover (Fig. 4).[2] Train-sheds appeared at the first Liverpool Station in 1830 and in the United States five years later at Lowell, Massachusetts (Figs. 5, 6). The latter was designed by P. Anderson, whose signed drawings, preserved in the Boston Atheneum, are the earliest surviving designs for a station.[3] It was a small temple with four columns under a pediment at each end and ten columns down the side— classical elements also employed in many European stations. A single track ran behind the colonnade and occupied one-third of the floor area. The balance of the space was devoted to the platform and offices, which are not detailed in the architect's drawing; perhaps the separation between architect

2. Tollhouses in England did not have this feature; there, the roof of the innyard may have been the prototype of the train-shed. If so, the inn had two distinguished offspring, the other being the Elizabethan theater

3. A view of the Lowell station was published by John Coolidge in his *Mill and Mansion,* Fig. 48. See my "Some Early Depot Drawings," *Journal of the Society of Architectural Historians,* 8 (1949), 33.

and engineer was already in effect, the architect being responsible for proportion and the engineer for utility.

Just as English engineers dominated the railroad field for the first half-century of railroading, so the English stations established patterns for the whole world. In that compact country with abundant capital, pioneer lines were lavishly built. The roadbeds were straight, level, and permanent; tunnels, bridges, and viaducts were constructed solidly of good masonry. Similar pains were taken over the terminal stations. Although no plan of the Crown Street Station, Liverpool, 1830 (Fig. 7) has survived, contemporary views and illustrations indicate that it embodied the basic features of the modern station in embryo. The passenger preparing to depart from Liverpool arrived by carriage or omnibus at a vehicle court—foreshadowing the covered driveways of later stations—which was separated from the street traffic by a wall. On entering the building he found himself in a room which combined the functions of ticket-selling and waiting, as in the great concourses of today's terminals. From the waiting room he passed onto the platform and into his carriage under the cover of a train-shed. The degree of protection was greater than it is in many recent stations, which have abandoned the shed for individual platform covers. Undoubtedly George Stephenson, the engineer of the line, advised the architect on this prophetic depot. The architect did not feel constrained to invent new architectural forms; he was content to solve his functional problem and clothe his solution in accepted contemporary detail. The engineering of the train-shed with a modest span of thirty feet did not demand unusual ingenuity either.[4]

The carry-overs from coaching practices into pioneer railroading were numerous and colorful. The guard, for instance, still survives in England (although his costume has been toned down); magnificently caparisoned, he formerly sat on the roof of the train coach and served as brakeman, and his horn was the signal for the arrival and departure of trains—as it still is in Portugal. The first passenger coaches were modeled, as their name indicates, on those built for the turnpikes. Each was named, as is still done with Pullmans, and those of each line were painted in the company's livery. It was soon discovered that smoke and cinders from the engines made it impossible to use the carriage roofs for passengers and luggage as had been done on turnpikes. Operating practices, however, were carried over: passengers could book specific numbered seats in advance; tickets were sold at inns. The first conductors were often former stage drivers who were well acquainted with the traveling public. Passengers were collected at centrally located inns and

4. See Henry-Russell Hitchcock, *Early Victorian Architecture in Britain* (2 vols. New Haven, Yale University Press, 1954), chs. 15 and 16, for an additional and valuable discussion of early British railway stations.

transferred to the more remote stations—the modern air-line practice. In 1839 French passengers assembled in a common waiting room in a gay mood of anticipation. When a bell sounded, the gates opened and the crowd streamed forth to the shed where the cars waited. Without confusion, they found their places according to the numbers of their tickets. When all was ready, the conductor in a fine costume, seated *à l'impériale* on top of the first car, blew his horn and they were off.[5] In some small English stations, first- and second-class passengers waited in separate pens on the open platforms, while the third-class passengers were perhaps taken aboard at the goods shed.

Some technical details reveal how thoroughly experimental the early decades were. In Germany, both horse and steam traction were in use simultaneously on the same tracks. Cars were hauled up steep grades by stationary engines in Liverpool in 1830 and between Johnstown and Hollidaysburg in Pennsylvania in 1834. Atmospheric railroads enjoyed a brief vogue in the 1840's: in this system, the cars were attached to pistons which slid in tubes parallel to the tracks. A vacuum was maintained in these tubes by engine houses at regular intervals. As the promoters rightly claimed, this made for smooth, clean propulsion. As the pistons slid along the tube, they pushed open flexible lips which closed behind as they passed, thus preserving the vacuum. Unfortunately, for lack of a strong resilient material such as vulcanized rubber, the lips wore out at an excessive rate and made the system too costly to maintain.

Since the first cars were short, light, and single-trucked, they could be moved by manpower alone without switching engines; hence early stations were equipped with two devices—the turntable and the traversing frame (Figs. 7, 48)—which had to be given up as cars increased in weight. The first device, taken over from mining practice, was the earlier one, and primitive station plans are adorned by numerous circles representing them. The traversing frame was a section of rails, long enough to hold a car, itself on rails. It moved laterally and enabled cars to be pushed sideways from one line to another without the use of switches.

Facing the New Problem

During the first few decades of the station's development, so many ingenious experiments were being conducted that the evolving station types elude ready classification. Some stations bore in them the patterns for the great terminals of the future, others proved abortive. César Daly, editor of the *Revue Gén-*

5. Charles Dollfus, *Histoire de la locomotion terrestre* (Paris, 1935), pp. 45–6.

A. EARLY TYPES OF STATION PLAN

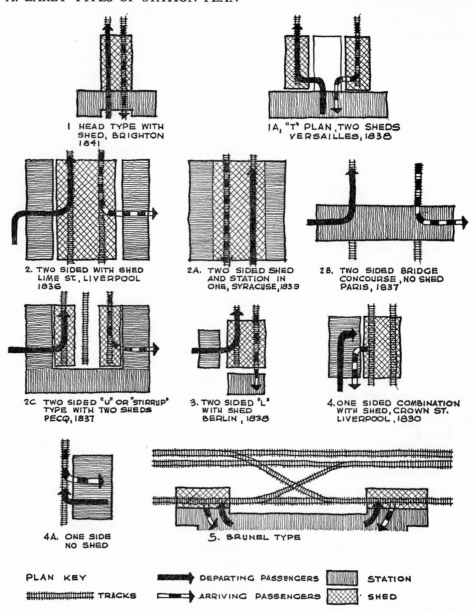

1 HEAD TYPE WITH
SHED, BRIGHTON
1841

IA. "T" PLAN, TWO SHEDS
VERSAILLES, 1838

2. TWO SIDED WITH SHED
LIME ST., LIVERPOOL
1836

2A. TWO SIDED SHED
AND STATION IN
ONE, SYRACUSE, 1839

2B. TWO SIDED BRIDGE
CONCOURSE, NO SHED
PARIS, 1837

2C. TWO SIDED "U" OR "STIRRUP"
TYPE WITH TWO SHEDS
PECQ, 1837

3. TWO SIDED "L"
WITH SHED
BERLIN, 1838

4. ONE SIDED COMBINATION
WITH SHED, CROWN ST.
LIVERPOOL, 1830

4A. ONE SIDE
NO SHED

5. BRUNEL TYPE

PLAN KEY

TRACKS

DEPARTING PASSENGERS

ARRIVING PASSENGERS

STATION

SHED

érale de l'Architecture, made the first attempt in 1846 to reduce to order the proliferating chaos of station types. He claimed there were only four, if stations were classified according to the arrangements for entering and leaving them: (1) head type, arrival and departure in a single building across the end of the tracks; (2) two-sided or twin type, with arrival and departure handled on opposite sides of the tracks; (3) "L" type, with arrival at the end of the tracks and departure at one side or vice versa; (4) one-sided combination type, with arrival and departure on one side of the tracks (Text Fig. A).

The one-sided combination type, at first used everywhere in the world, including Mount Clare in Baltimore and Crown Street in Liverpool,[6] has never become obsolete; in fact, most small stations are still built according to this plan. It was the most natural one to use, involving no break with tradition and almost no rethinking of the problem; furthermore, any other arrangement at a small station used by a few persons would be disproportionately expensive. Its operation is too familiar to all of us to require detailed analysis.

Isambard Kingdom Brunel (1806–59), the engineer whose reputation ranks second only to Stephenson's, was the inventor of a variation of the one-sided station which was used for a time at intermediate stations on the Great Western Railway (Text Fig. A, 5). It provided duplicate buildings for arrival and departure a short distance apart on the same side of the tracks, at towns such as Reading, where the principal part of the town lay on one side of the line. The purpose was to save passengers arriving or departing from either direction from having to cross the tracks. Instead, the trains were switched across the lines, a complicated business which worked well enough until the number of trains became too great. Evidently it was thought simpler or more ingenious to operate the trains in this fashion than to build an overpass or tunnel, as is done today.[7]

A more typical station of the one-sided type was built in Derby in 1839–41 (Fig. 8). Parts of this landmark stood until recently, though in sad condition. Begun only nine years later than the first railway stations, its formula is already mature and it was used for through stations without essential change until 1855, after which it died out in Europe. The long, thin station building stretched along the single platform for more than 1,000 feet. The ends of the platform were used for terminal trains which came in on spur tracks, the center for through trains. From the passenger's point of view, this was a convenient plan; the walking distance from train to waiting room was no greater than the width of the platform. Like Brunel's plan, however, this scheme worked only while trains were short and infrequent. Later, increased traffic was handled by using more of the existing lines under the shed (Derby had nine of these from the start, intended for freight and baggage handling), but as there was still only one platform, the hazards of walking across one line to reach another became notorious. The last monumental one-sided station was that at Newcastle built in 1855, and with this dinosaur, the type became extinct in England.[8]

The twin or two-sided type in its many variants was the preferred mid-

6. Other examples include Malines (1835), St. Petersburg (1837), Potsdam (1838), Vienna and Amsterdam (1839).

7. Stations at Slough, Windsor, and Gloucester were built this way.

8. See below, p. 59, for a description of the Newcastle station.

19th-century station on both sides of the Atlantic. Euston Station in London, 1835–39 (Fig. 9), the first important example of this type, provided a platform on each side—the arrival platform opposite the departure one. This meant that incoming and outgoing passengers were kept apart, so that arriving trains did not hold up departing ones and both could wait longer at the platforms. The principal buildings were on the departure side, since it was necessary to have booking offices and baggage and waiting rooms there. At Euston, passengers arrived through the great propylaea and were set down along a platform under a colonnade. The characteristic separation into classes begins here: first-class passengers entered through the north door and after securing tickets passed down a corridor into their waiting room, while second-class passengers entered a different door into a combined waiting room and booking office. Light baggage was carried by hand into the waiting room; heavy baggage was loaded at a dock at the end of the lines. For the first two years, 1837–39, cars were pulled out of the station as far as Camden Town by stationary engines; on the way in they coasted under their own momentum, controlled by a brakeman. This may have been done to keep the engines from frightening the horses, but it is also possible there was still some uncertainty about the adherence of locomotive wheels to sloping rails.

F. S. Williams provides a colorful description of the scene as it was in 1852 when the station was becoming rather inadequate for the volume of its traffic.

> Porters bustle about with luggage . . . one man endangers the heads of the public by the clumsy manner in which he conveys a huge box, . . . while another . . . seems to feel perfectly justified in knocking anyone down . . . if he has first sought their permission by muttering . . . "By y' leave." . . . The luggage is deposited in, on, or under, the several carriages. . . . The second-class passengers will joke about the engine, say that they prefer having their backs to the horses, talk about "a feed of coke" or when the engine whistles they will exclaim pathetically "Poor creature."
>
> The invariable old lady . . . is first found in great distress about her box, which is a thing perfectly unique; and which she is afraid may be pocketed by some one (though it weighs a good half-hundred-weight. . . . The inspectors . . . exercise a very refined discrimination . . . "Tickets, if you please, ladies and gentlemen!" are the euphonious accents which fall on the ear of the first-class passenger. This is modified, it is said, to the—"Tickets, gentlemen, tickets!" of the second class; while the appeal is shaded off into the—"Where's your tickets?" of the third.[9]

9. Frederick Smeeton Williams, *Our Iron Roads, Their History, Construction and Social Influences* (London, 1852), pp. 211 ff.

The gate to the right of the main one at Euston led to the carriage dock at the end of the lines. This was a luxurious feature designed to placate hostility to the new mode of transportation. Lordly clients would drive up to this dock in their own carriages, which would then be detached from the horses and put on a flatcar with the horses in a box car. The owner could ride in his own carriage or a regular one. At the destination the loading process was reversed, and the equipage was at hand for the next step of the journey. This feature had to be abandoned because of the inconsiderate behavior of clients who would drive up to the station at the last minute and by the time the loading was effected delay the train half an hour.[10]

The extreme right-hand portal at Euston was the exit from the arrival court. The train drew up along one edge of the platform and omnibuses along the other, so that the passenger passed directly from one vehicle to the other under cover. This degree of convenience exists today only in some of the surviving old terminals like St. Pancras and in small intermediate stations. The traffic flow in stations of this type was at right angles to the tracks, and it was limited to the two main platforms.

The head-type station plan, in which all passengers entered and left through the head-building across the end of the lines, proved to be the most long-lived scheme for terminals. Numerically important even in the experimental period, they were of continuing significance. A single building was erected across the ends of the tracks with platforms lying between the tracks and perpendicular to the building. This was the plan of the Brighton Station by David Mocatta, 1840–41 (Fig. 10). At York in 1840–41 a "U" or "stirrup" plan was employed with wings extending back from the head building to surround the end of the spur tracks on three sides (Fig. 11). Other variations occurred, even in large stations: "L's," for example, and a "T" plan at Stuttgart in 1863–68 (Fig. 85), where the returned wing lies between two sets of spur tracks.

York became famous for its railroad stations; each successive one was celebrated in its period. The first was opened in 1841. Unusual pains were taken because it was the pride of George Hudson, the "railroad king," whose home town it was. G. T. Andrews, the architect, had a complicated situation to solve since it was a joint station shared by several companies. Some through lines curved by at one side, others came directly in as spurs. The wings which enclosed the four central spurs were built first and a hotel was added across the end shortly after, thus making one of the first "U" plans. Across the ends of the spurs and parallel with the rear of the hotel was a wide cross-platform,

10. The carriage dock seems not to have been used in America; perhaps Americans in the 1830's and 1840's felt it inconsistent with democratic principles. It is still in use on the Santa Valley Railroad in Peru.

permitting passengers and company personnel to move freely among the four lines without having to cross tracks. The building was accessible on the exterior from three sides.

The three-storied railway hotel at York, the original drawings for which are preserved there, was the ancestor of the famous London ones and the first to form an integral part of a station complex (Fig. 11). It was unpretentious, of plain grey bricks. It provided complete comfort for the traveler: on the ground floor the coffee room, bar, and bar parlor were conveniently accessible to both the street and the cross-platform. Some features seen here, such as the "U" plan and the cross-platform, had been introduced at the Nine Elms Station in London by Sir William Tite in 1837–38.[11] In the next few years other large head stations followed, such as the first Gare du Nord in Paris.

Because of variations in level of the site, some early depots had to be multilevel stations, affording the ingenious designer opportunities for simplifying circulation. At that time, however, there was no need to exploit them, as was done in the 1870's.

Two of Brunel's Great Western stations—those at Bath and Bristol, where the tracks were on a viaduct above the street level—were two-leveled as well as two-sided. The more magnificent one was Temple Meads Station at Bristol, under construction in 1839–41. On the departure side, booking offices and waiting rooms were under the tracks, with stairs leading up to the platform. On the arrival side, an arcaded loggia alongside the carriage yard was similarly connected to the platform above. Facing the street and across the end of the tracks but detached from them stood a picturesque Gothic head-building containing the company's offices. Most of this station is still standing, supplemented by additions in a harmonious style.

Several stations showed the reverse organization, the stations being above tracks in a cut. One of the earliest was the Gare de la Place de l'Europe (Paris, 1837), where wide, easy stairs led down to the platforms on both sides of the cut from the main building on a bridge. Fig. A, 2B.

Railroads only two and three miles in length were sometimes built in metropolitan situations. The tracks were on viaducts, and head-type stations were appropriate to the constricted sites. Staircases led from the tracks down through the head-building to the street, as at the Minories Station in London. Ultimately, this type evolves into such great terminals as the Anhalter Bahnhof of Berlin, 1872–80 (Fig. 112). No early examples of it have been found in the United States.

11. This station is still in existence, though it was damaged during World War II. A proposal has been made to repair it and use it as a transportation museum.

Audacious Engineers

If, as Henri Focillon once remarked, the 19th was the most inventive century of modern times, then the train-shed can be said to typify the inventive spirit of the age. Such a view of its importance is not the creation of 20th-century historians looking backward but was held by contemporary observers. At the end of the century, for example, an American critic stated that the glass cages of the great railroad stations were the characteristic architecture of the time. He admired them for the following qualities: relation of structure to decoration, amplitude without bareness, and ornateness without confusion. Referring to a design by Normand for a railroad terminal, the critic brings his article to a conclusion by saying that this "brilliant design is our last word upon the evolution of architectural styles." [12]

A peculiarly 19th-century phenomenon, the train-shed was born—as we have seen—in 1830 at Crown Street Station, Liverpool. It died, for all practical purposes, in 1904 at Hoboken when Lincoln Bush introduced a less extravagant solution to the problem of sheltering passengers at terminals. In its prime, the train-shed owed its poetry and daring to the engineer as much as to the architect, and its demise was also engineer-contrived. As in the Middle Ages, technical demands led to new forms: structural invention in the form of iron truss construction was clearly dominant.

The train-shed in the first years of its development is of particular interest on two counts. The warfare between the points of view of the architect and the engineer was out in the open in much the same way as when the two professions are jointly employed on a bridge; [13] the harmonious collaboration which took place at Paddington II in the 1850's between Brunel and Wyatt was rare. In the second place, the train-shed as a special type of wide-span construction demanded and received the best engineering skills available. Time after time, engineers pioneered in the erection of new sheds: new materials and new methods of fabrication found in them a dramatic expression.

There was the competitive element too. Toward the end of the century, engineers rivaled one another with wider and more daring spans. The railroad companies took pride in their colossal halls and lavished their funds upon them, presumably motivated in part by considerations of publicity and prestige. The competition to build the widest single-span train-shed was won

12. J. R. Coolidge, Jr., "The Characteristic Architecture of the Nineteenth Century," *Architectural Review, 7* (Boston, 1900), 77 ff. Paul Normand's second grand prize of 1891 was based, significantly, on the 1889 Paris Galerie des Machines. See below, pp. 85, 114–15.

13. See J. M. Richards, "The Wrong Turning," *Architectural Review, 105* (1949), 107.

by the Pennsylvania Railroad in the 1890's at Philadelphia. Later this energy went into the competition to build the highest skyscraper.

To roof the largest possible unencumbered area was an ancient dream. Until the 19th century, each daring advance was a rare and costly thing, a phenomenon not to happen again for several generations. By 1846 wood spans of 100 feet had become fairly commonplace. Masonry spans of this width had occurred a few times: the widest vaulted span erected in the Middle Ages is that at Gerona of 73 feet; the nave of St. Peter's in Rome equaled the widest Roman span of 84 feet; the width of the domed nave of Hagia Sophia is 107 feet. Spans wider than this had also been domed in the Pantheon, the Duomo in Florence, and the domed area of St. Peter's—all with diameters in the neighborhood of 140 feet.

Nineteenth-century engineers seized upon the potentialities of iron, a new material, and achieved a clear, single span of 211 feet at the New Street Station, Birmingham, in 1854, and at almost the same moment a triple span with the combined width of 238 feet at Paddington Station II, London.[14] These occurred within twenty-five years of the building of the first train-shed, so rapidly did the new problem call forth new solutions.

The experimental nature of the first decades of station building appears with particular distinctness in the diversity of train-shed types. The gamut extends from a total absence of protection, through an intermediate stage of cantilevered porches, marquees, pergolas, and colonnades, to arched iron sheds flung over four lines of track and two wide platforms (Text Fig. B). At Kassel the train-shed, while wholly detached from the modest station building, was an elaborate three-naved wooden skeleton (Fig. 12). It looked like the framework for a church with the enclosing walls left off. The types destined to have a future were primarily three: the relatively short-lived wood-framed ones and the two principal types using metal as trusses and as arches. Each of these requires separate treatment.

At first and for some time, the natural thing was to lean upon centuries of experience and construct the roof supports entirely, or chiefly, of wood. Stephenson's first station, Crown Street, Liverpool (Fig. 1), had a modest wooden shed supported by a queen post truss about 30 feet wide. In 1836, when the terminus was moved to a more central location at Lime Street, the shed was constructed in the same way but the span was increased to 55 feet. The following year at Nine Elms a larger wooden shed, covering an area 74 by 290 feet in three spans, was raised on handsome iron columns with ornamental iron stiffeners (Fig. 13). The most elegant wooden sheds of the

14. There is an extended treatment of the Birmingham station with an integrated hotel by William Livock, and of the shed, in Hitchcock, *Early Victorian Architecture in Britain, 1,* 562–5.

B. EARLY TYPES OF TRAIN-SHED, WITH IDENTIFICATION

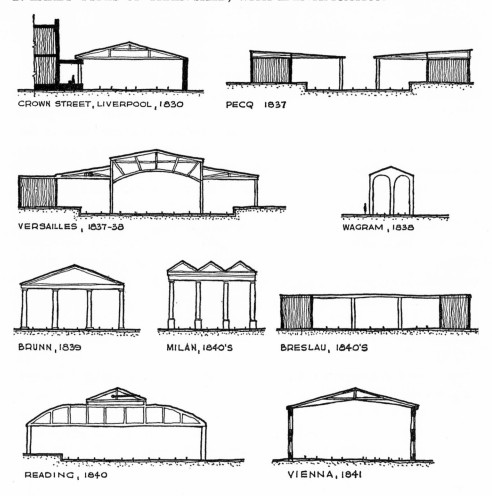

CROWN STREET, LIVERPOOL, 1830

PECQ 1837

VERSAILLES, 1837-38

WAGRAM, 1838

BRUNN, 1839

MILAN, 1840'S

BRESLAU, 1840'S

READING, 1840

VIENNA, 1841

period were Brunel's at Bath and Bristol. Because these stations stood on narrow viaducts, it was desirable to reduce the outward thrust of the trusses (Fig. 14). This was accomplished by building them like cranes: the uprights were iron columns placed at the outer edge of the platforms, the principals imitated hammer-beams.[15] At Bristol the span was 72 feet, four feet more than that of Westminster Hall. In less than a decade a handsome, if derivative, form had been devised for what was destined to become the most dramatic element of the station complex, the setting in which nervous travelers first came in contact with the marvelous contrivance by which they were to be hurled through space.

Wooden trusses, common at first, had ultimately to be abandoned because

15. The word "principal" refers to any of the main rafters on which rest the purlins that support the common rafters. In roof or bridge trusses the principals are the main compression members.

in busy stations wood deteriorated rapidly from exposure to sulphurous steam, if it did not burn down first; in any event, it required constant repair. In many cases, after a life of a decade or two a station with a wooden shed was torn down to make way for a larger station with Howe trusses or all metal ones.[16]

The engineers of the London and Birmingham line used metal in their sheds from the beginning. Both of their terminals had double sheds with five trusses entirely of iron resting on cast-iron columns. At Euston the span

C. HOWE TRUSS

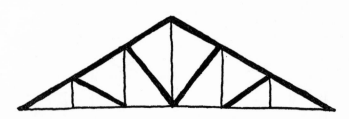

was 40 feet (Fig. 15), and at Curzon Street, "without a parallel" [17] in 1839, that figure was exceeded by 17 feet. At Euston the original sheds may still be seen, now resting on higher supports.[18] Their glory was short-lived, however, for the Derby Trijunct Station by Francis Thompson, completed the same year, had a splendid shed covering nine lines in three spans, of which the central one alone equaled Curzon Street's (Fig. 16). The whole covered area, 140 feet by 450 feet, was of "unequalled extent." [19] Contemporary views make the construction appear light and elegant. The interior supports were tall cast-iron columns in the form of a bundle of ribbon-bound fasces.

Numerous sheds were now rising, some of them remarkable for their functionally expressive struts which clearly showed their role as compression members. There were occasional difficulties: the shed of the Bricklayer's Arms Station in London, consisting of three parallel iron roofs, crashed in 1844 and again in 1850.

In the former year, the new Victoria Station at Manchester eclipsed the Derby Trijunct. Though not so wide, its shed was 250 feet longer, a remarkable

16. The Howe truss (Fig. C) was patented in 1840 by William Howe of Spencer, Massachusetts. A development of Ithiel Town's wooden lattice truss in which metal was substituted for wood in the tension members, it was widely used on American railways for many years. Richard Shelton Kirby and Philip Gustave Laurson, *The Early Years of Modern Engineering* (New Haven, 1932), p. 146.

17. Thomas Roscoe, *The London and Birmingham Railway* (London, 1839), p. 161.

18. G. R. Smith, *Old Euston*, London, 1938.

19. *Illustrated London News, 3* (July 15, 1843), 35.

increase in view of the fact that the original shed at Euston was only 200 feet long. The race was already being run at a swift pace, the chief contestants being the French and the English. In 1846 Eugène Flachat built the widest roof span in the world at the Entrepôt de Marais, a rigid four-centered iron arch 118 feet long. The next lap was to the English, who were designing one of 150 feet. Turner and Locke, assisted by William Fairbairn, were boldly trying to equip a new Liverpool Station, the third in fifteen years, with a shed which would not hamper any future revision of the track plans: experience had shown that such revisions were likely to be frequent. A "sickle girder" with cast-iron struts was chosen.[20] Although the first ribs had failed when tested at the foundry in Dublin, the shed was subsequently accomplished in one span 153 feet wide and 374 feet long. Nearly complete in 1849, and finally finished in 1850, it became the largest span in the world; it surpassed every earlier roof of any material of any type, including domes. The rapid and enthusiastic pursuit of the new wide-span idea was accompanied by changes in the architectural designs.

Chaos or Coherence: the Problem of Expression

The axiom that "a railroad station should look like a railroad station" would be subscribed to without question by any functionalist architect. In the early 19th century such dogmatism was impossible. In the 1830's the question was, "Which station has the right look?" A new building type was evolving. There were many approaches; which was the best?

As stations grew larger, they became too complex to be seen as a whole. Which element should dominate—the shed, the terminal, or, if there was one, the hotel? The engineers were building the sheds and the architects the stations and hotels. Who would consent to subordination? In the 1830's no one counseled, "Solve the problems of plan and structure and let the exterior take care of itself." The discussion was active. Romance has always endowed the railroad with a mixture of wonder, astonishment, and awe. Its buildings were becoming the symbol of the age.

A persistent idea was that the station was to the modern city what the city gate was to the ancient city. The directors of the London and Birmingham

---

20. The "sickle girder" is a truss with curved upper and lower chords connected by struts and ties. Its name comes from its shape, which resembles the blade of a farmer's sickle (see Fig. 54). The bowstring truss, also found in train-sheds, is a related form: its curved principal is tied by a light lower chord, resulting in a shape like a strung bow (see Fig. 87).

Railway and their architect, Philip Hardwick, believed in the symbolism of the gateway and used it at both ends of their line. Their propylaeum in London (Fig. 17) is still standing and has been a *cause célèbre* from the beginning. It was originally hoped to combine the terminals of the Great Western and the London and Birmingham on the Euston site, but the directors of the Great Western refused to come in because they were offered only a five-year lease. The great gate went up nevertheless, even though for the first decade it led anticlimatically to a ridiculously small building. The "grand entrance" was finished in 1839, two years after the line opened. It consisted of seven elements: the large central portal and six smaller pavilions used as coach, mail, and parcel offices, connected to one another by a fine iron fence and gates. Although it cost £35,000, it was money well spent from the point of view of publicity alone because it has provoked criticism and admiration ever since. Francis Whishaw, one of the early authorities of English railroading, said that "the Grand Doric Entrance to Euston Station is perfectly allowable since it is the key, as it were, to all the railways of London." [21] On the other hand William Cubitt, about to build a station some years later, said: "a good station could be built at King's Cross for less than the cost of the ornamental archway [*sic*] at Euston Square." [22] Henry Noel Humphreys compared the whole London and Birmingham line to the aqueducts of Rome: he found that it not only eclipsed the ancient undertaking but, more meritoriously, was built without slave labor. He questioned, however, whether magnitude alone made for architectural grandeur and he had doubts about the gateway being suitable. In a functionalist mood, he found Stephenson's engineering works superior to the architect's work at the termini on the grounds of "fitness." [23] When the great gateway was half a century old, Acworth commented: "The national character had been involved in the execution of the whole." [24] Some such thought must have been in the builders' minds when the enormous dimensions were agreed upon. The columns are eight and a half feet in diameter, or half again as great as those of the Athenian propylaea. The center intercolumniation is twenty-eight feet; the over-all height is seventy-two feet. The result is thrilling. "When Euston was first built, it was regarded not as a railway station but as a spectacle. Visitors used to

21. *The Railways of Great Britain and Ireland Practically Described and Illustrated* (London, 1840), p. 227 f.

22. Quoted in Wilfred L. Steel, *The History of the London and North Western Railway* (London, 1914), p. 66.

23. "Fragments from a Provincial Tour of Railways and Railway Architecture," *Architectural Magazine, 5* (1838), 677.

24. William M. Acworth, *The Railways of England* (London, 1889), p. 86.

flock to it in omnibuses and examine it with the careful scrutiny of sight-seers."[25]

There were also those who disapproved. The most violent attacks came from Pugin and Ruskin, who found nothing to admire. Pugin said:

> The architects have evidently considered it an opportunity for *showing off what they could do* instead of *carrying out what was required*. Hence, the colossal Grecian portico or gateway, 100 feet high [*sic*] for the cabs to drive through, and set down a few feet further, at the 14-inch brick wall and sash-window booking office. This piece of Brobdignaggian absurdity must have cost the company a sum which would have built a first-rate station, replete with convenience, and which would have been really grand from its simplicity.

In the same eloquent passage he attacks the Gothic design for the Rugby station as follows: "At Rugby, because Rugby School, as rebuilt lately, has had battlements and turrets, the old station had four half turrets with the best side turned out, and a few sham loop holes."[26] He proposed a design including Gothic vaults, buttresses, and massive walls which would hardly have failed to equal in expense the design he was ridiculing, and would have been no more appropriate. Ruskin offered a negative suggestion which might be taken as a plea for functionalism. In his *The Stones of Venice,* he treats the station as a necessity, like plumbing, unworthy of artistic effort:

> Another of the strange and evil tendencies of the present day is to the decoration of the railroad station. . . . It is the very temple of discomfort, and the only charity that the builder can extend to us is to show us, plainly as may be, how soonest to escape from it. . . . There never was more flagrant nor impertinent folly than the smallest portion of ornament in anything concerned with the railroads. . . . Will a single traveller be willing to pay an increased fare on the South Western, because the columns of the terminus are covered with patterns from Nineveh? . . . or on the North Western, because there are old English-looking spandrels to the roof of the station at Crewe? Railroad architecture has or would have a dignity of its own if it were only left to its work.[27]

25. Anon., *Round London* (London, 1896), p. 278.

26. A. W. N. Pugin, *An Apology for the Revival of Christian Architecture in England* (London, 1843), p. 11.

27. *The Stones of Venice, 1,* 110–11.

His contemporaries were not impressed by these remarks, which the *Builder* called "purely nonsense." [28] A Frenchman said, "he could not approve of it [Euston] since an arch [*sic*] of triumph of that sort had no connection whatever with the purpose of a railway." [29] For that matter, could any traditional motives appropriately be associated with the railway? The columned portico, whether Greek or Palladian, was liberally employed. This was at the moment when the portico was enjoying supreme favor as the means above all others for ensuring dignity. Wilkins had used a portico at the National Gallery and so had Smirke at the British Museum. The architects Stansby at Huddersfield and Dobson at Newcastle attached porticoes to their stations; it was as though they were claiming that stations were as monumental as museums. Eventually towers and domes were to be used impartially on both classes of buildings.

Whether building gateways or porticoes, English architects felt free to adopt almost any style. For small rural stations the style was often suggested by the locale (a kind of protective coloration). These little stations have been lovingly described and illustrated in many charming accounts. It has been remarked that during the last few centuries the English have excelled in domestic architecture. Perhaps this explains the charm of their small stations and the shortcomings of some of their urban terminals.

The French, as the English critic Fergusson admitted, attacked the problem of terminals more logically. Their system of architectural education emphasized monumentality. French architects successfully integrated their station complexes just as they also solved other new, 19th-century problems such as the library (Bibliothèque St. Geneviève), the market (Les Halles), the opera, and the department store (Le Bon Marché). Although the English handled the technical aspects of railroading brilliantly, the best architectural solutions were French. Perdonnet sums up the French point of view in the following passage:

> The Architecture of a monumental building should express its purpose. Peristyles are expressive of theatres, ancient temples and modern churches. Bell towers, flèches and pointed portals characterize the churches of the middle ages. Railroad stations, especially terminals, also have a distinctive architecture of their own. In terminals, as in all edifices which serve for the congregation of large groups of people, there are often peristyles behind which one finds semi-circular doors or windows of very large dimensions, intended to illuminate enormous vestibules or to pro-

28. *Builder,* 7 (1849), 230.

29. Auguste Perdonnet, *Traité élémentaire des chemin de fer* (3d ed. 4 vols. Paris, 1865, 1st ed. 1855–56), 2, 495.

vide egress for the crowds of travellers brought by each train. But what particularly characterizes the principal façade is a monumental clock, and when this façade is also the end of the station itself, a great arch or an immense pediment expressed the shape of the great roof which covers the trainshed. . . . The Gare de l'Est is the most striking example of this.[30]

This was written some time after the Gare de l'Est had been completed, when it had become easier to recognize the essential features of expressive station design. The English rarely built one on these principles; they tended to ignore the problem of expression and to let a hotel act as the façade for the rest of the station.

The Railroad Style and Alternative Modes

In response to the need for vast numbers of new buildings which could be cheaply erected and easily designed, the 19th century developed several styles in which the derivative elements were subordinated to the original traits. Among these, one, the "Italian villa" style, has become the subject of a long bibliography during the last decade.[31]

The presumed sources of the style are the minor rural buildings of Italy as depicted in the backgrounds of paintings by Raphael, Claude, and Poussin. The buildings were abstracted from paintings to serve as models for new buildings [32] or sketched from nature for the same purpose,[33] and the motives were adapted in pattern books by many others.[34] The earliest buildings in the style include John Nash's Cronkhill of 1802 on the Isle of Wight and Schinkel's

30. *Traité élémentaire, 2,* 492.

31. See my "Henry Austin and the Italian Villa," *Art Bulletin, 30* (1948), 145 ff., and "Form beneath Fashion," *Magazine of Art, 39* (1946), 378 ff.; review of Talbot Hamlin, *Greek Revival Architecture in America,* in *Art Bulletin, 26,* (1944), 283–6; Clay Lancaster, "Oriental Forms in American Architecture, 1800–1870," *Art Bulletin, 29* (1947), 183–93; Hawkins Ferry, "The Gothic and Tuscan Revivals in Detroit, 1828–1875," *Art Quarterly* (Summer, 1946), pp. 234–56.

32. See, for example, Gilbert Laing Meason, *On the Landscape Architecture of the Great Painters of Italy,* London, 1828.

33. Pierre Clochar, *Palais, maisons et vues d'Italie,* Paris, 1809; and Charles Parker, *Villa Rustica,* London, 1832, 2d ed. 1848.

34. For example, T. F. Hunt, *Architecture Campestre . . . in Modern or Italian Styles,* London, 1827; and Francis Goodwin, *Domestic Architecture,* London, 1833.

and Persius' Hofgärtnerei at Potsdam, all asymmetrical and picturesque. Sir Charles Barry, in his Travellers' and Reform Clubs, and certain Frenchmen, influenced by J. N. L. Durand, used a more formal symmetrical version for urban buildings. Both types were to be seen in stations everywhere.

Another source of inspiration, often mixed with Italian villa in a free and offhand manner, was the group of pre-Gothic styles. Round arches are common to all of these, whether the architect called his manner Norman, Lombard, or Early Christian—the nomenclature varied with the learning of the writer. The boundaries between one and another source were lightheartedly disregarded.[35]

For the designer of stations, the Italian villa style and its cousins offered the opportunity to build cheaply and impressively; there were hardly any rules to hamper him. A bell, to announce the arrival of trains, and a clock were normal station equipment, and they justified the expense of a campanile. It was not difficult to group picturesquely the necessary buildings and train-shed around a tower, provided that orthodox proportions were not demanded. Arcaded loggias, so adaptable for platform covers and train-sheds, were an integral part of the style.

Panofsky has said that technical progress tends to cause a stylistic throwback at the time of its introduction.[36] In a period as characterized by stylistic throwbacks as the 19th century it is difficult to disentangle cause and effect. Could it be that the whole series of revivals which begin to become significant just as iron is introduced for architectural construction can be thus accounted for? The introduction of the railway in 1830 was sufficiently influential and conspicuous to have similar consequences. Is it a coincidence that the Italian villa or "railroad" style should begin its rapid spread at this moment after two decades of slow incubation? The station architect had his hands full coping with the practical requirements, without trying to develop an original style. Unless we assume that there is an unlimited amount of creative energy available to any generation, we must recognize that much of the architectural talent available must have been absorbed in the practical aspects of the new problem.

One of the leading station architects of the experimental period was Francis Thompson. The important stations at Derby (1839–41) and Chester (1847–48) are his, as well as the architectural parts of the Britannia Tubular Bridge. As architect to the North Midland Railway, he was responsible for modest stations such as that at Belper (Fig. 18) and many on the Holyhead

35. See my "Romanesque before Richardson in the United States," *Art Bulletin, 35* (1953), 17 ff.

36. Erwin Panofsky, *Transition,* No. 26 (Winter, 1937), p. 132.

line. A few of these were Jacobean but most were restrained Italian "villas." Prints of them were made: Loudon reproduced four of the smaller ones in his *Encyclopedia* and demonstrated how easily they could be adapted for use as small villas.[37] He was one of the advanced spirits of his day and an enthusiastic advocate of the principles of picturesque design, which he did much to popularize. His influence was close and direct upon his friend and American counterpart, A. J. Downing. To all the proponents of the picturesque, its merit lay in dispelling monotony by means of variety, intricacy, roughness, irregularity, and movement.

Thompson's epoch-making Derby Trijunct Station illustrates the architectural problem involved in a long one-sided station (Fig. 19). The central motive is a pavilion with an arched recess framing the main entrance, something like Soane's terminal motives at the Dulwich Gallery. Once established, this motive is repeated at intervals and in diminishing sizes, sometimes with doors, sometimes with niches. The roundheaded motive was repeated along the sides of the train-shed. In spite of the unity and simplicity of the scheme, however, nothing could mitigate the fact that though the façade was 1,050 feet long, it was only forty feet high. Thompson escaped from this dilemma a few years later at his Chester station by multiplying the number of towers, a notable example of Vanbrugh's influence.

William Tite experimented with the new style at Nine Elms, 1838 (Fig. 20), where a tall arcade of five arches stands between projecting rusticated wings, surmounted by an attic. The detail tends to coarseness: the window frames are in high relief and the modillions have the visual impact of brackets. The iron work of his shed, however, is sure and solid. A bold, elongated capital was devised because the conditions did not permit him to follow classical proportions (Fig. 13).

The next step, the asymmetrical addition of a campanile, was taken by Thomas Turner at the London Bridge Station of the South Eastern Railway (Fig. 21). We are told that "the Italian Palazzo style . . . is the prevailing one in the company's buildings; the choice having been determined by the convenience of its general arrangement, its cheapness and the suitability of its picturesque decorations to the bustling character of a railway site . . . the campanile made here to serve the useful purpose of a clock tower—is

37. John Claudius Loudon, *Encyclopedia of Cottage, Farm and Villa Architecture* (London, 1833, supplement of 1842), §2299. He states that Francis Thompson published a volume called *Railway Stations* (London, 1842) consisting of nine plates, but no copy of this volume has been found; two of the plates, however, exist in the William Barclay Parsons Collection at Columbia University. These are handsome colored lithographs (see Figs. 16, 19). S. Russell made lithograph views of some of Thompson's other stations, copies of which exist at Harvard.

certainly a striking and appropriate feature." [38] Cubitt's station at Bricklayer's Arms had seven arched gateways twenty-two feet high with exaggerated keystones, cantilevered roofs of red Venetian tiles on sturdy brackets, and an arcaded belfry. There are reminiscences from *Villa rustica* in the details, though nothing is copied exactly. This station was described as being in the "Italian Style more properly called the 'English Railroad Style.' " [39] In the same year, 1844, a far more extensive station was completed at Leipzig by E. Pötsch in the same idiom (Fig. 22). The train-shed opened toward the street with four large arcades, and spur lines were continued through them to a turn-table in the open air, thus enabling the age-old fraternity of sidewalk superintendents to watch the still novel operation of moving cars and engines from one track to another. The Leipzig arcade was flanked by a pair of towers and, on either side, a triplet of arches connected the tower to office and apartment blocks. These were treated as small *palazzi,* creating a façade of considerable complexity, plasticity, and variety. To judge by old prints, the result was harmonious and functionally expressive. There were enough other stations in this style, both in Europe and America, to justify the claim that this was an international, rather than an English, railroad style. During the first decade of station building in Europe the styles were used in the following proportions: classic 3, Italian villa 2, Gothic 2, all others 1; whereas during the second decade, the ratios shift as follows: Italian villa 5, Gothic 2, and all others 3.

The railroad style was but one of many eclecticisms adapted for depot use at a time when only a tiny current of rationalism was detectable. Stations rarely exhibited the brilliant frankness of construction seen in the Hungerford Market or the Crystal Palace; one exception, Fox and Henderson's station at Oxford in 1851–52, used metal and glass like the Crystal Palace of the same years, but it was unique among stations.[40] Generally, as we have seen, such boldness was confined to the train-sheds; very occasionally, it was carried further as though in deference to Ruskin's admonition: "better bury gold in the embankments than put it in ornaments on the stations. . . . You would not put rings on the fingers of the smith at his anvil." [41]

The lessons of the train-shed—the most original and efficient part of railroad architecture, which might have induced a new aesthetic in which mass

38. *Illustrated London News, 55* (Feb. 3, 1844), 75.

39. *Illustrated London News, 55* (May 4, 1844), 284.

40. This station is illustrated in Hitchcock, *Early Victorian Architecture in Britain, 2,* 10, pl. 16.

41. *The Seven Lamps of Architecture* (London, 1849), pp. 110 ff.

would melt away and space would flow—went unheeded. Elsewhere, transparent enclosures, the attenuations inherent in metal, did not become acceptable until the 20th century; it was not possible earlier to escape from the tradition that limited architecture to masonry and massiveness.

There were those like Humphreys who asserted that it was the duty of railway architecture to "reassure the timid traveller." [42] This obligation could be fulfilled by using familiar shapes, often those with domestic associations. Such a point of view was reinforced by the growing cult of the picturesque: many stations looked as though their designers had cottages in mind; the Germans lined their tracks with chalets; the English often leaned toward Jacobean, as in Sancton Wood's stations in the eastern counties, and even the power plants of the Croydon Atmospheric Railway were disguised as Tudor villas to make them more acceptable. Cluysenaar, the Belgian railway architect, explained that his designs were intended to increase the variety of aspects and impressions which one seeks from travel; "too often ennui results on a route of which the succeeding structures are uniform." [43] Apparently the unassisted natural landscape was not considered sufficiently beguiling. He attempted to raise his red brick stations above mere utility by trimmings of bluestone, red, blue, and black slates, balconies, trellised gables, and brackets.[44] Such stations appealed to A. J. Downing: "the smaller ones are almost always built in the style of the cottage ornée—and, indeed, are some of the prettiest and most picturesque rural buildings that I have seen in England. They all have their little flower-gardens, generally a parterre lying open quite to the edge of the rail, and looking like a gay carpet thrown on the greensward." [45] The fascinating aspects of the vernacular stations, numbered in the tens of thousands, could easily beguile us from the main story. They remain to amuse and delight us today, a characteristic expression of the sentimental attitude toward rural architecture.[46]

Though it is difficult to recapture the train of thought which justified the use of Egyptian forms for the depot, one argument has come down to us. W. J. Short proposed the Egyptian style for a station at Kennington Common in 1836 because "it was most suitable for engineering purposes . . . its

42. "Fragments from a Provincial Tour," p. 677.

43. J. P. Cluysenaar, *Bâtiments de chemins de fer* (Paris, 1862), p. 6.

44. J. M. Richards has described the corresponding English stations: "Domesticating the Iron Horse," *Architectural Review, 91* (1942), 129 ff.

45. *Rural Essays* (New York, 1853), pp. 542–3.

46. Contrasting modern attitudes toward these small stations are recorded by Angela Thirkell in her novel *Before Lunch* (London, 1940), pp. 25–7.

few and bold details not requiring nice or expensive work or materials . . . not much knowledge of architecture would be needed to supervise the erection." [47] Similar arguments were used to justify the Italian villa style; in fact, they are likely to be heard whenever there is a shortage of craftsmen and an urgent need for buildings. Their "functionalism" is an unconvincing set of rationalizations cloaking emotional preferences.

Gothic, which in its more creative Victorian version would supersede the Italian villa as *the* railroad style, was not frequently resorted to for large stations; until the Houses of Parliament were well along, it was generally regarded as unsuitable for monumental purposes. Two exceptions—Brunel's major stations—are medieval, and his choice of Gothic for one of them, in Georgian Bath, was a curious one. The architect Goodridge, building the Lansdowne Tower there for William Beckford in 1826, used a classic mode even though Beckford had previously built the fabulous Gothic revival Fonthill Abbey; but apparently Brunel considered medieval Bath Abbey a more important precedent than the Georgian Circus and Crescents. At Bristol too Brunel used Gothic for what came to be known as the first large station to be well built and carefully planned. It is rich with turrets, buttresses, and battlements modeled after Rickman's recently completed St. John's College. The magnificent hammer-beam roof of the train-shed has been mentioned.

During two decades of rocket-like development, the new architectural problem had evoked scores of experimental solutions. Like those of nature, many were not destined for survival. Others were to prove fruitful by establishing patterns which would endure for the rest of the century.

Provincial America

In America the physical circumstances were wholly different. Miles of poorly built track connected the widely separated coastal cities and reached back into the Middle West. The available capital, much of it foreign, had to go into track, bridges, and tunnels. Huge terminals were hardly needed; the early stations were therefore much smaller than European ones. The station at Stratford, Connecticut (Fig. 23), is typical of those built in small towns throughout the United States during the whole of the railroad era. An architect was rarely employed. Generally the company engineer provided the plans, which were then used repeatedly, sometimes for forty years without change. Such shelter as was provided over the platform came from the over-

47. *Architectural Magazine, 3* (1836), 219.

hanging eaves extended much farther than usual; these eaves became an identifying characteristic of stations.

Chauvinism would tend to attribute some outstanding qualities to experimental American stations, but the conscientious historian fails to find supporting evidence. Even though some cities in the United States were about the size of provincial European ones, their stations were inferior in design, material, and convenience. It was not until the building of the old Grand Central Station in New York in 1869 that America had a single station capable of standing comparison with the finest European ones. The pictorial evidence, hardly controvertible, is supported, furthermore, by literary evidence. Perdonnet could properly say that most small American passenger stations seemed temporary: they were built of wood, were uncovered, and usually consisted of a single room; a whole station might be no more than fifty feet long.[48] Conditions seem not to have improved very much by the 1880's: Ringwalt reports that American stations "are, as a rule, conspicuous by the absence of the accommodation and convenience which characterize the stations on English or continental railways . . . little more than rough sheds giving shelter, while absence of platforms and railway officials tends still further to mark the characteristics of these stopping places." [49] The emphasis at first was upon the building of the lines, then upon structures to house the precious equipment, and finally—if funds permitted—upon passenger stations. A timetable of 1837 says, "A through train for the accommodation of western passengers will leave the vicinity of Broad and Callowhill Streets . . ." [50] As in England, often the only provision for the comfort of passengers was afforded by taverns. Illustrations of station taverns are numerous. One on the Philadelphia, Germantown, and Norristown Railway was a two-storied building, residential in character and scale, parallel to the line with a piazza for shelter. Such buildings continued in use without modification for decades. Elsewhere old houses were adapted to serve as stations. In 1835 the Baltimore and Ohio Company remodeled a three-story brick house to serve as the first depot in the national capitol. Tailor and cabinetmaker shops were moved out and the two lower floors were opened up into a single room. A belfry was added and a car shed was built nearby. This makeshift served Washington for fifteen years until it was replaced by a new building in the Italian villa style.

Wholly new stations were of several types: (1) domestic, (2) temple,

48. *Traité élémentaire, 2,* 403.

49. J. L. Ringwalt, *Development of Transportation Systems in the United States* (Philadelphia, 1888), p. 309.

50. Quoted in E. P. Alexander, *The Pennsylvania Railroad: a Pictorial History* (New York, Norton, 1947), p. 84.

(3) train-barn. An example of the first type was built at Frederick, Maryland (Fig. 24). These stations were domestic and vernacular in character, distinguished from the modest buildings among which they stood only by their belfries and clocks. If the company had more ambitious ideas, they adopted the second type and modeled the depots after small Greek temples.[51] The tracks ran through the side of the building under one gallery of the peristyle, and the remainder of the area was used for waiting rooms and offices. The third or train-barn type—stable for the iron horse—was popular in America, though comparatively rare in Europe. In this type also the station and train-shed were combined in one compact block, but instead of rolling along the side, the trains went through large doorways in the center. The engines were housed within the station at night and there seemed to be a fear that they might run loose unless secured. Some municipalities, for example Lynn, demanded that doors be provided; but too often the doors were demolished by rash engineers who either did not wait for the doors to be opened or did not stop their engines quickly enough. Except for the presence of trains instead of hay wagons, a train-barn was indistinguishable from a substantial farm barn. So simple and compact a structure was entirely adequate to the operating needs of early American railways, since there were only a few trains a day and none at all at night. The first station at Syracuse, New York, was typical (Fig. 25). It was built over the tracks, which ran down the middle of the main street (street-level tracks continued in use until recently). There it stood, an obstacle to local traffic, until one Sunday morning in 1869: a new station in a less inconvenient location had finally been provided, and a pair of engines were attached to the old one and pulled it crashing down.

This station and the double train-barn at Schenectady may be compared with a British example, the Great Western station at Exeter St. Thomas (Fig. 26). In all three, classic pediments and pilasters were adapted and modified to the new form. In the American ones, the roof ventilators were decoratively handled. The formal setting of the Schenectady station with its accessory buildings, pergolas, and ornamental gates is unusually elaborate for its time and place (Fig. 27). The train-barn type survived for many years as the much later example at Hanover, Connecticut, indicates (Fig. 28).

Wood, the most readily available material, was used for stations even though combining a wooden building and a locomotive was as risky as smoking in a hay rick. The Schenectady station burned in the winter of 1842–43 when it was less than a decade old, and a station in East Boston burned down the day it opened. Train-barns were later built in a less derivative and

51. One example of this type—at Lowell, Massachusetts—is described above, p. 27. Numerous other examples include stations at Salem, Haverhill, and Worcester, Massachusetts; Woonsocket, Rhode Island; and Utica, New York.

less inflammable manner. Their low shed roofs must have been oppressive; the engine fuel was wood until the 1860's, but even so the interiors became sooty and smelly; and the arrival of coal made conditions still worse.

Large cities received stations of a somewhat more permanent and ambitious character. Boston, the first railroad center in the United States, had six lines fanning out from it and six terminal stations. Even in the 1830's these were built of brick or stone with wooden sheds adjoining. The Boston and Lowell Station, 1835 (Fig. 29) was two-storied with arched openings across the front and a shed forming an "L." It may have been designed by Richard Upjohn, who did some unspecified work for the company in 1834–35.[52] Boston stations included several of the head type, of which the most splendid was the Haymarket Station, 1844–45 (Fig. 30). For its time and place it was enormous. Across the imposing façade ranged ten colossal Corinthian pilasters under a pediment. The architect may have been George M. Dexter, who had a busy practice in railroad architecture. His better known successor, Nathaniel Bradlee, enlarged the station in 1867.[53] In the original plan of 1845 two spur lines came into the building under a low wooden shed with a span of 78 feet. Planned for future growth, the upper floor of the main block was at first occupied by a carpet store.

The Boston station of the Old Colony Railroad on Kneeland Street, 1847 (Fig. 31) was the most completely equipped American station of its day. It had a lofty gaslit smoking room equipped with inside shutters, a popular barber shop, telegraph office, newsstand, lavatory, bootblack, and check room. It is possible that the architect was Gridley J. F. Bryant, though he may only have conducted the improvements of 1867. It was in this station in 1852 that the practice of paying a small fee for the privilege of checking baggage was introduced. It was expected that this would discourage the growing practice of leaving parcels for weeks at a time; instead, it led to a storm of protest and had to be abandoned.[54]

American stations showed as much diversity of plan as their European counterparts. All types were represented. A contemporary description of an example of the one-sided type is of interest. The Hudson River Railroad Depot at Tenth Avenue and 30th Street, New York (Fig. 32), was built in 1860–61

52. Everard M. Upjohn, *Richard Upjohn* (New York, Columbia University Press, 1939), p. 218.

53. See the discussion in my "Some Early Depot Drawings," *Journal of The Society of Architectural Historians, 8* (1949), 33 ff.

54. See Walter H. Kilham, *Boston after Bulfinch* (Cambridge, Harvard University Press, 1946), p. 66; and Charles E. Fisher, *The Story of the Old Colony Railroad* (Taunton, 1919), pp. 138 ff.

as the terminus of the line. It was described in the *New York Tribune,* February 19, 1861, as follows:

> The new depot of the Hudson River Railroad on 30th Street will be opened for the first time today. It is not a very imposing structure though well adapted for the purpose for which it was designed. It is of brick, is 200 feet long by 28 feet in width, with a roof projecting 15 feet over the platform in the rear. There are two entrances in front, one for ladies and one for gentlemen. In the center is the ticket office. At the east end is the ladies' sitting room and toilet occupying one third of the building. West of the ticket office is the gentlemen's room, telegraph office and baggage room. Over the ticket office is a spacious refreshment room.

It is surprising that a metropolitan terminal for a railroad which had been open since 1851 should be so primitive, lacking even a rudimentary shed. It ceased to be the line's principal station ten years later when the company moved into the (relatively) stupendous new Grand Central Station on 42d Street.

The type of station using two levels is illustrated by the first New Haven station in 1848–49 (Figs. 34–36). There was a shed, a bridge over the cut, and stairs down to narrow platforms. Although the street-level building with towers and pergolas was carefully studied and highly original, the operating parts, cramped and airless, were so inadequate that it was remodeled twice during its first two years. The inadequacies are shown by the reaction of a little boy, brought up in the Calvinist way, who got off the train there soon after it was opened. Finding himself engulfed in smoke and darkness, he clutched his father's hand and asked, "Is this hell?" "No, my son," his father replied, "New Haven." [55]

This station was the first important American example of the railroad style. Its architect, Henry Austin, was following the new European fashion, which was superseding the temple style. He designed two other stations in railroad style in 1847, small ones for Plainville and Collinsville, Connecticut. [56] All three of Austin's stations have Moorish details which he was introducing in other buildings at that time. These had been used only once before in railway architecture, in the Moorish arch on the Liverpool and Manchester Railway (1830). The Collinsville depot was the more massive of the two.

55. George Dudley Seymour, *New Haven* (New Haven, 1942), p. 291.

56. The drawings are preserved in Sterling Memorial Library at Yale. These stations were rectangular blocks 40 by 20 feet, set upon low platforms with lower blocks attached containing earth closets. The waiting rooms for ladies and gentlemen were separated by an office and vestibule. At Collinsville the platform was protected by a flaring cantilevered roof. At Plainville the roof was supported by closely spaced wooden posts.

There is a pleasant solidity and dignity about it. Its coarse detail and louvered cupola recall Francis Thompson's minor stations, which Austin may have known, since he owned a copy of Loudon's *Encyclopedia* in which they were published.

A contemporary description of the New Haven station expresses the enthusiasm of the period toward its new transportation and all that was connected with it:

> The beautiful edifice . . . is situated in Union Street and occupies the entire square from Chapel to Cherry Street being 300 feet in length. The style of architecture is Italian . . . with a tower at each end . . . that to the North rises to an altitude of 140 feet above the pavement. . . . In this latter tower are the Engineer's rooms, and the office of the company. . . . The Main or central edifice is a parallelogram, 100 feet in depth, with a floor or platform suspended from the roof by numerous strong iron rods. . . . The grand entrance for passengers is from Union Street, by a spacious doorway. . . . On either side of the main hall or platform, are extensive Parlors, that on the left side being for the accommodation of ladies and is furnished with a profusion of rich and costly sofas, divans, chairs, ottomans, mirrors, etc., with convenient dressing rooms attached. Obliging servants are always in attendance. The Parlor on the right is for gentlemen's use, and is to be furnished as a Reading Room. . . . The Ticket Office is on the left side of the grand hall, with ornamental windows of ground glass, one of which opens into the Ladies' Parlor. . . . In the North Tower, at an elevation of 90 feet above the street, is a clock, with glazed faces 8 feet in diameter looking toward the four cardinal points. This clock is to be illuminated with gas. . . . Twenty feet above the clock a large bell is suspended, the ringing of which indicates the arrival and departure of the trains or cars. A watchman being stationed in the building at night, this bell is usually the first to sound its note of alarm in cases of fire. . . . The design of this beautiful structure, which reflects the highest credit on the architect . . . was furnished by Henry Austin, Esq. . . . Its cost to the railroad was upwards of $40,000. Long may it stand as an enduring monument to the taste, the liberality and the enterprise of its projectors.[57]

While the plan was almost perfectly symmetrical, the elevation was not. Fantasy began above the cornice. Austin placed a campanile at one end (it was the first American station with a campanile), a truncated pagoda over

57. *Benham's City Directory and Annual Advertiser, 1849–50,* No. 10 (New Haven, 1849), pp. 7–8.

the main entrance, and at the far left an anomalous feature which synthesizes elements from the other two. To the conventional roundheaded arches and brackets of the Italian villa style he has added Indian and Chinese motives. Richard Upjohn had introduced a campanile in his King Villa at Newport in 1845–46 and since Austin kept up with the literature in his field and subscribed to the illustrated English journals, he probably knew of the earlier stations with asymmetrically placed campaniles.[58] Among the English architects, only John Nash would have dared to combine so many styles in one building. In spite of the exuberance of the detail, the long, low lines with extended eaves on robust brackets served to keep the whole in equipoise. A dramatic experiment, Austin's station was followed rapidly by other stations in the Italian villa style. But it soon became outmoded and was superseded by a second one in 1874, surviving as a market for many years before it met a violent end by fire in 1896.

There is a modest station at Norton, Massachusetts, by Richard Upjohn, for which the drawings dated 1852–53 are preserved at the Avery Library in Columbia University. The sturdy detail and proportions show its derivation from Francis Thompson's stations. The elevation is reproduced in Fig. 37.

The important railroad style was supplemented here and there by Egyptian or Gothic designs. Great latitude in the interpretation of these stylistic labels was tolerated. Perhaps the main idea was not scholarly accuracy but, as in Europe, to invest the architecture of the often frightening new mode of transportation with the reassuring garb of traditional forms. Several small stations illustrate this. The Greek formula of columns *in antis* was employed at New Bedford, Massachusetts (Fig. 38), built before 1840, and in Pittsfield (1846). In the former the columns were derived from Edfu and in the latter they were Greek. Both were designated Egyptian by their contemporaries.[59] Another instance of ambiguity of style is Gridley Bryant's station of 1847 at Salem, Massachusetts (Fig. 39). The flattened arch over the tracks is flanked by a pair of towers which can be interpreted as either villa or Norman style.[60] The polygonal masonry adds another curious note of historicism with its air of seeking after the primitive.[61]

58. Examples include London Bridge (1840–44), Dover (1844), Colchester (1846), and Victoria Station, Norwich (1849)

59. These monumental motives were executed in wood. Wooden buildings rarely fall into pleasing decay, and in its old age the New Bedford station merely looked battered. The Pittsfield one burned to the ground in 1854 in half an hour.

60. Compare the towers at Leipzig, Fig. 22; see also Figs. 65 and 66.

61. The design of this station is sometimes attributed to the president of the company, D. A. Neal, but as in so many similar instances his role was probably confined to instruct-

The Gothic style, so notably adapted by Brunel for use in British stations, was less often employed in early American ones. It will suffice to mention the station and warehouses in Charleston, South Carolina, and the Fitchburg station in Boston, Massachusetts. None of these was a serious Gothic exercise; the spirit was closer to that of garden follies. Gothic such as that which clothed the wooden station at Stratford, Connecticut (Fig. 23) was derived from the cottage ornée.

The experimentation of the 1830's and early 1840's was gradually replaced by slower, more orderly progress. Enough schemes had been tried. A few dominant types were beginning to emerge. The remaining decade of the early phase would witness the erection of more maturely conceived stations. Their architectural form, as distinguished from the engineering elements, would be closely integrated with 19th-century architectural trends as a whole.

---

ing the architect. The original wooden roof of the train-shed burned in 1882, and there were other changes with the years; nevertheless it is regrettable that this venerable station could not be preserved from demolition as a memorial to early American industry.

3. STANDARDIZATION

(THE 1850'S)

A Stable Situation

During the late 1840's and the 1850's the railroad station ceased to be a novelty. The experimental period had been relatively short. Station architecture fell into step with the current phase of the picturesque eclectic style. The railroad style was in the ascendant. It marked the transition from the period of the strict revivals to the period of synthetic eclecticism. The desired visual effects were admirably recorded in lithography by numerous British and French illustrators.

Conditions during the 1850's favored a tranquil progress in the arts. The reforms of the Peel and Gladstone administrations were bearing fruit. The Crystal Palace Exhibition of 1851 focused attention on the flourishing state of England. On the Continent, too, conditions were satisfactory: Leopold I was completing the modernization of Belgium; France prospered after Napoleon III came to power, to judge by the increase in the population of Paris and by the exhibits at the Fair of 1855; the unification of Germany was well under way. Stabilized governments ruled nearly everywhere, and the business cycle reflected this calm security. There was no major world-wide economic collapse until 1873.

The historians of the railroad hold that its second phase began about 1850. H. G. Lewin places the second period of British railways between 1845 and 1852 and calls it a time of consolidation following a period of speculative frenzy.[1] Vernon Sommerfield observed that in terms of technical advance a second period began in 1850.[2] In America the year 1850 also marked a turning point: the end of the experimental stage.[3] During the following decade,

1. *The Railway Mania and Its Aftermath, 1845–1852* (London, 1936), pp. xvi–xviii.

2. *English Railways* (London, 1937), p. xix.

3. John Moody, *The Railroad Builders,* Chronicles of America, 32, New Haven, 1920. See also Slason Thompson, *A Short History of American Railways,* Chicago, 1925.

the national wealth doubled—a more rapid rate of increase than in any sub-sequent decade. By this time the land east of the Mississippi was connected by long lines from Bangor to Savannah and from Chicago to New Orleans. The canal system was beginning to decline. Commuting by railroad was abetting the flight to the suburb.

Numerous mechanical improvements were introduced. Modern types of "T" rails were replacing the murderous strap iron ones which had too often worked loose to spring up and pierce unlucky passengers. The roadbeds were re-engineered with wider curves. Permanent bridges took the place of earlier makeshifts. Cumbersome, dangerous inclines were being abandoned as tunnels could be afforded. Headlight reflectors made night operation feasible. Wood-burning locomotives were being given up and the more economical coal was coming into general use, in spite of its filth. The horrors attendant upon the transformation of the countryside into industrial belts—"the cinder strip" —were about to appear.

Stations were becoming more standardized. Waiting rooms and offices were arranged in a thin ribbon parallel to the tracks. This practice was so stand-ard that in a station serving several companies the ribbon was unrolled far enough to provide each company with a section of rooms. Every major station now provided covered access to trains and to cabs by means of either arcades or marquees. Waiting rooms grew larger and more monumental.

The directors of the London and Birmingham Railway, who had set one precedent with their "Great Arch" at Euston, now set another: in the late 1840's they built a new "Grand Hall" at Euston (Fig. 41) on empty land west of the original building. The architect, Philip Charles Hardwick, was the son of the author of the Euston Arch. He built a richly decorated hall. Its Ionic columns were painted dark red in imitation of granite. The upper walls were adorned with low reliefs. An elaborate staircase led up to a gallery in front of the private offices. The adjoining booking offices alone were nearly as large as the original station. The imposing hall, which is still standing, was imitated almost at once in other stations. The needs of departing passengers thus handsomely taken care of on the departure side of the building, better provision for arriving passengers followed on the other side: they were accom-modated with enclosed waiting rooms, baggage rooms, and covered cab ranks.

The architects' problems were intensifying because even though freight traffic was no longer handled in the same building with passenger traffic, the passenger station was growing in size and complexity. Hotels and office buildings were coming to be housed in the same complex. New stations were gigantic compared with those of twenty years earlier. In the belief that a permanent size had been reached, these new stations were well and carefully constructed, with the intention of forestalling the need of future rebuilding;

but actually this goal was never reached. The most optimistic forecasts of the future volume of traffic always proved conservative.

We can judge the standards for station design reached in the 1850's from the observations made by a prominent engineer, Robert Jacomb Hood.[4] He recommended that platforms be from thirty to forty feet in width and as long as possible, paved, raised about two feet above the level of the rails, roofed, and free of columns. In a period characterized by two-sided plans, he argued that the head station was preferable. His sound reasons were to be borne out in the ultimate triumph of the type over its rivals. He conceded that the struggle to keep the classes of passengers separate had not been successful. He suggested that a charge be made for carrying luggage and that space for it should be booked in advance to save confusion and delay. He anticipated by half a century the modern criticism of wide-span train-sheds as extravagant and unnecessary and further suggested that the prevailing method of shifting cars and engines by means of turntables was inefficient and noisy. Switches were just coming into use for this purpose, but Hood advocated traversing frames which were adequate so long as the cars remained small enough to be managed by hand power. He was insistent that ample and convenient parking spaces, paved and roofed, should be provided. (It is doubtful if they were as badly needed then as they are today, or that he found any more receptive audience than today's planners find; private enterprise is still reluctant to bear the cost of adequate parking facilities, preferring to leave it to municipal authorities.) The ideal of keeping entrances and exits entirely separate seemed attainable then, but has never proved feasible. Hood's recommendations and criticisms show that high standards for railroad station planning had already been reached in thought, if less commonly in deed.

Ascendant Station Types

Three principal types of station were to be found during the last years of the pioneering period: one-sided, two-sided, and head. The merits of the two latter types were summed up in 1850 by the French architect and engineer Léonce Reynaud:[5] the advantages of the head station are that the building is

4. "On the Arrangement and Construction of Railroad Stations," *Minutes of the Proceedings of the Institution of Civil Engineers, 1857–1858, 17,* London, 1858. This paper was summarized in the *Builder, 16* (1858), 340 ff.

5. François Léonce Reynaud published *Traité d'architecture,* 2 vols. and atlas, Paris, 1850. The pertinent remarks begin on p. 464 of the 2d volume. Reynaud was the architect of two Parisian stations: the Gare d'Austerlitz (1843–47) and the Gare du Nord I (1845–47), and engineer for a third, the Gare du Nord II (1861–65). He was born in Lyon in 1803 and died there in 1880.

clearly visible, the entrances are clearly marked, the buildings are concentrated, the same vestibule may be used for arrival and departure, the concentrated services require less personnel, and the areas at the sides are free for expansion, while the principal merit of the two-sided station is that passengers and baggage move shorter distances without cross circulation. Reynaud gave general architectural advice to station builders also. All parts of a large station should be generously dimensioned: the platforms should err on the side of excessive width and be free of impediments, train-sheds should be bold and not require supports which would interfere with the activities underneath. Entrances and exits should be well marked, numerous, and easy to traverse.

He says nothing about the first type, one-sided, which was falling out of favor for terminal purposes because it had proved to be inferior to its rivals in convenience and flexibility. Under special circumstances, however, it was often the only feasible solution: the site at Newcastle-on-Tyne, for example, is on the edge of a bluff, thus limiting convenient access to one side. The one-sided station begun there in 1845 (Figs. 43, 44) proved to be one of the largest as well as one of the last of its type. It stands between an enormous vehicle court in front and curved tracks at the rear. There are three arched sheds each sixty feet wide resting on lofty, widely spaced columns. The effect of the glass-covered concentric vaults diminishing in the distance was new to the history of architecture.

The architect, John Dobson (1787–1865), had hoped to equal the works of Sir John Vanbrugh. The stone-built façade, 600 feet long, is interrupted by a colossal porte-cochere which projects boldly from it. The main order is forty feet high. When the design, including a model, was exhibited in Paris in 1855, it won a Medal of Honor for its author, though the original design was modified in execution to permit more office space and to cut costs. The existing porte-cochere with pilasters substituted for the intended columns was added at a later date by Thomas Prosser. Dobson apparently strove to arrange correct academic detail according to picturesque principles. Pavilions, towers, and arcades were used to animate the huge composition, which still seems impressively vigorous. The contemporary critic James Fergusson found a good deal to object to. He wrote:

> The Station at Newcastle, though very grand, and possessing some excellent points of design, is neither quite truthful nor quite appropriate. The great portico might as well be the entrance to a palace or theatre. The ornamentation has too much the character of being put there for ornament's sake alone . . . and what is worse, in order to give light to the rooms below, its roof must be either wholly or partially of glass, consequently its monumental forms at once become absurd. They are

such as would almost suffice for a vault—a few iron posts would have done as well for all they have to support.[6]

Modern critics, however, are kinder.[7] Actually, Newcastle station is one of Dobson's finest works and one of the most imposing stations of the period.

The second type, the two-sided station, predominated around the middle of the century. In fully developed examples, a range of buildings flanked each side of the lines, with each range including waiting rooms, baggage rooms, and a vehicle court. If these blocks were identical, the station belonged to a subgroup, the twin type. Usually the building for departing passengers was the more important one. It often had a monumental vestibule or booking office.[8] There is an exceptionally stately booking office at King's Cross Station, London. Separate waiting rooms were regularly provided for each class. Buffets and restaurants grew in size and popularity, and some of them became famous for their cuisine. Quarters of considerable size were often provided for royalty and customs offices.[9]

The chief defect of the two-sided plan appeared when the traffic could no longer be accommodated by one principal platform on each side. Intermediate ones were then added; but how could passengers safely reach or leave the inner platforms? Cross-platforms were rare and interfered with the movement of cars at the end of the shed. Some stations provided footbridges from the beginning and others added them. At Paddington, Brunel installed retractable drawbridges, which could be lowered and stored under the platforms when not in use. This was a clumsy device, since while in place they blocked the movement of trains; even so, passengers found them preferable to climbing over footbridges.[10] In the 1850's some stations had as many as fourteen lines under their sheds, the majority allocated to standing cars; but increased traffic required more active use of the whole shed. King's Cross, which at

6. *History of the Modern Styles of Architecture* (1st ed. 2 vols. London, 1862), *2,* 480–1.

7. Hitchcock, *Early Victorian Architecture in Britain, 1,* 521–2.

8. Its dimensions are 100 by 40 by 40 feet.

9. The list of important examples of two-sided stations includes: Liverpool, Lime Street II, William Tite, 1846–49; Paris, Gare Montparnasse, Victor Lenoir, 1850–52; London, King's Cross, Lewis Cubitt, 1850–52; London, Paddington II, Brunel and Wyatt, 1852–55; Leipzig, Thüringer Bahnhof II, Brandt, 1855–56; Vienna, Nord Bahnhof, Stummer and others, 1855–56; Vienna, West Bahnhof, Bayr and others, 1858–60; Paris, Gare d'Austerlitz II, Léonce Reynaud, 1859–62; Copenhagen, Central Station, J. D. Herholdt, 1863–64.

10. A cross-platform was not feasible at Paddington since the area at the end of the lines, between the shed and the hotel, was used for car storage. It was ironically called "The Lawn." Eventually this use of The Lawn was given up. Cars were stored in a separate yard far outside the station and a cross-platform was built.

first operated only thirteen trains a day, managed for some time with only outer platforms.

At this time the third type, the head station, was comparatively rare, although it was to become the dominant type during the next period. The French were the first to create a model station of the head type. This landmark was the Gare de l'Est in Paris, built in 1847–52 from designs by the architect François Duquesney (1800–49). In its prime, and long after, it was acclaimed as the finest station in the world, and there seems to be no reason even now to quarrel with this judgment. In 1865 it was hailed as "the most striking example of railroad architecture." [11] The English critic Fergusson, quoted above in reference to the Newcastle Station, said that the Gare de l'Est is "perfectly appropriate to the purpose." [12] But by the 1890's it was beginning to be regarded patronizingly. "It has long been considered a masterpiece. The scheme is direct, the vaulting of the hall looks very well. The management of the company has a great affection for it, and it has had its hour of fame." [13]

As has been mentioned, the plan owes its best features to the earlier Gare du Nord I (Fig. 47), completed in 1847 by Léonce Reynaud. This station is little known, since it was replaced within sixteen years by the present, larger Gare du Nord II. The great step is the provision of a *salle des pas perdus* —concourse or vestibule—in the head-building, through which passengers could move back and forth at will from one platform to another, entering or leaving without interfering with the operation of the trains and without crossing any tracks. In both stations, wings formed a "U" with the departure side on the left and the arrival side on the right (Figs. 47, 48). Each wing contained waiting rooms and baggage rooms and had its own vehicle court. The area between the wings was covered by wide sheds, neatly held in a lithic embrace. The plan of the second Gare du Nord in Paris is an enlargement and modification of the plan of the first (Fig. 49). The original waiting rooms had been proportionately small, implying that trains waited at the platforms long in advance of departure time. The shed of the second station was much wider, covering eight lines and four platforms; but the number of lines soon had to be increased, and the "U" plan did not permit new lines to be added parallel with the old ones. It was therefore necessary to move the offices and waiting rooms out of the wings, where space was made for them by cutting back the lines and platforms and increasing the depth of the head-house. Then, the platforms could occupy the whole width of the site, and the plan resembled that of the first Gare du Nord more closely.

11. Perdonnet, *Traité élémentaire, 2,* 492.

12. *History of the Modern Styles of Architecture,* p. 417.

13. Léon Benouville, in Planat's *Encyclopédie de l'architecture* (Paris, n.d.), *4,* Pt. II, 735.

The obvious merit of the plan led to rapid imitation of it. In Paris the old Gare St. Lazare was remodeled to incorporate a concourse and wider shed, so that Paris then had three stations of this advanced type.

The head stations represent the high point in station planning at the mid-century. What of the enclosing architecture? Reynaud's views express his rationalism and imagination. He recognized that the station was a new problem created by the new century; "it was the spontaneous consequence of one of the most admirable inventions of the epoch opening up new horizons, new materials and new forms." In his opinion there was no single station that could be called a model since they all lacked either good form or, more important, a good plan. He did not think the time had arrived for monumentalizing them. Stations should be built solidly but without excess. There was no reason why stone should be used or even be noticeable. "Iron," he said, "forms the rails and should have a part in the building they give rise to. It would be appropriate to glorify in some way the precious material to which industry has just given birth and which has, perhaps, endowed architecture with the most beneficial invention of the epoch." [14] Few stations made much effort toward the expression of the precious new invention excepting in their train-sheds.

Room-Streets

Reflecting the quality of station planning at this time, the train-shed too made notable advances. The arched train-shed of the Gare de l'Est which dominated the whole complex represents the ideal shed of the 1850's (Figs. 50, 51). Here, the traditional solemn character of vast halls was transformed at one stroke. Self-contained and almost semicircular, it created a static interior space. The glass of the vault allowed light to flood the interior as never before had been possible, so that the old distinction between a ceilinged room and an unroofed street was dissolved. From this moment on such "room-streets" became a familiar sight in great cities. The ratio of the width of this shed to its height approached that model of classic proportions, the Pantheon. The walls rose fifty feet to support the ribs—so high that the architect, fearing the ribs might exert a thrust which would push such lofty walls over, insisted that the danger be removed by tying the arches with rods (which, however, were so light as to be visually insignificant). The pure curve of the arched ribs defined the vault. This splendidly conceived and carefully preserved space is still impressive.

The favored arch of the mature period was semicircular in shape. Some-

14. *Traité d'architecture*, 2, 469.

times iron was used, as in the Gare de l'Est. Sometimes laminated wood was preferred, as in bridges at Ouseburn and Willington Dene. The wooden arches of the Crystal Palace in London spanned seventy-two feet; subsequently, at the Alexandra Palace, similar ribs spanned eighty-five feet. Both of these spans were surpassed by those of the twin sheds at King's Cross, which were 105 feet wide (Fig. 52). In 1869–70 the deterioration of the wood from the combined effects of steam and smoke was so advanced that the wooden ribs were replaced by arched steel ones, which were fitted into the original iron shoes and may still be seen in place. Wooden-arch train-sheds rose on the Continent also. That of the Hauptbahnhof in Munich spanned eighty feet (Fig. 53). Its principals flowed cleanly from one side to the other, starting and ending at the level of the platforms, and elaborately ornamented spandrels braced the ribs. Heavy and solemn in effect, the Munich train-shed fell short of producing the majestic effect achieved at King's Cross.

The practice of using wood for train-shed roofs was comparatively short-lived, since the double needs for greater permanence and wider span were better met by using metal. In the 1940's, however, when the war restricted the use of metal and new methods of fabrication in wood were available, wide-span arches of wood were revived for many purposes.

A century ago experimentation in trusses was as lively as it is today in space-frames. The sickle girder or crescent truss was one of the favorite types: an outstanding example was designed by the engineer E. A. Cowper for the shed of the New Street Station in Birmingham, 1854 (Fig. 54). Its widest point was 211 feet, but since the site did not permit this width to be continued throughout, some of the trusses were shorter. In France a somewhat different system for truss construction, the Polonceau system,[15] was widely used in Parisian stations. In most British-designed trusses the stiffeners or struts were perpendicular to the lower chord, whereas in the Polonceau system they were perpendicular to the rafters (Fig. 55).

Another French engineer, Engène Flachat (1802–73), built several fine train-sheds in Paris, including a new shed for the old Gare Montparnasse, which spanned 131 feet. There for the first time plates and angle irons were used instead of the rods and struts; ultimately this practice replaced all others. Flachat's sheds at the Gare St. Lazare were the subject of numerous paintings by Monet.[16] French train-sheds tended to be narrower and lighter looking than British ones. Reynaud praised the lightness of a cantilevered platform cover, but generally lightness was not admired as much as it is today. Rey-

15. Named for Antoine Remi Polonceau (1778–1847), the engineer who perfected it.

16. One, of 1877, is now in the Louvre. Another is in the Fogg Museum in Cambridge, Massachusetts.

naud complained that wrought iron trusses seemed "more amazing than re-assuring." He advocated instead the use of cast iron in trusses, which was no more expensive and of which the heaviness would be more harmonious with the bulk of columns in cast iron. He had proposed a single iron span of 110 feet for his Gare du Nord I; instead, two wooden spans, totaling 176 feet, were erected.[17]

The arched roof truss was aesthetically superior to these triangular trusses. Comparison of two roofs of nearly equal width, those of Paddington II and of Gare du Nord II, illustrates this (Figs. 55, 56): the stiff angularity of the latter is less pleasing than the graceful vaults at Paddington, where the inter-relationships of five elements—three naves intersected by two transepts—display a masterful handling of form and space. Arched principals were not economical; each part had to be fabricated individually, and standardized parts could not be used, although at a time when standardization was in its infancy this objection was less serious than it became later.[18] The use of arches persisted beyond the end of the century, encouraged by competition between rival railroads seeking to eclipse one another's spectacular train-sheds. The architecture of the whole station shared in this contest. Higher standards of design and greater splendor resulted.

In these new stations the main motive was sometimes an arch, sometimes a tower.

Arches and Towers

The new stations abounded with either arches, reflecting a conservative tendency, or towers, reflecting a progressive one. The arches were primarily semicircular, like those of the train-shed vaults, and the towers were stumpy and lacked spires. Horizontal and vertical elements were harmoniously balanced, but the undisturbed unity of the previous decades had been abandoned. In the search for more plasticity the building mass was fractured into subordinate parts which were then pulled, pushed, or piled together. This manipulation of form reflected the midpoint of the movement toward verticality. At this transitional moment, architects neither were entirely independent of academic rules nor yet dared to be as fully exuberant as they became in future decades. The influence of the picturesque doctrine had now

17. *Traité d'architecture, 2,* 465–575, and pl. 75 in the atlas.

18. The Crystal Palace, London, 1851, was the first dramatic demonstration of the economy and speed of erection obtainable from the use of standardized, interchangeable parts.

advanced to the extent that S. H. Brooks, the architect-author, could write: "It is evident that to introduce irregularity of form in building is an architectural refinement of the present age." [19] Regularity was thus marked down as the first of the academic rules to be overthrown. At this moment a combination of academic forms and picturesque composition was the limit of inventive possibility. The railroad style was one such combination.

All buildings of these years had a common configuration, whatever stylistic detail was employed; a practiced eye can often date a building accurately by its general shape. It seemed that man "needs some special shape to echo the harmony which, at that period, inhabits his spirit." [20] One of the obligations of the architectural historian is to identify the typical shape of each period—periods which occupy shorter and shorter units of time as they approach the present—and the typical shape of the period under consideration may be described as a group of blocks over which a grid of horizontal and vertical motives has been superimposed. The grid is made up of cornices and string courses interwoven with pilasters, buttresses, and chains of quoins, and it often frames and isolates various arched motives.

This configuration can be observed in five outstanding stations: the Gare de l'Est and the Gare du Nord II in Paris, King's Cross and Paddington in London, and the station at Chester in Cheshire. The most striking feature of the Gare de l'Est is the piercing of the façade by the end of the train-shed in an enormous arched window (Fig. 50); thus the finest and most important element of the plan is allowed to give character and meaning to the architecture. The arcade which stands below it marks the location of the *salle des pas perdus*. The wings end as a pair of flanking pavilions, and the gable over the axial window forms a splendid climax. At King's Cross, twin sheds were allowed to pierce the end wall as windows separated by a small tower (Fig. 57). Fergusson thought the Paris station clearly superior to the London one: "From its higher degree of ornamentation and its more artistic arrangement it becomes really an object of Architectural Art and one perfectly appropriate to its purpose without too great an amount of imitative features borrowed from any particular style." [21] To our eyes the sculpture, which receives part of this encomium, detracts from its worth, rather than increasing it as an object of architectural art, and is little superior to oversized mantel ornaments, which are more effective in malachite and ormolu than in stone.

The composition of the Gare de l'Est was adopted, somewhat timidly, at Munich (Fig. 58), with a small rose window replacing the more expressive

19. *Designs for Cottage and Villa Architecture* (London, 1839), p. viii.

20. Clark, *The Gothic Revival*, p. 253.

21. *History of the Modern Styles of Architecture*, 2, 417.

lunette. Both stations in their original form symbolize the ideal composition of the period, a clearly expressed dominant flanked by plastic lesser parts; but a century of rebuilding has marred the clarity of the original conceptions. At Munich as it was before World War II, the original parts remained on axis, with harmonious additions symmetrically disposed. At Paris the only space available for enlargement lay to the right; accordingly, the original composition was duplicated at the right end. The old and the new units became end pavilions connected by a long and uninteresting block, a composition characteristic of the late 19th century.

French, English, and Swiss stations featured commanding arches on the exterior. Two of the best are Victor Lenoir's (1805–63) Gare de Montparnasse (1850–52) in Paris and its exact contemporary, Lewis Cubitt's (1799–1883) King's Cross Station in London (Figs. 57, 59, 60). Lenoir's composition, gradually rising and exactly symmetrical, climaxed by a pylon rising above the twin arches, is more sophisticated than Cubitt's, but the main elements of the composition are the same and one wonders which design came first. The London one has some peculiarities. There is no preparation for the axial tower, which may have been an afterthought because it contains the clock made in 1851 by Lord Grimthorpe for the Crystal Palace Exhibition. The wings do not match. Both semicircular and segmental arches are used. Lenoir's design dramatically expresses his flat-roofed sheds by arched windows and gables, but Cubitt, whose vaulted sheds were among the finest ever erected, slices off the end of the building as though the windows lighted a flat-ceilinged hall.

Because King's Cross is the only large London station to reveal its sheds on the main front, it has received a disproportionate amount of praise from modern critics; in its day it had no influence. When it was new, Fergusson felt that "it suffered by comparison with Westminster Hall" and that insufficient attention had been paid to architectural effect, which reduced it to "engineer's architecture." [22] In line with the growing demand for more emphatic contrasts of light and shade, he also objects to the shallow reveals of the arches. In 1879 a number of changes were made, including a new carriage way across the end, thirty feet in height, adorned with blue and white cresting. By that time, taste having changed, the new feature was considered to "somewhat relieve its heavy and monotonous character." [23]

Arches became common on station façades. Hittorf's Gare du Nord II (Fig. 61) is a striking illustration of the manner in which the typical configuration of the period could be achieved without ostensible towers.

22. *Ibid.*, p. 413.

23. *Builder, 38* (1879), 1157.

Pairs of colossal pilasters supporting sculpture separate the arches, introducing strong vertical accents and breaking up the outline. The motives of the façade are arranged in the following sequence from left to right: pilasters, arch "a," pilasters, wing, pilasters, arch "a," pilasters, and a larger arch "b" on the axis. The sequence is repeated in reverse on the right-hand end. The three central arches stand before the three naves of the shed. Since the roof of the shed was not curved, the arches had only symbolic and associative value. To reflect the exact form of the shed on the façade would have required a pediment 238 feet wide, and so grotesque a distortion of a classic motive was too alarming to contemplate; nor was it possible at this time to invent a wholly new motive. The final result is not unlike the stucco-covered confectionary of a world's fair. Hemmed in by adjoining buildings, the front of the station cannot easily be seen as a whole. Its large scale and robust detail, however, make a powerful and often admired spectacle.

The multiple arches of the Gare du Nord II are recalled in the Zurich station of 1865–73 by J. F. Waner, originally called the Nordostbahnhof and now simply "the Bahnhof" (Fig. 62). The main entrance is a triumphal arch flanked by pavilions, each equipped with an individual roof. The shed rose up behind. Each of the nine major bays of its ridge and furrowed roof ended in a gable surmounting an arched window. Across the narrow end three towers frame a pair of gabled arches, a variation of Lenoir's composition. As it is today, the original one-sided layout has been changed: seven bays of the old shed form the present concourse, and new low sheds over spur tracks have been added. This basically classic station had been given variety and movement by combining and emphasizing standard motives.

These terminals, because of the nature of their plans, were long and low. The picturesque aesthetic condemned length and lowness as tending to monotony. Arches alone, whether spread over the whole extent or used as accents, were not able to supply sufficient variety and movement; but towers met the need.

The application of towers to his Chester Station (1847–48) rescued Francis Thompson from the difficulties he had experienced with his Derby Station (Fig. 63). Both buildings were over 1,000 feet long. In the later one the academic principle of emphasizing the central axis was dropped and the interest diffused over the whole length by the application of high and low blocks, each with its own pair of towers; this device brought about an amazing gain in variety and picturesqueness over the earlier Derby station. Congruent with the change in taste during the eight years which had elapsed since Derby was begun, the detail is richer and the arched forms are manipulated more freely, so that the result is more picturesque.

Thompson was perhaps overenthusiastic about the usefulness of towers, but the mania was spreading rapidly. In London, towers of a different origin were soon to adorn the façade of Paddington Station: the architects of the station and train-shed, Brunel and Sir Matthew Digby Wyatt, had set out valiantly "to avoid any recurrence to existing styles, and to try the experiment of designing everything in accordance with the structural purposes, or nature of the materials employed, iron and cement." [24] The laudable goal was not achieved, for the detail was borrowed from almost every ancient style, but it was recombined in an interesting and vigorous manner. Just how the collaboration was effected is not known; perhaps Wyatt had a share in determining the shape of the magnificent triple shed. The Praed Street frontage, reserved for the Great Western Railway Hotel (Fig. 64), was designed independently by a different architect, Philip Charles Hardwick, and is not connected to the station it hides from view. The hotel has French towers and is the one English railroad building of the 1850's which shows the influence of Lefuel's additions to the Louvre.[25] Hardwick used mansard roofs, both curved and straight, huge dormers, balconies, triplet-windows, and a tower seven stories in height. The result is very nearly as striking as its Paris prototype. Both buildings are as picturesquely managed as any in the Italian villa or Gothic idioms. If Lefuel had disapproved of the picturesque aesthetic, he could have modeled his work on Perrault's wing of the Louvre instead of Lemercier's. In Lemercier's and Lefuel's pavilions on the Louvre, caryatids continue the vertical rush of the superimposed orders which act like buttresses. The abundant detail, elongated proportions, and vertiginous roofs are the embodiment of picturesque principles. So striking a manner is hard to struggle against: Wyatt's and Brunel's station is found lurking ignominiously in the shadow of the dazzling hotel.

Towers came into general use all over Europe. They formed two of the five elements in the façade of the second Thüringer Bahnhof at Leipzig, 1855–56 (Fig. 65). There are fewer parts in this design than in that of its predecessor. The central motive, a block flanked by towers, recalls a composition published by Durand fifty years before in his textbook on architectural composition (Fig. 66).[26] Many early stations had already been outgrown, and in their rebuilding towers played an increasingly important role.

The new configuration was adapted for small stations, too, in which neither

24. *Builder, 12* (1854), 41. The story has been told recently: see Nikolaus Pevsner, *Matthew Digby Wyatt,* Cambridge, 1950; and Henry-Russell Hitchcock, "Brunel and Paddington," *Architectural Review, 109* (1951), 240–6.

25. Henry-Russell Hitchcock, "Second Empire *Avant la Lettre,*" *Gazette des Beaux-Arts,* ser. 6, *42* (1953), 115–30.

26. J. N. L. Durand, *Précis des leçons d'architecture* (2 vols. Paris, 1802), *1,* pl. 8.

arches nor towers played a part. The anonymous designer for the small station at St-Germain-en-Laye (Fig. 67), for example, had felt the influence of the new taste; he has combined several blocks in such a way as to emphasize their picturesqueness and diversity while maintaining symmetry.

The important European monuments of station building in the period of its coming of age include a number of still serviceable stations. The simpler American ones of the same era, however, have rarely survived, since they were replaced by larger, more permanent buildings; at that time American railroads were not ready to invest in structures of comparable quality.

American Depots

The first major American railroad station was the work of the prodigy Thomas Tefft (1826–59). He was only twenty-two when in 1848 he designed the Union Station at Providence, Rhode Island (Fig. 68). The site was on filled land near the Old Cove. The tracks made a loop, with the station tangent to them. It was a large one-sided station used only as a terminal. Wings at either end, containing sheds over spur tracks, were bent back toward the tracks to form a half-hexagon. Although some of the original drawings have been preserved, these unfortunately do not include the plan; but we are told that there were large and comfortable waiting rooms and that the second floor was reserved for future use as offices when the need should arise.[27] As late as 1885 this station was voted one of the twenty best buildings in the United States—a rare distinction for any depot, let alone one thirty-seven years old.[28] Shortly thereafter it burned down.

It was the first station in this country in the new Romanesque manner introduced by Renwick in New York and Washington, anticipating by one year the publication of the American bible of the new style, Robert Owen's *Hints on Public Architecture*. In a lecture given in 1851 Tefft correctly ascribed the origin of the style to Germany: "The round arch school of Germany is employing much invention and originality in their design and we hazard but little in predicting a favorable result." [29] Since Schinkel had used this style in some of his parish churches in the 1830's, it had been widely taken up and applied to such stations as the Karlsruhe Bahnhof of 1842.

27. Quoted by Barbara Wriston, "Thomas Alexander Tefft," unpublished Ph.D. thesis, Brown University, 1942.

28. *American Architect, 16* (June 13, 1885), 282.

29. Wriston, "Thomas Alexander Tefft."

Tefft's building at Providence strengthened the hold of the new mode. Related to von Gärtner's Ludwigskirche (1829–40) in Munich, the combination of light arcades, octagonal baptistry-like blocks, and five-story campaniles was unique in this country. The slender elegance of the campaniles is noteworthy. Although Pugin had been writing for some time about verticality in design, it was several years before Lord Grimthorpe noted "the modern passion for the foreign characteristic of height." [30] Tefft's gracefully roofed towers show that he was avant garde.

The unknown architect of the Troy, New York, Union Railroad Depot of 1857 lacked the subtlety of Tefft, but using the railroad style he achieved a remarkably mature one-sided station (Fig. 69). Since Troy was then a more important rail center than Albany, seven companies joined to build the union station. Four of them had independent duplicating suites of rooms for passengers: each consisted of baggage room, gentlemen's waiting room, ticket office, wash room, ladies' reception room, and ladies' drawing and toilet rooms. The suites were strung out in a long, narrow row alongside the shed. The stupendous shed roof, sheltering ten tracks, formed a graceful reverse curve which flattened out into spreading eaves. The one-sided plan may have been antiquated, but the picturesque composition was not. Blocks and towers were ranged to contrast with the shed roof. The three-storied main block containing offices and refreshment rooms supported an axial tower which rose four stories more and ended in a burst of crenelations Shorter towers at the ends were connected by a continuous marquee that echoed the horizontal line of the shed. Vertical and horizontal motives were interwoven here more boldly than in any earlier American station. Five years after completion it burned down and was immediately rebuilt, without the towers; these towers, however, had been necessary parts of the composition, so that in its second, denuded state the shed and offices made an ugly appearance.

One-sided stations gave way, as they had in Europe, to the more functional two-sided type. The Hartford Union Depot of 1850 was typical of medium-sized ones. It reflected the English railroad style somewhat crudely, mingling Lombard and villa elements. One roof covered the central shed and the flanking twin buildings. The most celebrated station of the two-sided type was the pride of the Atlantic and Great Western Railroad, built at Meadville, Pennsylvania, about 1865 (Figs. 70, 71). With lavish backing from British investors, it was generously planned. By the *New York Herald* it was considered "to rival in the style and beauty of its surroundings any of those you may notice in the best railroads of England; charming cottages for the officers of the road, a park at the rear with winding walks, fir trees, rose and

30. Grimthorpe, 1st Baron, *On Some of the Grounds of Dissatisfaction with Modern Gothic Architecture* (London, 1859), p. 15.

jessamine bushes." There was a hotel of over a hundred rooms and "a dining room as long as a train" (Fig. 72), said to be the finest in the United States, windowed and roofed like the nave of an English cathedral.[31] Judging by the extant drawings, the reality seems less remarkable to us than it did to our great-grandfathers: the dining hall was somewhat sketchily embellished with thin pilasters supporting trusses on cusped brackets; the shed, built in the French manner with hollow iron struts (Fig. 71), was sixty-six feet wide and spanned three tracks, occupying half the total width; and since the platforms were each fourteen feet wide, the offices were confined to narrow strips. Nevertheless, some features not previously mentioned were included—train-men's room, dispatcher's office, water supply, car repairs, storeroom, and vaults. The hotel and the fireproofed kitchens were detached from the main station building, which was made of wooden boards and battens—a system unknown to the builders of the Middle Ages but one which was frequently and creatively used for Gothic revival buildings, including many stations of the 19th century.[32]

Americans also built some head-type stations. The two principal examples were in Baltimore—a city that often set the pace in things connected with railroads. Both stations were closer to their Boston predecessors than to the grander European ones.

One of them, Calvert Station by Niernsee and Nielson, was completed in 1848. The well-built shed, the width of the head-house, covered five lines and three platforms. The design recalled Tefft's station at Providence but with the detail coarsened. Calvert Station has recently been torn down and with its going went one of the few American stations which was permitted to live out its century.

The builders of Camden, the second Baltimore station, 1852–53 (Fig. 73), hoped to surpass the famous English ones. They were defeated by the depression of 1853 and failed of their objective; even so, they were able to claim for it the swiftly circulating title "largest station in the United States." A spacious hall for general entrance and exit—an early concourse—led to waiting rooms, refreshment salon, and the usual minor offices. The company offices, in accordance with the custom, were on the second floor. A "temporary" wooden shed over two lines was not replaced until 1869; wings were added at that time also. The newer wood and iron shed is still in service as a freight house. An additional arched shed in steel was added in 1895.

31. *New York Herald,* Feb. 6, 1870. Quoted in Edward Hungerford, *Men of Erie, a Story of Human Effort* (New York, Random House, 1946), p. 191–2.

32. See Vincent J. Scully, "Romantic Rationalism and the Expression of Structure in Wood; Downing, Wheeler, Gardner, and the 'Stick Style,' 1840–1876," *Art Bulletin, 35* (1953), 121–42.

Some American stations followed the European precedent of having attached hotels. Those at Schenectady and Meadville have been mentioned. A hotel formed the head-house of a station in Pittsburgh which was destroyed in the railroad riots of 1877.[33]

Whatever type of station he was dealing with, the American architect took enthusiastically to the use of towers; both of the head stations in Baltimore had them. There was a short stubby pair at Calvert Station, the Camden Station had three: the central one reached a considerable height and sat above a massive pediment. The lowest story, with groups of free-standing columns at the corners, remains, but the second story—ornamented with pilasters and arches—and all the superstructure have been taken down. The final octagonal stage ended in a dome. We are told that the design was to be "Norman," like the recently completed Smithsonian Institution in Washington,[34] but no trace of that intention remains; everything is Italian villa.

Whether by accident or by design, the Harrisburg, Pennsylvania, station (Fig. 74) belonged even more justly than the Baltimore ones to the picturesque canon; it was a larger, more elaborate version of the Hartford Union Depot. The station was shared by two companies, each of which had its own sheds, separated from each other by a stalwart tower. Considerable pains were taken to vary the detail from one part to another. The smaller left-hand pavilion featured a triplet of round-headed windows, while the larger right-hand one displayed a group of four pedimented windows. A second, shorter tower marked the center of the right wing.

The least successful towers of the period were designed by Otto Matz, a German-born architect, for the Great Central Station in Chicago, 1855–56 (Fig. 75). The main front was an ill-assorted complex of disparate elements: too many different sizes of window, and towers that were merely enlarged buttresses. The shed end was better. Three unequal arches stood below the wide, stepped gable. This remarkable shed, destroyed in the fire of 1871, will be described later. The head-house burned in 1874. Partially rebuilt, it continued in use until 1893, although the shed remained entirely roofless.[35]

The cities of Boston and Lowell also acquired new stations at this time.

33. Following the Civil War, railroads became active in the development of resorts; they financed the construction of many hotels as part of the program, placing them close to the depot if not making them part of it. President Garrett of the Baltimore and Ohio Railroad sponsored a series of which the Queen Hotel at Cumberland, Maryland, was a luxurious example. See Edward Hungerford, *The Story of the Baltimore and Ohio Railroad, 1827–1927* (2 vols. New York, G. P. Putnam's Sons, 1928), *2*, 124. The later series of hotels built by Canadian railways is well known.

34. Hungerford, *Story of the Baltimore and Ohio, 1*, 286.

35. C. H. Mottier, "Great Central Station," *Illinois Central Magazine*, Jan. 1937, p. 27.

The 1850's

These were symmetrical, with axial towers whose mass constituted half the total bulk; this equality produced an equilibrium between the horizontal and the vertical elements. A somewhat different type of composition was applied to the New Haven and Harlem Depot (1857) at Madison Square, New York (Fig. 76). As yet New York's insular position had been breached only from the north, so that there was no need for stations as large as those in Boston or Baltimore. The Harlem Depot, in the railroad style, had a stepped-up silhouette; the eye was led from a one-story block up to the two-story main block and finally up to the tower, so that the building appeared to grow up out of the site.

Such towered stations set a fashion. In Jersey City, a small station consisting almost entirely of shed was nevertheless flanked by a pair of stubby towers. Functionally gratuitous, the towers were apparently necessary to self-respect. Much the same point of view accounts for the towers which were added to the Susquehanna, Pennsylvania, station during its modernization. Two water tanks were disguised as a pair of Lombard towers.

Fashionable as towers were, the arch was not entirely ignored. Amid the swirling, blending currents of eclecticism, one family of American stations featured the arch of the train-shed. In these lay undeveloped the possibility of producing a truly American railroad style, straightforward and appropriate to an unsophisticated country; but like so many other American false starts, this one too died young, smothered by newer fashions imported from the other side of the Atlantic. The type may be called the "arched train-barn." It was a development from the plain train-barn of the first decades. Its arched train-shed roof also covered the waiting rooms and ticket offices, which were ranged along the platforms rather than in separate blocks. Stations of this compact, unified type were to be found throughout the United States, and their images appeared in the periodicals of the day as the scene of historic events, such as receptions for the visiting Prince of Wales or the silent throngs mourning by the side of Lincoln's funeral train. From one to seven openings perforated the ends of the train-sheds. The trains, led by the bell-shaped stacks of their gaily painted engines, left the depot under straight or curved lintels. The gable sometimes occupied half the total height of the building, though usually less. In 1854 Cincinnati possessed an example (Fig. 77).[36] The shape of its conspicuous arch was not semicircular but segmental, and this shape was repeated by the ends of the building. The arched train-barn of the Fenchurch Street Station in London (1852) is the only European instance of this date I have encountered, perhaps an instance of an American invention sending its influence eastward.

As late as the 1850's and 1860's enlarged versions of the simpler train-barn

36. This was built by the Cincinnati, Columbus, Cleveland, and Erie Railroad and was 465 feet long, 90 feet wide, and 30 feet high.

73

without arched roofs were still being built. In general appearance these were scarcely more ambitious than those of the 1830's and 1840's; the great change was in size. The Union Depot at Columbus, Ohio (Fig. 78), of 1862 was such an overgrown train-barn. It was constructed of boards and battens, and the wide, low roof covers three lines of track and the two platforms, together with their offices. Like the Meadville station, it aspired to be Gothic, as evidenced by the drip molds over the windows, particularly those of the octagonal ventilators; but these Gothic touches do not disguise its Greek revival proportions. The old Louisville station of 1858 resembled the one at Columbus. It was designed by German-born Albert Fink (1827–97), chief engineer of the Louisville and Nashville Railroad and inventor of the well known truss which bears his name. It was a combination freight and passenger station, with a roof covering six tracks and three platforms.

Roofs of this width presented a considerable problem to American engineers of the 1850's. Their solutions, while not so bold as those of European builders, were no less ingenious. There was almost no structural metal, and although stone was readily available, competent masons and surplus capital were not; American engineers therefore were forced to use wood. They fell back on an invention of Ithiel Town, the New Haven architect. In 1826 and 1835 he had patented a lattice truss (Fig. 79), using readily obtainable small planks. It had been widely adapted for highway and railroad bridges and could also be used for the wide-span roofs needed for efficient operation in train-sheds;[37] in arched form such trusses were both convenient and pleasing. The train-shed of the Philadelphia, Wilmington, and Baltimore Depot in Philadelphia, with a span of 150 feet (Fig. 80), has such a truss. The Town truss was later refined by William Howe into the metal lattice truss named after him [38] and used impressively at the Great Central Station in Chicago in 1855 (Fig. 75). Here, the Howe truss arches spanned 166 feet and rose 36 feet from their springing.[39] Horatio Greenough's compliment to American ingenuity applies to the builders of this kind of roof: "The mechanics of the United States have, by their bold and unflinching adaptation, entered the true track and hold up the light for all who operate for American

37. The connection between bridges and sheds is no doubt due to their being built by the same men.

38. William Howe of Spencer, Massachusetts, patented his truss (Fig. C) in 1840. The verticals are tension members in wrought iron; the rest is of wood. Steel eventually replaced the wrought iron. See Kirby and Laurson, *The Early Years of Modern Engineering,* p. 146. See also note 16, Chapter Two.

39. This was erroneously considered to be the widest roof span constructed up to that time (see Mottier, "Great Central Station"); actually, the 211-foot span at New Street Station, Birmingham (Fig. 54), was both earlier and wider.

wants." [40] The railroad metaphor makes the compliment particularly appropriate.

More ample budgets were soon to coincide with more pretentious ambitions, so that such simple stations, resulting more from economy than from taste, did not last long. A few of them still stand, but most were doomed to destruction or converted to other uses: many became freight houses, and one in Philadelphia, built in 1850, became the Wanamaker store. The Chicago and Boston fires of the 1870's destroyed many more.

The situation in the United States at the end of the early phase of railroading, just as the Civil War was approaching, is summarized by Henry Holly, author of the first American pattern book to include a design for a depot. [41] In his opinion the Italian style introduced from the London clubs was "appropriate for stations in rural settings, where they set a good architectural example and result in improving the taste of the community." He contrasted British and American depots: "In Britain, stations are beautiful and tasteful just as their trains are safe and luxurious"; most American stations, on the other hand, were "uninviting or ridiculous, beggarly or pretentious, the Egyptian ones, mere sheds constructed of rude boards." As was to be expected after such an attack, he proposes as a remedy a design of his own (Fig. 81). His "Design 34" offers an asymmetrical Italian villa "improved" by the addition of the steep roofs and barge boards of the English Victorian Gothic style. Another improvement in the direction of increased safety is the separation of the up and down lines by a fence; the crossing from the station to the lines beyond the fence was to be accomplished by a complicated series of steps and bridges which crawl steeply up one end of the depot, wind along at the second floor level, jump across the lines, and finally descend to the far platform. This device adds to his mixture another stylistic flavor, that of the Swiss chalet.

Holly hoped to enlist support for his design from partisans of all three fashions, and as a matter of fact it seems to have influenced at least one station, built at Taunton, Massachusetts (Fig. 82) in 1865—the year Holly's book was published—and still standing. The unusual tower terminating in a steep pyramid is very close to Holly's massive one, and the rest of the station, though more somber than Holly's design, shares similar Victorian Gothic details. The train-shed, now removed, made the exuberant features of Design 34 unnecessary. The architect of the Taunton station is not known; if it was

40. Quoted in James Marston Fitch, *American Building* (Boston, Houghton Mifflin, 1948), p. 76.

41. *Country Seats,* New York, 1865. (This book was actually written in 1861, but publication was delayed by the outbreak of the war.) Quoted material is from pp. 170–1.

not Holly himself, at least his influence was felt. In any event, both the design and the Taunton station were prophetic: they heralded the next phase of the 19th-century style, in which picturesque tendencies were to become more marked—a combination of styles which was not revivalism but synthetic eclecticism.

4. THE MIDDLE PHASE:

SOPHISTICATION

(1860-1890)

Innovations and Improvements

The middle phase of the picturesque style lasted about thirty years. It was around 1860 that the new Victorian Gothic style was beginning to reign, under Ruskin's aegis, and by the 1890's it had run its course; a renewed interest in nonmedieval forms was superseding it. There are signs that these thirty years had a degree of unity in other aspects of life as well. The beginning of the period was marked by an extraordinary production of masterpieces in literature and music. By the end of it, basic beliefs about the universe which had dominated late 18th- and 19th-century thought had become untenable.[1] During the period three new world powers emerged: Germany, Japan, and the United States. It was a time of world-wide prosperity, marred by only one serious depression in 1873; this prosperity was reflected in lavish building programs characterized by opulence.

During these years the changes in railroad technology were directed primarily toward increased luxury, safety, and speed. This trend was reflected in costly bridges and tunnels, and in addition, more comfortable types of passenger cars were introduced. The first Pullman car appeared in 1872, and the first successful sleeping car, "The Pioneer," was built in 1865; an American invention, it was born from the necessity of longer trips here, and was then adopted in England in 1873. Formerly trains had been halting to permit the passengers to eat at stations, but as faster runs became desirable, time could not be spared for such stops. In 1879 dining cars had been tried on the run

1. L. Price, *Dialogues of Alfred North Whitehead*, pp. 119, 131.

from Leeds to London, and in 1882 meals were being served to the passengers in their seats en route. In 1883 dining cars ran between Detroit and St. Thomas, and the West Shore Railroad introduced buffet parlor cars. In 1887 a car-vestibule, invented by H. H. Sessions, was tried out on Pullman cars, and Bruce Price, the architect, patented a bay-windowed parlor car.[2] By this date cars seventy feet long were mounted on six-wheel trucks.

In the interest of safety, and in response to public outcry stimulated by a series of appalling disasters such as the one at Revere in 1872, new devices were adopted—reluctantly, because of the cost. Westinghouse airbrakes invented in 1869, and Miller couplers and buffers invented four years earlier, were belatedly installed. An efficient system of interlocking switches and signals was in use at Camden Town in 1860, and thirteen years later there were 18,000 of these in England; but in spite of the fact that they were indispensable to the efficient and safe operation of large terminals, the first American one was not installed until 1881. Low passenger platforms had been very common, although highly dangerous; in England twenty people a year were killed by rolling off them under the carriages, but it was not until a prominent member of Parliament was killed in this way that remedial steps were taken.

As money became more plentiful, a series of tunnels was undertaken; one of these was the Hoosac Tunnel, bored in 1868. Great bridges took the place of train ferries across the Mississippi and the Firth of Forth. American rails were extended all the way to the coast in 1869, 1881, and 1883. The Trans-Siberian line was begun in 1891.

Comfort as well as efficiency was served by experiments with electricity. First used for motive power on the Baltimore and Ohio Railroad in the 1840's, it had to be abandoned then because the enormous batteries ran down quickly, were slow to recharge, and could not pull a pay load. Electric lighting had been tried at Newcastle and King's Cross Station and became common in German stations in the 1880's. In 1884 electric foot warmers, operated by axle generators, appeared. The earliest old steam line to be electrified was the Nantasket Beach Branch in 1895, although local trolley lines had come a decade earlier.

While these mechanical and physical ameliorations were being adopted, no completely new type of station was developed; instead, a parallel process of modification and improvement of old types occurred. The large room we call the concourse became more general during this phase. Its early appearance at Euston has been remarked. Later ones grew out of the restudy of three features: vestibule, waiting room, and cross-platform. A vestibule had always been customary, sometimes combined with the booking office. Wait-

2. *American Architect, 18,* No. 503, Aug. 15, 1885.

ing rooms had been lavishly provided for three classes in England and four in Germany, all duplicated for each company serving the station; these now were being consolidated. The cross-platform, or "midway," widened to thirty or more feet, was used as a waiting area adjacent to the train gates; with exits at its ends, it permitted direct egress for passengers who did not have to claim baggage. In- and out-passengers mingled there and the long struggle to provide architecturally for their complete separation was given up as platforms had to be used for both arriving and departing trains; instead, some of the functions of these three features were combined in a vast mixing chamber, the concourse, serving as a self-adjusting traffic center. Travelers and porters were left to find their own way to ticket windows, baggage rooms, restaurants, or platforms. Once the function of the concourse was comprehended, it became possible to abandon the midway altogether and to provide separate quiet waiting areas while all moving traffic was handled in the concourse. This was the principal development in station planning during the middle phase.

The one-sided station survived; tunnels beneath the platforms and rails made this possible. By extending the use of this device, even large stations could be built on the one-sided plan. The Germans were the first to capitalize on this possibility; a French observer commented in 1886 that it was consistent with the German character to develop borrowed notions.[3] The new station at Hanover, 1876–79 (Fig. 84) used tunnels extensively: a series for passengers was supplemented by a second series connecting with the baggage platforms.

The two-sided type of station also continued to be built for terminal stations through the 1870's in central Europe and Italy.[4] During this phase a more unified appearance was desired, so an additional block was built across the end of the lines to connect the two long wings, forming what we may call a pseudo head-building. The Stettiner Bahnhof in Berlin (Fig. 83) is an example. The main entrances and exits remain in the wings, and only in superficial appearance was there a resemblance to a true head station.[5]

3. Felix Narjoux, *A Journey of an Architect,* trans. John Peto (Boston, 1877), pp. 250–1.

4. In Zurich, Hauptbahnhof (1865–73); Berlin, Ost Bahnhof (1866–67), Schlesischer Bahnhof (1867–69), Potsdamer Bahnhof (1868–72), Lehrter Bahnhof (1869–71), Stettiner Bahnhof (1876); Vienna, Nord-West Bahnhof (1870–72); Turin, Stazione di Porta Nuova (1866–68); Milan, Stazione Centrale (1873); Rome, Stazione Termini I (1874); Naples, Stazione Centrale (*ca.* 1880); Budapest, West Bahnhof (1873–77), Ost Bahnhof (1881).

5. The Nord-West Bahnhof in Vienna was one of the most elaborate stations of this group. Its two sides were clearly differentiated. The departure one was marked by a colossal polygonal porte-cochere 60 feet in diameter and 45 feet high. Waiting rooms occupied most of the interior. A large restaurant was supplemented by dining terraces. On the ar-

Stations of this type were, however, proving inadequately flexible. Just as the one-sided type had been made more efficient by the use of two levels, so the two-sided type was given a renewed value by raising it on stilts. Elevated two-sided stations were no longer limited to terminal stations but were extremely practical as through stations. The name "island" is appropriate to such stations because they are isolated on viaducts completely surrounded by streets. Island sites, however, even when especially contrived, are always limited in width; this is their chief defect. In order to have as many lines as possible, the whole width at track level is devoted to them, with the waiting rooms, ticket offices, and services often concentrated in a single block at street level. This distinguishes them from the parent two-sided type. The first notable examples occur in Berlin in the stations of the Stadtbahn, a steam-operated belt line connecting the scattered main-line terminals They were derived from such two-sided stations as the one at Montparnasse in Paris, 1850–52 (Figs. 59, 60) and a hybrid one at Stuttgart, designed by Georg Morlok in 1863–68 (Fig. 85). Morlok's "T" plan stretched back of a narrow head-house on the Schloss Strasse, pierced by carefully separated entrances and exits. The main entrance led to a narrow central hall terminating in the distance in third-class waiting rooms. The hall was flanked by duplicate facilities for two lines, each with its own 100-foot-wide shed. Back of them lay a garden with pergolas, high above the street, across which passengers could walk from the end of one shed to the other. Excellent plan that it was, it was not a pure example of the island type, since only the rear was elevated above the streets.

Johann Eduard Jacobsthal (1839–1902) was prominent among station builders of the period in Germany. He built stations in Berlin, Metz, Strasbourg, and Marienburg and part of the important one at Cologne. He may have been the inventor of the island type; if so, he sired a distinguished progeny. The Alexanderplatz Bahnhof in Berlin, 1880–85 (Fig. 86) is typical of his fine designs. The shed *is* the station. A gigantic glass tunnel stands on the viaduct, with subsidiary rooms either within or below the train-shed. These structures are as unmistakably stations as the Gare de l'Est. Nothing is permitted to detract from the fine sweep of the elevated crystal palaces. Once invented, the type flourished, reaching a climax at the end of the century at Dresden and Hamburg. Stations of this type were so modern and rational that they seem to belong more to our century than to the belittled one which actually created them. They may contain, in their simplicity,

---

rival side, a long veranda permitted many carriages and omnibuses to load simultaneously. The Austrian court had its own facilities on both sides, one of them with an enclosed garden. The façades ran for 800 feet. The interior was correspondingly imposing.

the germ of a solution to less complicated, cheaper stations in the future; but for many years the head-type station was to triumph over all rivals.

In this period, for the first time, the head-type station overtook the others in number and distinction. In some instances the head-building was a railroad hotel. The towered forebuilding, closely resembling nearby post offices and city halls on which the marquee and tower also appeared, became a familiar part of the urban scene. The shed, which might have served as a distinguishing feature, was seldom visible from the front, since the head-house had become a huge multistoried building. The purpose of this increase in its size was to accommodate the increasing clerical staff; already the record-keeping mania had begun to clog our civilization with tons of carbon-smeared paper.

Splendid head stations eventually rose in America too, but during the middle phase other types of plan prevailed. As late as 1892 Walter Berg, writing his station manual,[6] did not realize that the head station was supplanting the old two-sided type; neither was he aware that the space-consuming one-level station was doomed by the rising values of urban land. He heartily recommended the two-sided plan with the proviso that extensive sites be acquired for gradual use as needed. His arguments are not materially different from those of Reynaud forty years before.

The disadvantages of the two-sided station which Reynaud had pointed out were the ones which actually proved fatal to it. The superiority of the head station had already been recognized. One of its advantages was flexibility: any track can be diverted to in- or out-traffic, as the schedule requires, so that as many trains can be operated simultaneously as there are lines. Tracks can be used for car storage without tying up the platforms. Crowds can be easily handled. The chief disadvantage is that the passengers have to walk much longer distances. These points which seem a matter of course to us today were still being debated fifty years ago.

Some American stations of the primitive one-sided type at one level have continued in use down to the present day;[7] they manage to operate several tracks simultaneously with no more modern device than a continuous planked platform laid between the rails, sometimes supplemented by footbridges. Elsewhere the use of two levels solved the circulation difficulties, as at the Grand Trunk Station built at Toronto in 1892 and the huge Illinois Central Station of 1892–93 in Chicago (the latter lay between the train-yard and the city and therefore was accessible only from one side). The second Providence Union

6. *Buildings and Structures of American Railroads.*

7. These relics include Taunton, Massachusetts; Richardson's Union Station at New London, Connecticut; and the Union Depot at Concord, New Hampshire.

Station (1892–99) is typical of many medium-sized depots in which the buildings are concentrated on one side of the through lines. Communication to the farther platforms is by ramp—perhaps the first use of them in an American station. This station was architecturally undistinguished to begin with; and the train-shed, which was its most striking feature, has just been pulled down.

The two-sided plan also endured, The Romanesque one at Springfield (1888–89), once the best known twin depot in the country, was the last American one. It stood on an island site with raised tracks, and accessibility from each side was so nearly equal that buildings on both sides provided maximum convenience. An asymmetrical, picturesquely composed group, it was designed by Richardson's successors in the style he had created. Its possession in 1889 of a generator for electric lighting was considered noteworthy.

The older related type, the train-barn, with shed and twin buildings under one roof, died out and head stations began their ascendancy in a tentative way. The most conspicuous American example, the first Grand Central Station in New York (Fig. 120), was a combined head and one-sided station. Modest stations like that built for the Centennial in West Philadelphia by Joseph Wilson, one of the architects of the Fair, or Louis Sullivan's later one in New Orleans, merely moved the traditional low block from one side to the end of the tracks. Three large maritime stations were built in Jersey City within the span of five years, all head stations following the same scheme: a sequence of train-shed, head-house, and ferry house (Fig. 101). The traffic flow was direct and unimpeded; waiting rooms and restaurants were off to the side.

Some curious features appeared in the United States. A unique refinement was introduced in the Detroit station of the Michigan Central (1882)—a separate ladies' entrance, on a side street with its own marquee. The Erie station at Rochester had a veranda around three sides like a suburban mansion. Carriage courts became more frequent, not within the shed as in England but in front of it or beside it. On the whole, however, these developments were minor compared with the dramatic new train-sheds.

Apogee of the Train-shed

The refinements of the head-house paralleled the structural advances in the train-house. Compared with the more standardized sheds of the decades before, the new ones were bolder and more varied. Beginning in the 1860's with the shed at St. Pancras Station, the climax was reached in the 1890's with the 300-foot span of the Broad Street Station in Philadelphia.[8]

The intervening years saw new shapes, ranging from the pointed arch to the reversed catenary. The cheaper, less challenging triangular truss was used only infrequently. The unremitting pressure to shelter larger and larger numbers of tracks and platforms was not always met by building new sheds of greater span; sometimes more small sheds were added alongside the existing old ones, as at St. Lazare in Paris.

Some new sheds—for example, the twin sheds at Stuttgart—used wooden sickle girders. The lower chords have a marked curvature of considerable grace. In the same decade iron sickle girders were constructed for the shed of the Schlesischer Bahnhof in Berlin (Fig. 87). The use of relatively few struts and ties gave the shed a light appearance, and it seemed unusually lofty because its height was more than half its width. The iron shed at the Nord-West Bahnhof in Vienna (Fig. 88) was both wider and higher. Its truss was nearly triangular but does not appear to be of the Warren type,[9] as is some-

D. DIAGRAM OF A TYPICAL WARREN TRUSS

times asserted; in this instance the lower chords were slightly cambered and the rafters slightly curved. These deviations from straightness gave the roof the same subtle vitality as similar refinements gave to Greek temples. Gustave Eiffel, the famous French engineer, designed the roof of the West Bahnhof in Budapest, 1873–77 (Fig. 90). This had a triangular truss built according to the Polonceau system: the lower chord and struts were exceedingly light and curved brackets added grace. A sensitively designed truss supported the roof of the train-shed at the Liverpool Street Station in London (Fig. 89). This is a highly refined version of the earlier Gare du Nord II shed. It spreads over four spans for 278 feet and, as in the Paris station, the girders are supported for part of their length on brackets; in London, however, the curves continue smoothly from one column to the next with almost weightless elegance. The ratio of height to width, 3:4, is relatively lofty and imposing.

Trussed roofs were less common than tied arches. The tied arch is a transitional form coming between the triangular truss and the pure, clean

8. The dimensions of the significant new sheds are given in the Appendix.

9. The Warren truss (Fig. 88; Text Fig. D) was patented in 1848 by James Warren and Willoughby Theobald Monzani, both of London. The compressive members in this form of truss are the girders. Kirby and Laurson, *The Early Years of Modern Engineering,* p. 160.

arch without visible ties. There are trusses of this type at Victoria Station, London (Fig. 91). The twin sheds are spanned by arched lattice girders tied by cambered lower chords. Radial struts connect the girders and chords. In spite of a clear height of 43 feet and an over-all height of 63 feet, the chords tend to create a low optical ceiling.[10] This type of truss, related to the bowstring type, was used a few years later for the train-shed of the Queen Street Station at Glasgow (Fig. 94). There the number of radial struts was reduced, although the span was greatly increased. A variation of the bowstring truss was designed by John Hawkshaw for two new terminals in the city, Charing Cross (Fig. 93) and Cannon Street. In the first of these the segmentally arched ribs leaped 164 feet and in the second, 190 feet. All the principals, resting on handsomely arcaded walls, were curved and gave a feeling of strength without oppressiveness, and the abundantly lighted interiors had an exceptionally gracious air. From the Thames one could clearly see the enormous spandrels with their glass screens.

In some cases, several small sheds were combined to give a more complex spatial effect, recalling Paddington Station. One of these was at Hanover, where the two principal sheds, not unlike those at Victoria Station, London (Fig. 91), were separated by a smaller one (Fig. 149g) and all three were linked by transverse sheds. At Lime Street Station III in Liverpool, a new shed was added side by side with an old one; each was 200 feet wide, but the new one made a finer effect because it was arched.

Using the same type of construction, German engineers achieved other variations in interior effect. At the Potsdamer Bahnhof in Berlin forceful ribs of segmentally curved "I" beams rested on stout walls. The roof, which was completely glazed, looked by contrast with the walls like a temporary cover; it was another glazed street like the shed at the Gare de l'Est. The illumination of the larger shed at the Anhalter Bahnhof (Fig. 113) was better balanced; here, large roundheaded windows admitted enough side light to blend with the top light. The lighter ribs were more closely spaced and rose in a steeper curve, giving unity and distinction.

The semicircular profiles of the early train-sheds harmonized with the surrounding architecture just as pointed arches suited the configuration of the middle period. The most celebrated shed of the middle period was built at St. Pancras Station, London, 1863–65 (Fig. 92), by the engineers W. H. Barlow and R. M. Ordish.[11] It was 243 feet wide, 100 feet high, and nearly

10. This station was remodeled in 1881 and again in 1904–05.

11. Ordish was also the designer of a train-shed fabricated in England and erected at the Central Station in Amsterdam in 1863. Tubular members were used in the truss, which spanned 120 feet. The present station building was erected 1881–89 by P. J. H. Cuypers, in a picturesque manner.

690 feet long. The curved latticed ribs met at a point at the apex. The rib ends were tied below the tracks and platforms by iron rods three inches in diameter—not essential for stability but added as an extra measure of safety. This structural system had been used a few years before by Frederick Peck in the much smaller Royal Agriculture Hall nearby, and its application so soon afterward to the far larger span at St. Pancras shows how rapidly technical inventions were seized upon in those creative years. Important as an engineering contribution, this shed also made an important aesthetic advance. The conventional distinction between wall and ceiling had been abolished; the ribs continue in an unbroken rising line from the floor up and over until they meet at the ridge. This epoch-making event anticipates by a quarter of a century Dutert and Contamin's similar and better known Galerie des Machines in Paris. The magnificence thus generated did not go un-recognized; contemporary testimonials mingle awe with admiration. It was one of the great achievements of the century.[12]

Pointed arches became more frequent thereafter as aesthetic and structural currents merged. As we have seen, tied arches could be used effectively, but far more striking sheds were created using pointed arches without ties.

Ten years later Mr. Cudworth, the engineer, built the most Gothic of train-sheds at Middlesbrough (Fig. 96). There were two sheds. The main one has a 5:4 ratio of width to height, the most vertical proportions ever applied to a train-shed. The significance of this is not minimized by its relatively small dimensions—74 feet wide by 60 feet high; as in the 13th century, the most characteristic examples of a style are not necessarily the largest. At Middles-brough, Cudworth built the Sainte-Chapelle of train-sheds.

In the 1870's two experienced station architects, William Peachy and Thomas Prosser,[13] were at work on York's third and present Central Station (Fig. 95), using curving lines which required concentrically curved sheds. A refined version of the Newcastle naves was employed. The total diameter was considerably greater but only the central span was wider than those at New-castle. The width to height ratio is 8:5. Extra height gives added dignity to buildings, if not always to man. The sheds at York are unusually handsome. The five-centered ribs are carefully scaled and the tie rods barely noticeable. These sheds were built at a time when single-span sheds were widely used on the plausible pretext that they permitted greater flexibility. The multiple-span

12. St. Pancras' metal work was at first painted brown in view of the dark deposits which were expected eventually to encrust it, but Mr. Allport, a director, ultimately persuaded Barlow and Scott to repaint it sky blue. Why did the latter have to be persuaded? Had the brown decades already come to England? There was nothing drab about Scott's ad-joining hotel.

13. Prosser had added the portico to Dobson's station at Newcastle.

shed at York proved that that type, too, was capable of producing great beauty. It is more beautiful than either of the older ones at Newcastle and Paddington. We should be grateful that these three exist to delight us by their intricate luminous spaces. It is regrettable that so few of them were built.

It is possible to single out only one or two more British train-sheds of this period. That of St. Enoch's Station at Glasgow was built by the Midland Company. They did not attempt to equal their triumph at St. Pancras Station. The Scotch shed was 45 feet narrower and its arches were not pointed; instead, the curved lattice ribs were given the refined shape of a five-centered arch. Considerably later a shed was built at the Prince's Street Station in Edinburgh of a type which does not often achieve great beauty. In this station, under certain conditions, the deep trusses take on a spidery look which recalls drawings by Paul Klee or Saul Steinberg (see title page).

Two British stations, like the island ones in Berlin, made the shed the dominant feature. The first was the Liverpool Central Station (Fig. 97), built by the engineer John Fowler in 1874, and the second was the Manchester Joint Central Station, begun two years later. Both sheds were arched and without visible ties. They are striking examples of refined technology. The profiles are reversed catenaries in shape, exceedingly subtle and worthy of their prominent role on the exterior. The high sheds reduce the wings and marquees to inconsequence, thereby reminding us of the earlier Fenchurch Street Station in London and of the numerous American arched train-barns. Coming so long after the Crystal Palace, they can hardly be considered an example of its influence, though they represent the lesson which might have been learned from it.

The new types of European sheds had American counterparts, of which the earliest was built in New York (1869–71). Commodore Vanderbilt's Grand Central Station (Fig. 98) was a deliberate attempt to emulate St. Pancras. The question of who designed it—Joseph Duclos or R. G. Hatfield—was being argued in the 1870's. Both men were employed by the fabricators, the famous Architectural Iron Works, and since no conclusive evidence has appeared, we may assume that both should share the glory. The shed, of imported metal, covered the largest interior space on this continent and was a sightseers' attraction second only to the Capitol in Washington. Imposing though it was, however, it was inferior to the English prototype, even from the standpoint of dimensions:

	Grand Central	*St. Pancras*
Width	200	243
Height	100	100
Length	600	689

While both sheds used arches tied out of sight below the tracks, Grand Central's were conservatively semicircular in shape.

Efforts were made to keep the Grand Central shed clean and quiet. The engines of arriving trains were cut off at 45th Street and the cars brought in "flying"—rolled in by gravity, with brakemen controlling them—and the engines for departing trains were kept standing outside the shed until the last minute, when they were backed in and coupled on. These precautions kept the shed nearly free from smoke. The ringing of engine bells was forbidden and the use of the whistle permitted only in emergencies. About the train-house, however (more of a house and less of a shed in those days), there were several gaucheries of detail. The great arches cut awkwardly across the masonry of the head-house, juxtaposed but not integrated, while at the other end there was a clutter of arcades, gables, and pediments (Fig. 121). The glazing of the roof, distributed in three narrow bands between wide opaque bands, conflicted with the rising curve of the arches. Furthermore, big as the shed was, it soon proved inadequate and long trains had to be broken into sections to get all the cars under it. In spite of its shortcomings, however, it continued for twenty years to be the most impressive shed in this country.

Smaller sheds, less imaginatively handled, rose here and there. One of the best of these still surviving is that of the Grand Central Station in Chicago (1889–90). A modest 119 feet in span, it is elegantly proportioned and harmonizes with the concourse and capacious porte-cochere.

The earliest American train-shed to imitate St. Pancras' pointed arch was built at the Park Square Station in Boston in 1872 (Fig. 100); but it fell far short of its model. Not only was it much smaller, but its narrow glazing strips, like those at Grand Central, interrupted the curve of its ribs. For maximum interior effect glazing strips should not cancel or overwhelm the main structural lines.

The inferiority of American to European stations is further revealed by comparing the stations of their elevated railroads. The solemn dignity of the spectacular island stations of the Berlin Stadtbahn, mentioned earlier, is in marked contrast to the frivolous Swiss chalets huddled precariously on the skeleton of the contemporary New York elevated lines. Sheds like the noble twin ones at Worcester, Massachusetts (Fig. 124), well integrated by an overall architectural treatment which included the head-house and a slender tower, were exceptional. The Worcester sheds ended in massive masonry arches and the surmounting gables were stepped as though to express the monitors, or clerestories, which rode the roofs. Since there was very little glass, the interiors must have been obscure. More typically American, the shed of the Louisville, Kentucky, station of the 1880's (Fig. 99) was attached to an unrelated head-house in the Romanesque style, from which projected an equally inharmonious iron marquee in front. The architect and the engineer could hardly be considered collaborators.

Massive forebuildings with returned wings concealed the train-sheds of two new Chicago stations, the Chicago and North Western and the Dearborn Street Station. Both sheds were over 100 feet wide but were timidly low in proportion.

The situation in Jersey City was similar. Two of the three maritime stations made no great effort at size or dignity. There was little need to make a great architectural show, since all three stood in an industrial neighborhood and served primarily as a transfer point for travelers whose eyes were on more remote objectives. The earliest was built for the Erie Railroad. Its main span was constructed in the French manner. The Central Railroad of New Jersey built a train-shed with a modest central span of just under 150 feet and supplemented this with two lean-tos.

The Pennsylvania Railroad executives, under the leadership of George B. Robert and A. J. Cassatt, favored huge sheds and lavished the company's resources upon sheds that eclipsed all previous American ones. Their extravagance has continued well into our century with the building of their colossal modern terminals in New York and Philadelphia. At the time we are writing of, the Pennsylvania company alone built three of the four spans which eclipsed Grand Central's. The one at Jersey City, for example (Fig. 102), spanned 252 feet. C. C. Schneider designed its three-hinged arch. The "I" beam ties were concealed beneath the rails, but in order to satisfy the eye, false bases in cast iron were wrapped around the ribs at platform level. Today we would prefer to see the ribs frankly piercing the platforms, but the modern concept of the interpenetration of parts was not then aesthetically satisfactory. The width-to-height ratio, 3:1, was wide compared to classic examples; at the same time its reversed catenary shape made it more dynamic. Three years later the Reading company at its Philadelphia terminus constructed an almost equally wide shed (Fig. 103) using the same system of ties and pins and a similar shape. Apparently spurred by this challenge to its supremacy, the Pennsylvania company set about enlarging its nearby Philadelphia station, only ten years old, and at the same time they built a new shed (Fig. 104) with the widest single-span train-shed ever built anywhere at any time: 300 feet wide, 108 feet 6 inches high, and 595 feet long. This proportion of width to height, 3:1, seems to suit sheds of this general shape, where height is less necessary for grace because of the elegance obtained from the subtly changing curvature.[14] In 1898 this princely company began its

14. The Reading shed still stands, but the Pennsylvania one succumbed to flames in a spectacular fire in 1923. By that date the expense of such monsters was no longer considered justifiable and it was never rebuilt.

third huge train-house, in Pittsburgh. It was proportionately loftier than its predecessors—240 feet wide and 110 feet high—as though anticipating its historical role as the last of the noble American train-sheds. A device new to train-sheds was employed: the ribs were fixed at one end and rested on rollers at the other.[15]

Two markedly different sheds were sponsored by the Illinois Central Railroad. The chief engineer, J. F. Wallace, combined an arched center span with cantilevered lateral extensions. His earlier shed forms part of Louis Sullivan's station at New Orleans, 1892 (Fig. 105). The symmetrical arrangements consisted of five parts linked smoothly together in a continuous flowing curve: an arched central shed, two lower, narrower sheds, and two cantilevered wings. Earlier than any important example of Art Nouveau architecture, this shed is nevertheless related to that curvilinear style. Louis Sullivan's connection with the station is suggestive, since he made a major contribution to the Art Nouveau in his original system of ornament. The Illinois Central's second significant shed was at their Chicago terminus (Fig. 106). A similar form was used but with only three elements, each greatly enlarged. In profile, the upward curve begins at the extremities of the wings, continues steeply over the arch, and flattens toward the apex. Possibly the shed was designed to funnel smoke off more effectively than conventional sheds, but the result looks like a delicately poised pavilion.

The great days of the train-shed were coming to a close. The railroad companies, finding them very costly to maintain, began to feel toward them as an elderly gentleman feels toward the fading but still extravagant mistress of his youth. This attitude grew up at the moment when the justification for such heavy expense was suddenly eliminated by Lincoln Bush's new type of shed. Another contributing factor was the reappearance of electrification, which permitted tracks and platforms to be depressed directly underneath the head-house, thus eliminating the need for any shed whatever; and as we shall see, only a few more were built.

Towers Triumphant

The stations of the middle period, as well as their train-sheds, remind us by their splendor and magnitude of Henry Adams' cynical comment: "Just as

15. The spans achieved in train-sheds were surpassed by others, for example the 362-foot span of the Galerie des Machines built at the Paris Exposition of 1889. Here the low, pointed profile and the ratio of width to height, 7:3, were close to those of the St. Pancras and Frankfurt am Main stations.

the French of the nineteenth century invested their surplus capital in a railway system in the belief that they would make money by it in this life, in the thirteenth they trusted their money to the Queen of Heaven because of their belief in her power to repay it with interest in the life to come." [16] Some such highly charged attitude on the part of investors is required to account for the lavishness of the new stations which so often reminded their contemporaries of medieval cathedrals—stations which embodied the triumph of the pictur- esque eclectic aesthetic in complex massing, bolder asymmetry, pointed vaults, and towers. Eclecticism had escaped from the control of the revivalists into its more creative synthetic phase. Verticality was in unchallenged supremacy in England and America. On the continent, station architects tended to be more restrained than their English-speaking colleagues, more prone to arches than towers, but they were not unaffected by the new aesthetic and clung to it longer.

The question of whether railroad stations were architecture or engineering continued to be discussed. The pages of the *Building News* recorded some of the anguished debate. The quotation on the title page of the present work comes from this source and shows how high feelings ran: "Railway termini and hotels are to the nineteenth century what monasteries and cathedrals were to the thirteenth century. They are truly the only real representative building we possess. . . . Our metropolitan termini have been leaders of the art spirit of our time." [17] Recent stations were compared to struggling monsters trying by every architectural device to attract public attention. The Paddington and Cannon Street Station hotels were condemned as "palatial" stage scenery.[18] Older stations were judged by some to be less inferior than newer ones; for example, it was argued that Tite's Italian villa stations had the merit of not being "gigantic blunders of taste." [19] Also, King's Cross was a noteworthy effort, and the newer Liverpool Street Station, though far from blameless, did essay to blend the unyielding materials brick and iron, and the color scheme of its shed—dull green roofing on chocolate-colored iron framework—was commended. St. Pancras and Liverpool Street Stations were allowed the merit of breaking monotony. Monotony was anathema to the whole century, perhaps fortunately, since their architects gave them so little of it.

If railway stations were not properly architecture, perhaps it was a matter

16. *Mont St. Michel and Chartres* (Boston, Houghton, Mifflin, 1904), p. 90.

17. *Building News, 29* (1875), 133 (source of the title-page quotation); *33* (1877), 547; *34* (1878), 430; *36* (1879), 332.

18. *Ibid., 34* (1878), 439.

19. *Ibid., 29* (1875), 133.

of choosing the right style, or a new style. The optimists who had dubbed the Italian villa style the "railroad style" were now less convinced of its promise. Revived Gothic was considered for a while to be "consistent with modern requirements," as Russell Sturgis argued.[20] A few believed that a new architectural style was forming in the despised work of the engineers. Viollet-le-Duc maintained that a civilization possessing railways should find appropriate methods of building just as the Greeks had.[21] We do not know whether or not he recognized that this had been partially accomplished in some of the Paris stations. Street's was the more common view: he scoffed at the idea that "a brand new Victorian Style might be invented, whose birth should rival that of Athena springing fully armed from the brain of some king of architects."[22]

The editors of the *Building News* suggested that new stations might be in a style bordering on the Japanese—light, free, and open—since these qualities would be more appropriate than the Queen Anne style.[23] How far in advance of the time these sentiments sound! Stations conceived as light pavilions were still seventy years off. Mass, whatever it might be in engineering, was still an inherent part of architecture.

Iron, which might have been the key to a new style, was still mistrusted and abused. Ruskin had admitted that a fresh system of architectural laws might be evolved from it, but on the whole it embarrassed him as much as it did the leading architects. Though Street admired metal in pure engineering, he was more alive to the possibilities of brick and marble in architecture. He reviled the commingling of architecture and engineering in façades which seemed to be supported by sheets of glass "as if nothing could be more satisfying to the eye than such an inversion of the natural order of things." He felt that as construction in iron became more scientific, it became artistically more unsatisfactory.[24] The naked use of iron had enjoyed a short, premature reign during the 1850's, but by the 1870's a strong reaction had set in and iron was, if possible, concealed from view.

In spite of the few who discerned some new qualities in the buildings around them, most observers were not sharp enough to see that new silhouettes, new coloration, new spatial effects, and new massing constituted a truly new style, picturesque eclecticism. Nor were they aware that "engineer's architecture" contained the ingredients of another novel, original manner.

20. *The New Path* (June 1863), pp. 4 ff.

21. *Discourses on Architecture, 1,* 343, and *2,* 53.

22. A. E. Street, *Memoir of George Edmund Street, R.A.* (London, 1888), p. 86.

23. *Building News, 36* (1879), 332.

24. *Memoir of George Edmund Street, R.A.,* pp. 111–12.

The bolder the engineers grew in designing metal train-sheds, the more timid the architects became in designing the head-house. Instead of accepting the proffered challenge, they fell back upon safer commissions: churches, public buildings, mansions. Only large dwellings might be handled in a free manner, since their respectability was assured by their owner's social or financial position.

There can be no doubt that the vast head-houses now demanded made the integration of them with the enlarged train-shed more and more difficult. Often the architect's responsibility was limited to the station itself, while the shed was reserved for the company's engineers, to be built simultaneously if funds permitted, otherwise to be added at some later date. Some architects felt that the two elements were so discordant in character that unification was impossible, and that no relationship more subtle than contiguity could be attempted. St. Pancras was unique in that its shed was designed before the architect of the station had been selected. Whether or not the architect was concerned with both, the outcome was that a masonry forebuilding usually emerged victorious, with the alien metal shed hidden behind it, visible only from the sides.

The architect was subjected to another major torment: how to provide for the crowds? Churches and theaters, the principal prototypes for a building serving large numbers of people at one time, were not much help to him: in these, the worshipers and the audiences flowed inward at stipulated times and outward at others, so that entrances could be used as exits when the leisurely flow reversed its direction. But at stations people were arriving and departing continuously, anxious to make their connection or seek their destination, burdened with luggage. How could all of them be taken care of without confusion? Many attempts have been made, but who will claim that a perfect solution has even yet been found? Perhaps a century is not long enough to solve so complex a riddle. The 19th-century architect had to work to a new kind of large scale necessitated by the vast urban crowds swarming through newly created buildings which were partly monumental, partly commercial—exhibitions, markets, department stores, railway stations—a scale which can be called demomorphic. So many new problems naturally upset the orderly traditions of architecture, and few men were big enough to meet the challenge.

Some interesting attempts were made, however, particularly in the new field of railroad hotels. Now these are dingy and out of date, so that it is hard for us to imagine their quondam appeal, but in their prime they were modern, luxurious, and fashionable. Each of the large London stations had one, usually as the forebuilding. Their central location was in their favor, particularly before the days of sleeping cars, and the premises were well kept up.

The dirt and noise which so distress us were minor factors then, since there were fewer trains and engines rarely stood long in the shed. Trains themselves still seemed partly miraculous and wholly delightful, like new toys; our great-grandparents enjoyed the novel experiences associated with trains, including the varied noises toward which our eternal urban roar has made us so blasé. The factor of convenience of the first station hotels is operative to this day, as in the group of hostelries which attached themselves to Grand Central and Pennsylvania Stations in New York; these too are in direct covered communication with the platforms. Convenience alone might have insured the success of the early ones; but when in addition no expense was spared to make them the last word in luxury, they were irresistible.

The early railroad hotels at Euston and York were comfortable, no doubt, but not opulent. P. C. Hardwick's Great Western Railway Hotel at Paddington (1853), described above,[25] pointed the way to increased grandeur. It was followed five years later by James Knowles' (1831–1908) singularly monotonous one, the Grosvenor, containing rooms of palatial size. E. M. Barry at Charing Cross (1864) and Cannon Street (1863–66) aimed at more display. The former hotel, with six stories between the street and cornice, has a "stripy pile-of-sandwiches" façade, according to Goodhart-Rendel, who does not give its architect due credit for compensating above the cornice for the unfashionable horizontality of the lower part.[26] At Cannon Street (Fig. 107), where the hotel was only four stories high, its ends were brought forward as pavilions sliced into vertical strips, the outer strips crowned by turrets. Moving inward toward the center of the building, the next strip ends in dormered mansards, and the third ones, still taller, terminate in spire-capped towers. The connecting roof is interrupted by banks of chimneys and punctuated with dormers. All this makes it more pronouncedly High Victorian than Barry's earlier one. Alfred Waterhouse finished a hotel at the Lime Street Station in Liverpool in 1869 (Fig. 108) which was both more luxurious and more Victorian. Its plumbing, lavish for the time, included thirty-seven water closets and eight baths. The main block—it is impossible to provide 200 rooms without building a block—erupts with twinned towers, some with pyramidal spires, some with conical ones. This is the Chambord *parti:* decorum is preserved to the cornice line; above it restraints are off. How much gaiety has been lost by taking the cornice as a full stop instead of a colon!

Gustave Lisch (1828–1910) used a restrained version of Waterhouse's scheme when, in 1885, he wrapped a hotel around the assorted sheds at the

25. Page 68.

26. H. S. Goodhart-Rendel, *English Architecture since the Regency* (London, 1953), p. 106.

Gare St. Lazare and frosted it with mansards, gables, and chimneys from the Tuileries. Such buildings were comparatively timid expressions of the desire for increased verticality.

This desire found opportunities for more complete fulfillment in what amounted to a rage for towers. In the English-speaking world the virile tower rose from every building of importance, including stations, in response to contemporary fashion; at this same time man was adorning his person with a towering beaver hat. Later when towers went out of fashion and the dome was revived, he made a parallel substitution of the lower, more spherical bowler for the top hat; the latter he reserved for special occasions, just as towers were still resorted to from time to time. Still later when the idea of monumentality was in temporary eclipse, man's preferred headgear became the shapeless soft felt hat.

Nowadays, to the man in the street an elderly building with a tower is automatically Victorian; but in the late 1880's, America was second only to England in her enthusiasm for them. In pre-Civil War days the competition to build the tallest church tower in the area was fought out as bitterly as the 20th century has fought to build the tallest skyscraper.[27] Christian Barman attributes the use of towers in railway stations to their hieratic function.[28] Goodhart-Rendel called the British indulgence in them at this period a "national mania," [29] and although he does not explain their ubiquity at this time, the word "mania" does recognize their emotional appeal and supports my claim that the demand for verticality coincided with the middle phase of the picturesque.

Perhaps we can account for the mania having its peak at this time. The generation in control had been born during the Regency and had, so to speak, been nurtured on towers. Each bewhiskered gentleman would have heard his nurse gossiping about the collapse of Beckford's celebrated tower at Fonthill in 1825. His reading of the Waverley Novels would have saturated every tower he knew in romantic associations. Each visit to a collection of paintings would make him realize that ruined towers were pictorial above every other subject. His drawing teacher would have encouraged him to sketch them. Henry James tells us that the sight of a ruined tower, seen one day as he was crossing the Alps, suddenly made real to him the whole glorious tradition of European culture.[30] The step from seeing towers through such an aura—one which we can never recapture—to building them was almost inevitable.

27. See my "Romanesque before Richardson in the United States," pp. 17–33.

28. *An Introduction to Railway Architecture* (London, 1950), p. 30.

29. *English Architecture since the Regency,* pp. 172–3.

30. Leon Edel, *Henry James, the Untried Years* (Philadelphia, 1953), p. 121.

Some process parallel to the conditioning of young birds would have been operative: whatever creature the fledgling first notices makes an irreversible and ineradicable impact upon its emotions, a conditioning called "imprinting." A similar conditioning may have resulted from so many-faceted an indoctrination into the lore of towers.

The allegedly insular tower mania was in fact intercontinental. Leopold Eidlitz scornfully indicated its power in this country: "how many are there who are willing to forego a tower simply because it is not needed either physically or aesthetically, . . . if by an ingenious argument it may be justified?" [31] To judge by the results, architects were capable of most ingenious arguments to support Sir Uvedale Price's belief that a tower always strikes and pleases the eye.

The models for 19th-century towers came from every past age, but one easily recognized shape was specially favored. Pugin seems to have introduced it at Scarisbrick Hall, Lancashire, in 1837. Some years later he built a much larger version that was destined to become a symbol of the whole Victorian era: Big Ben in Westminster. That striking silhouette, with its overhanging upper stage surmounted by a steep pyramidal roof interrupted by a lantern or belfry, is familiar to millions. It reappears throughout England and the United States and here and there in India and Australia. William Burges was fond of it too, though his version was generally rectangular rather than square.

Scott used it at his St. Pancras Station (Fig. 109); the train-shed and waiting rooms lie behind an unrivaled, uninhibited display of towers. The booking offices and waiting rooms are parallel with the platforms on the departure side, approached under the left-hand tower (Fig. 110). There is direct egress from the arrival platforms through a tall archway which pierced the head-building. The public rooms of the hotel were conveniently reached from the cross-platform and supplemented the facilities of the station proper. Scott, who achieved here the most extravagantly picturesque of all railroad stations, tells in his *Recollections* how he had to be persuaded to enter the limited competition after more than once declining. The directors of the Midland Company were ambitious to secure the best available talent. Among the other competitors were E. M. Barry, architect of the railroad hotels at Charing Cross and Cannon Street, who placed third; Mr. Darbyshire, Messrs. Hine and Evans, Mr. Owen Jones, Mr. Lloyd of Bristol; Messrs. Lockwood and Mawson, famous for their public buildings; Mr. Walters, Mr. T. C. Sorby, and F. P. Cockerell.[32] Scott relates that he worked out the design at the seaside (he never took a real holiday) "in the same style which I had almost originated

31. *The Nature and Function of Art* (London, 1881), p. 42.

32. *Builder, 23* (1865), 896, and *24* (1865), 35, 105.

several years earlier for the government offices [the Foreign and India Offices, Whitehall, which Palmerston had dictatorially rejected], but divested of the Italian element. The great shed-like roof had already been designed by Mr. Barlow, the engineer, and as if by anticipation its section was a pointed arch. . . . This work has been spoken of by one of the revilers of my profession with abject contempt. I have set off against this, the too excessive praise of it which I receive from other quarters. It is often spoken of to me as the finest building in London; my own belief is that it is possibly *too good* for its purpose." [33]

As Scott himself pointed out, the apparent harmony between the shed and the hotel was fortuitous though nonetheless admirable. The *Building News* acclaimed it: "The harmony that is apparent in all parts of this great work is a practical proof, if any were wanted, of the advantages that accrue from the united working of architects and engineers." [34] What if some other architect less determinedly Gothic had won the competition? Since it took place in 1865, the design would have been High Victorian anyway.

In confirmation of its author's immodest opinion, St. Pancras was admired for many years. In the 1890's "this splendid Gothic pile . . . is ornate to a degree seldom seen in such structures, and is of a rich red well calculated to defy the begriming aspects of the London atmosphere. . . . The lofty clock tower is the finest feature of the façade." [35] In 1913 it was enthusiastically praised by M. S. Briggs: "[It is] typical of Sir Gilbert Scott in his happiest vein, is one of the greatest works of the Gothic Revival . . . [and] preserves a freshness usually lacking in buildings of its age. In the writer's opinion no important English station of the nineteenth century surpasses St. Pancras in general excellence." [36] Today, converted to the less glamorous uses of an office building, the towered silhouette is still of remarkable beauty; seen in the dimming light of a late afternoon, it evokes visions of enchanted floating castles.

No other station was to cast such a spell. In London it seems to have been conceded that St. Pancras was unsurpassable, and no one even tried to surpass it. At Liverpool Street Station, Edward Wilson in 1874 did what he could with an awkward site chiefly below street level, using pavilions and one small tower. The *Building News* praised it. It was ingenious but not spectacular.

33. Scott, *Recollections*, pp. 270–2.

34. *Building News, 16* (1869), 135–6.

35. *The Queen's London* (London, 1897), p. 369.

36. *Architect* (London, Aug. 8, 1913), p. 156. One is reminded by all this praise of the joke "C'est magnifique, mais ce n'est pas la gare." The station is the chief one for trains to the Highlands; there is a saying in London, "St. George for England, St. Pancras for Scotland."

The Midland Company, as though exhausted by St. Pancras, built a lesser station, St. Enoch's, in Glasgow in 1874–78. Here the costly towers were omitted, but even without them a good deal was possible; the skyline was animated with banks of chimneys and pointed dormers, and the walls were subdivided by pavilions and bow windows. Thomas Prosser at York added another chapter to each of two stories: that of the arched train-shed and that of the celebrated series of York stations. The great beauty of the sheds has been praised earlier; [37] but it was not communicated to the insignificant buildings which accompanied them, plain to the point of bareness. The hotel by William Peachy, for example, finished in 1878, was entirely detached and contributed little to the external effect of the whole; indeed it would have been difficult to design a building in masonry to equal the superlative one in iron and glass. Architects were on the whole too ready to mask the grandeur of the engineer's work with the more questionable products of their eclectic imaginations.

The times called for richness and display and architects answered the call enthusiastically, particularly in Britain. Ultimately, the example of the great English stations of this period was felt on the Continent; but during the early part of the middle period German architects, indifferent to the extremely picturesque British mood, created a second railroad style of their own. They clothed plans derived from French stations in an idiom developed from their own Romanesque. Perhaps there was an element of chauvinism in the choice of style, but national pride was not strong enough to insulate them entirely from the typical configuration of the period. The charming Emden Station of 1856–63 (Fig. 111) is an illustration of the way these forces were operating. Only two stories high, it has a seven-part composition which has been handled more plastically than at Munich. The main theme is established in the end pavilions: tall pilasters frame two unequal stories, the lower story being pierced by a single thin roundheaded window and the gabled upper story having three such windows. This theme is modulated in the five bays of the wings and again in the larger pavilions of the central mass. In this way a long, low, complexly articulated building has been enlivened by numerous thin vertical details.

Toward the end of the decade, Berlin began rebuilding its numerous depots in a similar style. The prominent ends of the sheds were perforated by large windows. At the Ost Bahnhof (1866–67) their level summits lay below a horizontal attic. At the Schlesischer Bahnhof (1867–69) the end wall was curved upward above the windows to follow the outline of the shed roof. At the Stettiner Bahnhof, 1876 (Fig. 83), the climax of this type is reached in one of the finest of Berlin's stations: here the three arches at the end of the

37. Page 85.

shed are graduated in height under a curved gable flanked by thin towers, with low wings at the side emphasizing the majesty of the shed block; the curvilinear theme is subtly varied and graduated. At the powerful Anhalter Bahnhof (Fig. 112, 113) the same stylistic elements are used on a mass which has been given more movement. Here Franz Schwechten (1841–1924) designed the finest head station since the Gare de l'Est. From the streets which converged toward it, the traveler was able to see from afar each of its main elements and so understand how he should proceed after entering. The porte-cochere projected to invite him in; the waiting rooms lay conveniently at either side; behind soared the shed. The elements of the French model had been rearranged more expressively. Marianna Van Rensselaer, the subtle architectural critic, endorsed the station's reputation and praised its independence from time-honored models.[38] Other German stations at Karlsruhe and Hanover developed the formula of the Emden Station. Their long-drawn-out façades were broken into many small parts, each with its own roof, and intricacy was accomplished by interweaving horizontal and vertical motives.

The Berlin Stadtbahn stations constituted a radically different family. Architectural detail was confined to the lateral walls on which, rather needlessly, considerable effort was sometimes expended. Brick and terra cotta decoration, Renaissance in inspiration, contributed to the desired variety and roughness. The gratuitous elaboration of these walls recalls Fergusson's criticism of the London Crystal Palace: after it had been re-erected at Sydenham, he commented that "it could have been raised from mere engineer's architecture to monumentality by sheathing the lower stories in brick." [39]

Elsewhere on the continent there was little inventiveness at this time. The French made no important advances between their great head stations of the 1850's and the Laloux stations of the 1890's. Their energies were absorbed in repeatedly enlarging their terminals—each time inadequately.

As though to celebrate the unification of Italy, new stations were begun at Turin, Trieste, Genoa, Milan, Naples, and Rome at this time. Italian architects, drunk on the wine of nationalism, tended to ignore the new architecture in other countries and to rely on their own traditions; but unfortunately this spirit was not well suited to the solution of station problems. At Turin, Carlo Ceppi (1829–1921) built the Stazione di Porta Nuova in 1866 (Fig. 114) at the south end of the Piazza Carlo Felice, closing an unrivaled monumental vista. The arched train-shed was the axial feature, but the long wings at either side of it were so nearly the same height that the shed lost effectiveness, and a superfluity of colossal arches along the whole extent further tended toward

38. *American Architect, 18* (July 25, 1885), 51.

39. *History of the Modern Styles of Architecture, 2,* 421.

monotony. As rebuilt since World War II, the shed has become an imposing concourse preliminary to a range of great halls. In Genoa the site of the main station (Fig. 115) lies constrictedly at the corner of the Piazza Acquaverde, below one hill and looking down over another toward the crowded port. A triumphal arch was placed diagonally between colonnaded wings, each of which originally ended in another triumphal arch, but the western one became an obstacle to traffic and has been removed. The Milan station was begun in 1873 by the active railroad architect J. L. Bouchot (*b.* 1817). Since Milan had so many French episodes in its history, the employment of a French architect was natural enough. Bouchot supplied mansard roofs and pavilions derived from the new Louvre. Each of the five main elements had its own roof: the wings hipped ones, the end pavilions square mansards, and the central one a curved mansard. Except for these commanding superstructures, however, there was little attempt at fashionable verticality; movement and variety sufficed, as they usually did in Italy. In Rome, Salvatore Bianchi's (1821–84) Stazione Termini I (Fig. 116) presented a curious mixture of forms: it was a two-sided pseudo head station. From the vast Piazza dei Cinquecento the shed appeared as a pointed arch recessed between a pair of *palazzi.* Bianchi seemed undecided about which of his elements should dominate and was indifferent to stylistic purity. The influence of the Gare de l'Est was potent but its motives were recombined in an original and uncouth manner. In Naples, the *parti* of the Roman station was followed by Nicolo Breglia, who surrounded the lower floor with a stately arcaded portico (Fig. 117) providing covered access on three sides as welcome in the torrid heat as in the bitter winter. The shed was destroyed in World War II, but the remaining parts still serve their original function.

In the same year the renowned French firm of Eiffel and Company constructed the shed of the West Bahnhof in Budapest described above.[40] This was a two-sided station with a pseudo head-building. The glass-filled gables of the shed were flanked by an amazing exhibition of "architect's architecture" by A. de Serres. We may presume from the richness of the building with which he surrounded the simple shed that he was following the law of contrast. He supplied elaborate pavilions roofed by curved mansards and four towers ending in pointed, octagonal domes.

A second large station at Budapest (Fig. 118) went up in 1881, designed by Julius Rochlitz (1827–86). Although there were only three principal parts to the main façade, their relationships were unusual: the arched end of the shed pierced the pseudo head-building, framed by an enormous triumphal arch which fitted over it like a nut on a bolt. The columns flanking the arch were raised not on the conventional single podium but on a double one, so

40. Page 83. See Fig. 90.

that their bases stood level with the cornices of the wings—a more audacious than skillful device. The wings, smaller in size and scale than the giant arch which separated them, incongruously wore curved mansard roofs. It was an infelicitous reworking of Viel's entrance motive for the Paris Exposition of 1855; in no way could it be considered a refinement of it. Rochlitz' station was also derived from the Lehrter Bahnhof of 1869–71 in Berlin, where the same motives had been harmoniously integrated. Height, it is true, was achieved, but only by violence. It was in such compromises with the picturesque aesthetic that continental stations reflected English leadership.

Victorian America

In the United States there were compromises too, but they were due less to spiritual than to economic obstacles. American architects could not yet compete with their European colleagues on equal terms. On the new western lines, where the tepee fires had barely cooled, conditions were as primitive as they had formerly been in the East; in 1871 Indians were still burning lonely stations on the Santa Fe. Buildings were so crude that they were lined with buffalo hides in the winter. In 1873 the depot at Dodge City was turned into a citadel in a battle between the mayor and the populace over the closing of the red-light district. Stations improvised of old freight cars were intended to be temporary, though some remain today, as at Tabernash, Colorado. Until the 1890's, even the bigger stations were only relatively superior, though Ringwalt boasted: "On many lines and at many times, station accommodations have kept pace with the improvement in cars, elegant and commodious edifices taking the place of rude sheds, and some of the finest structures in the land being placed at the service of railway passengers. The aggregate outlay for such purposes represents such a large sum that many of the companies have never secured an adequate return." [41]

Only Grand Central in New York (Figs. 119, 120, 121) failed to disappoint visitors from abroad. In 1869, architects Isaac C. Buckhout and John B. Snook endeavored to realize Commodore Vanderbilt's dream of being the first American to sponsor a station that would rival the celebrated European ones. The "L" shaped block of the head-house concealed the tremendous shed from both Vanderbilt Avenue and 42d Street. The main front on the latter street was a long block three stories in height, but it was not possible in the 1860's to leave it at that; it was given three square-domed pavilions. The inspiration for all this clearly came from the Louvre, and the Commodore,

41. Ringwalt, *Development of Transportation Systems in the United States,* p. 255.

as an empire builder, was undoubtedly vain enough to feel that there was nothing incongruous in transplanting a palace to serve as his personal head-quarters. The two considerations of economy and fireproofing determined that all of the ornamental work (coins, cornices, and window frames) should be cast iron painted white; this was one respect in which Grand Central failed to equal the standards of Paris. There were others. The boxy elements lacked the elegant French verticality. Contemporaries accused the architects of clapping slated mansard roofs onto a Renaissance design, and indeed that was the impression it gave: possibly these flourishes were afterthoughts.[42] The rear façade of the shed was more delicate in scale but was marred by a bewildering variety of curves. The one noble curve, that of the shed itself, was ignored in favor of a meretricious confection. The pavilions of the main façade were steps on the road to true towers with Victorian Gothic habili-ments.

The earliest direct influence of St. Pancras Station was shown in the Park Square Station in Boston (Fig. 122)—one of the masterpieces of the 1870's —for which Peabody and Stearns won the competition held in 1872.[43] It was a head station on one level with excellent circulation. The design, materials, and finish were comparable to those at Memorial Hall in nearby Cambridge. The lofty general waiting room was provided with rose windows and clusters of gaslights. There was a reading room and a billiard room. Delicate iron tracery screened the steam radiators.[44] On the exterior the asymmetrically placed prominent tower, gables, and polychromy responded perfectly to the canons of High Victorian taste. If it had survived to the present day this station would have come in ultimately for the obloquy which now falls to the lot of most buildings of that period, but it did not last so long; in 1899 it was torn down and its services transferred to the new South Station. Its obituary was in the tone appropriate for a man cut down in his prime: "It was long the show building of Back Bay. . . . Its gentle English Gothic exterior, its finely proportioned clock tower, its graceful façade were the pride of our town, and the atmosphere of elegant social intercourse which pervaded its waiting rooms, its exclusive barbershop and even its refined

42. An extensive modernization was undertaken along baroque lines thirty years later under the direction of Bradford L. Gilbert. Unfortunately the consequences were even more ungainly than the clumsy original building. Twelve years later the whole was demolished to make way for the present third station—now in its turn threatened with destruction.

43. Its shed has been described above, p. 87. See Fig. 100.

44. Justin Winsor, the librarian, stated in the *Library Journal, 4* (1879), 222, that the plan of this station would make a better library than any in existence. The sketch (Fig. 123) shows how he would adapt the station to library purposes.

washrooms was wonderful." [45] The tower was generally admired, even though a New York newspaper voiced some reservations: "The new depot . . . resembles more nearly a church edifice . . . rising above the roof and aiding still more to mislead the spectator as to the nature of the edifice is a well-proportioned tower 125 feet high." [46] It was in the height of fashion, particularly in its varicolored roofs. Scott had stated the proper attitude toward roofs and his words had not fallen on deaf ears: "If the roofs be shown, they should rise fearlessly to the proper pitch, not seem to draw in their horns like a snail, as if dreading the touch of criticism." [47] Slates of a single color would have run the risk of seeming monotonous. Ruskin had emphasized the desirability of using varicolored materials in building—the principle of constructive coloration—and again it was Scott who specified how this should be done: "I would . . . endeavor to give warmth and richness . . . by the introduction of materials of varied color, and in some places introducing a kind of simple mosaic of colored materials to heighten and brighten the effects." [48] These last words are an amplification of the picturesque doctrine, an idea which had not occurred to Price but which exactly captured the taste of Scott's generation. Moderation, reticence, or understatement meant less to them than the bold and striking.

Of an exceptional station built in Worcester, 1875–77 (Fig. 124), only the tower has survived; this was preserved as a memorial to a building of outstanding quality after the rest of the station was demolished. The plan of the station was somewhat peculiar: some trains entered the shed obliquely while others went through directly, so that there was only one corner which could be occupied by the head-house. Part of this was slid in under the sheds and part projected from the corner, identified by an arrow-like tower. From a battered base the tower rose as a straight shaft for 160 feet, completed by a slate-covered wooden spire bringing the height to 212 feet. It would have gone higher if the architects, Ware and Van Brunt, had had their way—they always said it appeared too short—but the directors were firm. The sheds, tower, and rounded head-house, all faced in stone, formed a remarkably well integrated group called "the most picturesque structure of the kind which has yet been erected." [49] The stone facing of the metal sheds lacked structural logic, yet according to the prevailing point of view the end justified the means.

45. Quoted in Kilham, *Boston after Bulfinch,* p. 76.

46. *New York Daily Graphic,* Friday, June 4, 1875.

47. Scott, *Remarks on Secular and Domestic Architecture,* p. 210.

48. *Ibid.,* pp. 198–9.

49. *Railroad Gazette* (Dec. 18, 1875), p. 522. For a description of the shed, see above, p. 87.

Such towered stations with their Gothic seasoning were to be found throughout this country—at Washington, D.C. (Fig. 125), in Chicago, at Lynn, Massachusetts, and in many other cities. A few of them remain today.

The Broad Street Station in Philadelphia (Fig. 126)—launched in 1881 on a building program which was to continue nearly to the end of the century—stood for more than fifty years, receiving a dwindling volume of praise which turned gradually to downright abuse. In 1881 the Pennsylvania's spur lines into the city at Filbert Street were raised on a viaduct terminating at an ambitious station. Fifty years later it was decided to withdraw from that central location facing the city hall and construct a more imposing station on a more ample site at Thirtieth Street. Despite its colossal dimensions, the new one does not seem fated to enjoy as much praise as its predecessor. The Broad Street Station (Fig. 126) was full of fresh ideas and abreast of the fashions, but the Thirtieth Street Station (Figs. 176, 177) was old-fashioned before it left the drafting board. The trains approached the older station on the famous "Chinese Wall," now demolished, which made a two-level scheme inevitable. Part of the ground floor was used as a convenient protected carriage way connected to the platform level by massive elevators. Seven years later additions larger than the original building were begun. The modest twin-span sheds were removed and a new shed (Fig. 104) as wide as the site allowed—300 feet—was begun. This was destined to be the winner of the 70-year-long race to construct the largest single-span train-shed in the world. The architects were Joseph Wilson and Arthur Truscott for the earlier parts and Frank Furness and Allan Evans for the later additions in 1893.[50] The treatment of the public spaces was original, particularly in the waiting room (Fig. 127). Its roof was supported on a novel type of pier. Square in section, ornament began to enliven it halfway up, culminating in pairs of flattened brackets which flared outward to hold the beams. Either the upper half or the upper third of the piers can be understood as capitals; this ambiguity is in the mannerist spirit which seems also to pervade Karl Bitter's famous "relief paintings" in the waiting room—a rare combination of two media.

The interiors of the Broad Street Station flowed into one another with a minimum of impediment and with dynamic effect. The flat ceiling of the main

50. William Campbell, "Frank Furness, an American Pioneer," *Architectural Review, 110* (1951), 310–15; and Theo B. White, ed., *Philadelphia Architecture in the 19th Century* (Philadelphia, 1953), p. 32. Furness has lately received well deserved commendation for the freedom with which he composed masses, space, and ornament. He seems to have gone very far in throwing off the shackles of eclecticism. He contributed to the formation of Louis Sullivan's style, and his own style in turn was influenced by that of Viollet-le-Duc. Both of the older men had a sense of structural candor which outran their capacity to give it refined form.

rooms contrasted with the vault of the shed beyond. Furness' staircases were as baroque as 18th-century German ones. The stairs and attendant elevators rose openly from the floor below, their dignified up-and-downness complementing the in-and-out movement of the nearby trains.

Externally, the building played down station character in favor of office building character. Both older and newer sections bore towers, but the later one by Furness (at the left of the photograph) is so elaborate and intricate that it eclipses Truscott's earlier, St. Pancras-inspired one, as Lillian Russell eclipsed Jenny Lind. How did either architect have the temerity to challenge the stupendous tower of the city hall across the street with their comparatively puny ones? Perhaps it was done in the spirit which led David to challenge Goliath; perhaps rugged individualism was so much a part of their make-ups that they were totally oblivious of the neighboring giant. To the pedestrian the visual unit includes all the buildings on both sides of the street, but the designer of each section of this station behaved as though his work would always remain in the isolation of his drawing board.

The mood which made such an attitude possible was waning. At this same time, F. H. Kimball built a station (Fig. 128) a few blocks away for the Reading Railroad without any towers at all. It is like a wide, level cliff with a cave at its base. The verticals and horizontals derived from the Renaissance precedent are interwoven over its façade. It was too early for a flat slab treatment, but movement and intricacy were beginning to congeal. Something like this had already happened in England at the Midland Hotel in Manchester of the 1890's, where the Gothic idiom had been supplanted by the Queen Anne and variety of motive was more important than movement.

Overlapping in time with the Gothic group described above was a second, almost equally picturesque family in the Romanesque idiom. Popular as round arches had been earlier in the century (as seen in Tefft's station of the late 1840's and numerous German ones), fresh impetus was given to the use of Romanesque forms when H. H. Richardson began to manipulate them in his personal manner. So influential was his new version that it supplanted Victorian Gothic. By 1885 the ten best buildings in America, as chosen by the members of the American Institute of Architects, included five by Richardson: Trinity Church, Boston, first; the Albany City Hall, seventh; Sever Hall, Cambridge, eighth; the New York State Capitol, of which he had built a considerable part, ninth; and his town hall in North Easton, Massachusetts, tenth.[51] The only classical building considered worthy of inclusion was the Capitol in Washington, as much for sentimental as for aesthetic reasons. Nine of the ten selected were medieval and picturesque; eight had towers; half were by one man in his new style. There was no Victorian Gothic building among

51. *American Architect, 16* (June 13, 1885), 282.

them! How could a new style become so popular so quickly? Probably because it did not break violently with the established aesthetic tradition; the same picturesque principles continued in force. There was change without revolution.

The wave of 19th-century form was beginning its descent toward another trough. When it had begun its rise, classical and Italianate round-arched motives prevailed. When it reached its crest, the tall, thin, pointed arches of the Victorian Gothic had been favored. Now as the wave was subsiding, round-arched motives returned, but this time the motives were derived from Romanesque sources; presently classical arches would reappear and the cycle would be complete. Towers followed the same sequence: from short, stubby ones to thin, elongated ones with tapering spires, and then to short, bulky ones. Eventually they would be omitted. The second revival of Romanesque forms might have enriched the eclectic vocabulary of High Victorian Gothic; instead it replaced it. The process was the gradual substitution of static forms for exuberant ones. Towers were not suddenly abandoned: they gradually shrank down to be absorbed in the main mass. In the new configuration, a single massive tower became the focus of the composition, whereas previously several were used as accents. The transition from the old to the new began at the base of the building as though a fancy-dress costume were being lifted off to reveal more and more of a stout body underneath. The first step is illustrated in C. L. W. Eidlitz's stations (Figs. 129, 133), where fantasy, eliminated between the basement and the cornice, remains at the summit. The next stage is illustrated by S. Beman's Grand Central Station in Chicago (Fig. 130), where the costume has been lifted still higher and the tower stretches upward as though to grasp its vanishing hem.

The slight change involved in the new mode can be seen by comparing two stations built about 20 years apart: the earlier is the Park Square Station in Boston, the later is the Chicago and North Western station in Milwaukee (Figs. 122, 131). In both stations the mass of the head-house is about the same size. In both, the roofs are clearly seen; gables break up the skyline, and clock towers stand to the left of the central axis. Arched entrances penetrate the ground floors; towers dominate the building. The general resemblances are strong. The transformation has been one of detail—from the sharp, thin, and agitated toward fewer but more substantial elements and a calmer tone.

Similar changes can be traced through other stations. Joseph Wilson's Victorian Gothic Baltimore and Potomac station in Washington, D.C. (Fig. 125), has the restless polychromatic character of the Park Square Station. Boyington's Chicago and North Western station in Chicago has Queen Anne detail (Fig. 132). C. L. W. Eidlitz in his Dearborn Street Station in Chicago

(Fig. 129) moved further toward the newer configuration; only his tower preserved some Victorian exuberance in its complex roof, which is almost a spire. His Michigan Central station in Detroit (Fig. 133) is more restrained, although its picturesque qualities were very marked, as the description quoted above indicated.[52] Isaac Taylor's Union Depot in Detroit a few years later (Fig. 134) moves still further from the earlier mode toward the more restrained later manner. The towers no longer clearly dominate the gables but are in competition with them. Both that station and Thomas Rodd's Indianapolis Union Station (Fig. 135) still place their towers at the most conspicuous corner and the adjoining façades climb up toward them motive by motive. The impressionistic effects of previous decades have been replaced by more plastic ones composed of groups of robust blocks, each preserving a degree of independence yet fitted together in an articulated pyramid. At Indianapolis this seems to happen almost by accident, since each façade is symmetrically composed about a central axis of its own, with only the corner tower making the whole building asymmetrical. In the Detroit example the tower has been distended; it is half tower and half skyscraper. As though to point up its huge bulk there is a miniature copy of it at the end of the right wing. It would have been more natural to design a different tower for that location. Spencer Solon Beman composed his Chicago station in a similar manner but with exaggerated proportions. His Chicago Grand Central Station (Fig. 130), referred to above on p. 105, has a tower 247 feet high. Unbroken vertical masses on each of the main façades step gradually up to the climactic tower, thus conforming to the new configuration.

Beman's towers and arches incorporate huge blocks, an innovation of the period. These were derived from H. H. Richardson's enormous quarry-faced stones or boulders used for textural contrast. To Sir Uvedale Price, roughness had been largely a matter of deterioration of the surface through age and neglect. He would, however, have appreciated the positive contribution of Richardson's device over the small-scale materials of Victorian Gothic or the uniform bricks of the earlier round-arched style. Richardson made use of his innovation in his famous stations for the Boston and Albany Railroad in the neighborhood of Boston. His North Easton station (Fig. 136) typifies his use of large voussoirs combined with widely overhanging roofs. The ends of the beams are buried in masonry worthy of a fortress. Railroad officials deplored his impractical plans, excessive costs, and interior gloom, but the cultivated Bostonian was impressed. The dramatic grandeur of these small stations was in marked contrast to the wooden structures they replaced. How would Richardson have designed a really large station? How would he have coped with the train-shed? The largest station he designed, that for New

52. See above, p. 5.

London (Fig. 137), was only commissioned in 1885 and hardly begun before his death. There, as in Sever Hall, he used only brick, but the desired massiveness was accomplished by battering the walls of the lower story and letting the second story overhang. There was no shed; instead, the platform was protected by a massive timber veranda quite as overwhelming as the roof of the main building. Since this proved too expensive to repair, it has recently been removed, thus ending the dense gloom within.

The ponderous Richardsonian manner was followed by station architects for many years. Bruce Price used it at Montreal in 1888, Strickland and Symonds at Toronto in 1892–94, Theodore C. Link at St. Louis in 1891–94, and Bradford Gilbert in several places. Only two more stations of this type will be considered in detail. They are transitional, belonging in some respects to the third phase. The first of these is Theodore C. Link's Union Station in St. Louis (Fig. 138). It was St. Louis' pride. For a brief moment it enjoyed the title of "largest depot in the world." Its enormous shed made no aesthetic contribution; it covered several acres but was broken up into five spans, none of them very wide and all of them low. The station is a head station technically on one level, since it is possible to enter and leave at the track level, entirely bypassing the Grand Hall and waiting rooms on the second floor. There is a cross-platform seventy feet wide which, in the terminology of the Chicago Fair of 1893, was dubbed "the Midway." The Grand Hall (Fig. 139) is the best feature; it is an enlarged version of the dining room in Adler and Sullivan's Auditorium Hotel in Chicago, roofed by a semicircular barrel vault which seems to spring from the floor itself, so low are the side walls. No previous age had used this proportion of wall to ceiling, which is related to the tunnel spaces previously discussed.[53] The sense of enclosure is overwhelming. It is cavelike and induces a feeling of awe but, unlike the vestibule of the station at Frankfurt am Main, does not make the spectator feel insignificant, because the portals are in human scale. The exterior is less successful. The elements include a hotel, a powerful tower, and many smaller parts too numerous to be successfully fitted into a Romanesque formula. Although the Romanesque was frequently applied to vast buildings, it was better adapted to relatively small ones. Nevertheless, the St. Louis station is effectively picturesque from a distance and now forms a scenic background for Milles' operatic fountain.

The second late Romanesque station to be considered is Bradford Gilbert's Illinois Central Station in Chicago, begun in 1892 (Figs. 140, 141), whose train-shed has been described.[54] Gilbert had already completed a number of successful stations. He was the second architect since Francis

53. See above, p. 23.

54. See above, p. 89, and Fig. 106.

Thompson to publish a book of his railroad buildings; his *Sketch Portfolio of Railroad Stations* first appeared privately in 1881. The Chicago station is his masterpiece. The metropolitan site and an ample budget permitted him to surpass his previous efforts. There are four main elements: train-shed, tower, office building, and waiting room. The latter, in the form of an arched train-shed, is a clear instance of the metamorphosis of the train-shed into another element of the station complex. This noble room is placed on the second floor over the tracks, so that passengers are required to climb up to it and then descend again to the tracks. Louis Sullivan made an apt criticism of this type of plan, presumably with reference to this station: "My son, here is the place—perhaps a unique spot on earth—holy in iniquity, where, to go in you go out, and to go out you go in; where to go up you go down, and to go down you go up. All in all it seems to me the choicest fruit yet culled from that broad branch of the tree of knowledge, known as the public-be-damned style." [55] The waiting room was elaborately decorated, perhaps partially to compensate for this inconvenience. It had a mosaic floor, marble wainscoting, and stuccoed ceiling "studded with incandescent lights." [56] At the end toward the lake there was a huge arched window recalling that of the Gare de l'Est but transformed with "cathedral glass set in rich and glowing colors." [57]

Richardson's influence is paramount in exterior detail and massing, but the master would have been able to avoid the disjointed look of Gilbert's design. The thin tower and stout office block compete for attention. Both masses house continuous floors of office space, perhaps justifying the undifferentiated fenestration, which, however, also obscures the individuality of the two parts. The windows make the tower seem insubstantial and the office block irresolute. These weaknesses were less marked in his first project (Fig. 140).

These two stations mark the end of the second phase of station building in the United States. Better operating practices, palatial stations, luxurious Pullmans had made railroad travel as comfortable and secure as the pioneers had predicted would come to pass. The previous decades had witnessed the climax of the High Victorian style, during which arches were given new profiles and towers were believed to lend hieratic significance. Eclecticism was becoming more and more independent of the past. The picturesque aesthetic, now rounding out a century-long domination of man's way of seeing, had absorbed new idioms. It was losing some of the vitality of its youth but was not yet moribund. Its influence would be felt for two more decades.

55. *Kindergarten Chats* (New York, Wittenborn, Schultz, 1947), p. 23.

56. *Chicago Inter-Ocean*, Nov. 1893. Quoted in B. L. Gilbert, *Sketch Portfolio of Railroad Stations and Kindred Structures,* New York, 1895.

57. *New York Observer,* Nov. 1893. Quoted in Gilbert, *Sketch Portfolio.*

5. THE THIRD PHASE:

MEGALOMANIA

(1890-1914)

"No New Problems"

The peaceful years which were brought to a tragic conclusion by the catastrophe of 1914 exhibited the positive and negative qualities of a late period. Elephantiasis overtook every aspect of railroading, including the terminals, now built to dimensions never before approached. Aesthetically, the obviously striking effects of the previous more romantic decades were replaced by the equally obvious appeal of unprecedented size. The love of towers was now too deeply rooted to be entirely overthrown; but towers became less frequent and less picturesque. Domes often took the place of spires. The creative element in the eclecticism of the Victorian Gothic grew stronger and in movements such as the Art Nouveau freed itself entirely from derivative details. Eclecticism, "that principle of the highest value," [1] was capable of many permutations, and in this period it led to marked independence from the alleged prototypes of the Renaissance or classical storehouses. When these unmedieval idioms were first readopted, the tendency was toward exact copying, but for two reasons they did not last long. In the first place, familiarity with the newly introduced forms led not to contempt but to confidence, and the details were manipulated and interpreted as freely as the designer willed. In the second place, the historic *partis* could not be stretched to clothe the vastly greater bulk required by the new buildings. No chateau or temple could be reused without violent distortion or tedious multiplication. The State, War, and Navy Building in Washington and the Philadelphia City Hall bear witness to this;

1. Scott, *Remarks on Secular and Domestic Architecture*, p. 265 n. See above, pp. 13 ff.

in both there are more pavilions and more stories than in any ancient chateau. The increase in size also forced an increase in scale. Direct imitation of the model became impossible so that its clear image faded and blurred; this can be so easily confirmed that the charge of "copyism" falls to the ground. The University Club in New York is not a copy of any particular Renaissance building; the Tiffany Building, though Venetian, is like no specific palace; the Union Station in Washington, while classical, is not a facsimile of any classic building.

The increase in the scale of building echoed the tendency of the era to increase the absolute size of everything from empires to transatlantic liners. The number of tracks on the main railroad lines was doubled and in two instances increased to four parallel lines: the New York Central in the 1890's between Albany and Buffalo, and the Pennsylvania in 1903 from Pittsburgh to Philadelphia. The average distance traveled was increasing, and the speed of operation picked up. Short independent companies were consolidated into large systems or nationalized into still larger ones, as in Italy. France was doing the same thing more gradually as the original private leases expired. It is not surprising, therefore, that the largest stations in history were built during this period. The second Grand Central in New York (1903–12) had 67 tracks and accommodated 600 trains and 110,000 passengers a day; the new station at Leipzig, with 36 lines, had 400 trains a day. In older, rebuilt stations in London and Paris 1,000 trains and 200,000 passengers per day were becoming common. The new leviathans stood 70 feet high to the cornice, with façades 1,000 feet long and concourses to correspond. There was a grave concomitant: travelers were required to walk interminable distances through the marble wastes—in five instances it was more than 1,000 feet from street to train—and the situation was not improved by the lengthening of trains, which extended into the yards beyond the platforms. Veblen's attack on public buildings could be applied to terminals: "It would be extremely difficult to find a modern . . . public building which can claim anything better than relative inoffensiveness in the eyes of anyone who will dissociate the elements of beauty from those of honorific waste."[2] Whatever such a critic might feel, the common man loved palatial surroundings, and dedicated, sensitive architects supplied them.

Since the shed, which had been the largest element, was becoming old-fashioned, the tradition of vast interiors was transferred to the concourse: at Grand Central, New York, this is 125 feet wide, 375 feet long, and 120 feet high; at the nearby Pennsylvania Station it is even higher—150 feet. Such opulent dimensions were not functionally necessary; the companies could afford magnificence and enjoyed their munificent role, as princes had in predemocratic ages.

2. Thorstein Veblen, *The Theory of the Leisure Class* (New York, 1899), p. 154.

It was alleged that no new solutions to station planning appeared because there were no new problems. Although this was an exaggeration, it is true that no radically new principle of station planning appeared then, nor has any appeared since the mid-19th century; the monstrous new stations merely revised traditional schemes. The chief modification was toward multiplication in depth, going beyond the simpler two-level scheme of Hanover to three or four levels. There was also a decrease in the use of stub tracks; it was found that a stub track could handle only about two trains an hour compared to three for through tracks, so that the former were used only in situations so constricted as to admit of no alternative. When new sites could be selected, those permitting the lines to run through freely—even if only for a few miles to a train-yard—were preferred. At Washington and Chicago, through lines supplemented the spurs. In South Station, Boston, and Grand Central, New York, loop lines were introduced (Fig. 142). Not all the spurs could be connected to the loop lines, since some of the resulting curvatures would be unnegotiable; loops were therefore a compromise with the engineer's ideal of a full complement of through lines. At Victoria Station, London, an extra line between two spurs helped solve some of the difficulty (Text Fig. E).

E. London, Victoria Station. Diagram showing third track added between two older ones.

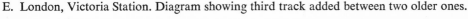

The present Grand Central Station in New York (Figs. 142, 169, 170), now nearly half a century old, was and is one of the outstandingly successful stations of history. The use of multiple levels to handle the complex circulation problems was carried further than in any other station; the credit for this is to be divided between the company engineers and the architects, Reed and Stem. The engineers devised the track layout with express trains above and suburban trains below, each set of tracks being provided with a concourse of its own, so that in effect two stations are superimposed. Unlike the earlier loop lines at South Station, Boston, those provided in New York functioned admirably. Ramps were used lavishly, not only to get passengers to and from the platforms but also to get them in and out of the station. There are connections to all the neighboring streets and to subways and shuttle trains. All of this was achieved without forcing passengers to walk excessive distances. The history and operation of this terminal are well described in a recent monograph.[3]

The one-sided scheme, as always, continued to be the only feasible solution

3. David Marshall, *Grand Central,* New York, McGraw Hill, 1946.

in some locations. The ways of connecting the waiting room with the outlying platforms included subways and bridges varied by an occasional ramp. When the tracks were at a lower level than the street, the bridge waiting room could be used. At New Haven's first station, Austin had hung a gallery over the lines. At the Kansas City Union Station (1910–13), Baltimore Union (1910), and Richmond, Virginia (1919), this gallery was developed into a fully enclosed waiting room, connected by stairs with the several platforms immediately below, so that the passenger waiting there has the comfort of being Johnny-on-the-spot. This device is still current in such very recent stations as those at Toledo and Akron. From the viewpoint of the traveler, the most regrettable arrangement is one in which the tracks are above street level and the connection from the waiting room is by staircases. This unfortunate arrangement persisted in stations like the North Western in Chicago (1906–11) and culminated in gigantic flights of stairs at Milan. The problems attendant in moving 100,000 people a day vertically by mechanical means are not easily solved, but abundant elevators and more escalators offer welcome ameliorations.

The source of these new variants lay, as had been so often the case, across the Atlantic in Paris, where Victor Laloux had built a new, more central station for the Orleans lines (Fig. 143) at the Quai d'Orsay, 1897–1900, timed for the opening of the Exposition of 1900. The lines had been prolonged for two miles from the Gare de Lyon in a tunnel built along the bank of the Seine and consequently were sometimes flooded. The new station rose over the tracks. Since electric engines were used, the absence of smoke and fumes made it possible to dispense with the traditional train-shed. Vestibule, waiting rooms, and concourse were combined in one space. They were originally disposed at street level around open wells, through which one could see trains standing at the platforms below.[4] A graceful vault with ample skylights made a majestic canopy. Externally, enormous glazed archways signaled the entrances. The total bulk was increased by a large hotel. Laloux had put his Beaux-Arts precepts to good use, just as he had done on a more modest scale two years earlier at Tours (Fig. 144). When new, the latter was as extravagantly admired as the old Gare de l'Est had been, as a perfect expression of a station. Twin arched portals were held to reflect the clear separation of arriving and departing traffic, an interpretation only partly justified by the internal arrangements. The Gare d'Orsay became a model station, destined to influence many others. The Exposition was spectacularly successful and the new station, widely publicized, was considered one of the attractions. It influenced the two stations at New York as well as the less remote Hamburg one of 1903–06.

4. The open wells were subsequently floored over to increase the circulation area.

112

The old Central Station in Copenhagen of 1863–64 by J. D. Herholdt (1818–1902) had long been outgrown, so an international competition was held in 1900 for a new one. The present building was begun in 1906 and finished in 1911 on a plan which recalls Laloux's Paris one, since the tracks run below the head-house, which stands like a bridge over them (Fig. 145); even the plaza in front is over the lines. In the original station the trains ran through an arched wooden shed spanning eighty feet, the arches closely spaced, and not unlike the design of 1850 proposed by the building committee for the Crystal Palace Exhibition of 1851.[5] In the new station by H. E. C. Wenck (1851–1936), the old shed—which has now been moved to a different site and preserved as a sports hall—is recalled in the twin halls of the new head-house. The old red brick building with its big arches had a dignified monumentality which is lacking in the new one. Wenck seems to have been strongly influenced by the romanticism of the early 20th century: his station is polychromatic, picturesque, small in scale, and modest in effect. This exterior clothed one of the best organized stations of the period, with six passenger platforms, seven separate luggage platforms, and clear separation of incoming and outgoing passengers.[6] These new versions of old plans were characteristic of the prewar period.

Meanwhile the train-shed was coming to the end of its career.

Glass Cages, the Shattering Blow, and Metamorphosis

The twenty-seven years covering the last period of great train-sheds began in 1888 with the completion of the magnificent triple shed at Frankfurt am Main and ended in 1915 with the completion of the eight enormous sheds at Leipzig. The momentum acquired from the superlative Frankfurt am Main achievement kept Germany securely ahead, with America second. France did nothing after the great effort of 1900 in Paris. England had an adequate number of urban terminals. British journalists deplored the utilitarian aspect of the occasional new ones, constructed usually by the railroad's own staff. Marylebone Station in London (1899–1905), alterations to Victoria Station, London (1905), and the Snow Hill Station at Birmingham admittedly fell below the standards of St. Pancras and Paddington. Considerable humiliation was

5. Henry-Russell Hitchcock, *The Crystal Palace, the Structure and Its Immediate Progeny, an Exhibition* (Northampton, 1951), pp. 18–19.

6. See Steen E. Rasmussen, *Nordische Baukunst* (Berlin, 1940), p. 51; *Schweizerische Bauzeitung,* Oct. 20, 1900; *Génie Civil,* Aug. 23, 1913; and *Railway Gazette, 68* (1938), 1108.

expressed at their absolute inferiority to the Parisian ones and especially to what was being built in North America. Not only was the architectural quality declining, but the wide-span shed was being employed less and less frequently, so that by 1914 it was almost extinct. Instead of one or two vaults of enormous width and magnificent effect, the number of subdivisions was being increased and the spans and height reduced.

It was not only in train-sheds that iron and glass roofed enormous areas; such roofs had been applied for decades to other types of demomorphic building—markets, arcades, and temporary exposition buildings. In the latter, even vaster dimensions were attempted. For other purposes a repetitive bay system was all that was required. The well known London markets had shown the way: Hungerford (1835), Smithfield (1867–68), Covent Garden (1830 and later). Paris had its numerous and colorful *halles*: the Temple (1863–65), and Les Halles (1853 ff.) with its 100 by 100-foot bays. Giuseppe Mengoni had amazed Italy with his Florentine Mercato Nuovo of 1874, in which glass louvers were used. In his Galleria Vittorio Emanuele in Milan (1865–77) all four arms as well as the crossing bore iron and glass vaults. Smaller galleries enriched Genoa (1871), Turin (1889), and Naples (1887–90). In these room-streets the lateral walls were differentiated from the utilitarian roofs by sumptuous architectural confections recalling those that Palladio had installed on the stage of his celebrated theater at Vicenza. But such arcades did not contribute to the aesthetic expression of iron and glass. This was left to the exhibition buildings.

Viel's Paris roof of 1855, masked in neoclassical costume, contributed less than the London Crystal Palace. The roof of the Paris Exposition of 1878 was more poetic, and it was also more metallic; the forms were curved and bent in new and graceful ways. The scale was small, the structure was light, the cantilever was used freely, and a flashing many-faceted pleasure dome was achieved. By the 1880's spans such as that of St. Pancras could, as we have seen, easily be duplicated when called for—which was infrequently, since the expense was usually not justified by the occasion. For this reason, audacious projects such as Calvert Vaux' for the Philadelphia Centennial rarely advanced beyond the paper stage. Even the greenhouses which had started the great series of glass houses had ceased to be the engineer's testing ground; only exposition buildings could rival train-sheds in audacity. In 1889, Contamin in his Galerie des Machines at Paris eclipsed all previous roof spans by hurling his arches for an additional breathtaking 100 feet to reach a total width of 362 feet. Three years later engineers were working in Chicago on the Manufacturer's and Liberal Arts Building, planned as a series of galleries surrounding large courts. Informed that the demand for space would exceed the estimates, they changed their scheme and vaulted the whole area, equaling

Contamin's span. The next year Lyon proudly added a third giant of equal width, another Exposition Palace, to the supreme trinity of 19th-century glass cages. Their joint record stood for twoscore years, until 1934, when it was equaled in the Grand Palais at Lille, which stretched its width in a single flight to 362 feet. The Lille hall was the only building of the 20th century to dare so much. Its record still stands, unbroken by any building for any purpose. We are tempted to think that our century has perhaps not wanted to compete in this way, being more interested in conquering gravity by reaching upward, Tower of Babel fashion. We should, however, remind ourselves that the prototype for our skyscrapers, the Eiffel Tower, whose 1,000-foot height has been surpassed only twice, was built for the same Fair (1889) in which Contamin set his wide-span record. (See Table 3.) Notice the con-

Table 3: Single Roof Spans of over 250 Feet

City	Building	Width of Greatest Span	Date
Jersey City	Penn. Station	252	1888
Paris	Galerie des Machines	362	1889
Philadelphia	Reading Station	256	1891–93
Chicago	Mfr. & Lib. Arts Bldg.	362	1892–93
Philadelphia	Broad St. Station	300	1892–93
Lyon	Exposition Hall	362	1894
New York	Kingsbridge Armory	308	1912–17
Orly	Dirigible Hangars	285	1916–24
Akron	Airship Docks	325	1920–23
Lille	Exposition Hall	362	1934
Brussels	Exposition Hall	282	1935
Chicago	Indoor Stadium	262	1939
Renton, Wash.	Boeing Plant	300	published 1946
Milan	Exhibition Hall	310	1948
Chicago	American Airlines Hangar	257	*before* 1949
Montgomery, Ala.	Livestock Coliseum	286½	*before* 1952

centration in the decades beginning 1888 and 1934. Steel accounted for those in the first of these decades and reinforced concrete started another cycle beginning in 1922. Still more recently an improved type of the latter material, shell concrete, seems to be well launched. The period so disparagingly known as the *fin de siècle* seems to have been, from the point of view of structural boldness, exceptionally stirring and creative. What an intoxication the engineers must have felt! These milestones followed rapidly upon other feats: the St. Gotthard Tunnel (1872–80), the Brooklyn Bridge (1867–83), and the first Simplon Tunnel (1898–1906). Translucent vaults were the engineer's poetry, an outlet for tense brains after the drudgery of viaducts and wharfs. Some extraordinary drive must have lain behind the urge to build ever wider and higher, so far beyond the limits of utility or economy. No wonder that in 1900 it was being said that stations were the original characteristic architecture of the age! With such accomplishments and potentialities it is one of the tragedies of history that this family of stations was allowed to die out, to be succeeded by a conventionally lithic architecture. It is the more imperative to record them here before even their memories fade, vanquished by fire, bombs, and the demands of new city plans.

Architect Georg P. H. Eggert began the most significant station of the latter part of the century in 1879 at Frankfurt am Main (Figs. 146–8). It took nine years to complete, so that its influence was not felt until 1888. It was one of the stations which Eliel Saarinen visited in 1906 while working on his famous one at Helsinki. Frankfurt am Main had been served by three separate stations. When it was decided to combine their services in one new one, it was found that the only adequate site lay in the outskirts; but this proved to be no disadvantage, as the city obligingly grew to surround it. A triple shed was built to cover 18 stub lines, luxuriously equipped with separate platforms for passengers and baggage. The triple shed perpetuated the identity of the three regions formerly served separately, and the single head-house symbolized the unity of the German state. Between the sheds and the head-house extended a capacious midway which could accommodate huge crowds—even armies, for military considerations lay behind the lavishness of this layout, extensive far beyond the needs of civilian traffic. Direct exits at either end of the cross-platform meant that arriving passengers did not necessarily have to pass through the head-building. This provision was subsequently introduced into other large stations—at St. Louis, Washington, and Leipzig. The departing passenger entered through a monumental domed hall flanked by ticket windows. He could then turn right or left to waiting rooms and restaurants or proceed forward to the cross-platform; where he caught sight of the stupendous sheds 549 feet wide divided into three equal spans of 183 feet and stretching away from him for 610 feet. The tapered ribs began at the floor and ended at apexes ninety-three feet overhead in points so refined as to be barely visible. Glass covered all surfaces except the bottoms of the valleys. The effects of multiple soaring spaces, so memorable in Paddington and York, had been surpassed.

No medieval cathedral was more spectacularly calculated to exploit the properties of its materials. The five luminous volumes—three sheds, cross-platform, and domed vestibule—formed a graduated sequence of ascending heights and crossing axes. Externally these glass cages, rising above low wings framed by domed pavilions and slender towers, commanded attention. The rather elaborate ornament of the masonry portions served to emphasize the

116

simplicity of the vaults as a boxer's fancy shorts set off the lines of his torso. The piling up of the parts in a logical sequence is a brilliant variation on the theme of the Anhalter Bahnhof and inaugurates a new family of stations which includes Cologne (1889–94), Hamburg (1903–06), and the Bundes Bahnhof at Basle (1904). Their soaring glass cages make them instantly recognizable as stations. To a European the word "station" conjures up the collective image of these examples, just as the word "depot" is likely to mean to an American a drab, dingy building with wide eaves.

In the following year, 1889, the second largest station in Germany was completed at Bremen; this was the Hauptbahnhof, designed by Professor Hubert Stier, the architect of the earlier Hanover Hauptbahnhof in 1876–79. The long conventional building in brick lies parallel to the shed and nearly obscures it from the plaza. One large arched shell, the shed spanned 193 feet (Fig. 149 *l*) and thus nearly equaled the span of the Anhalter Bahnhof. At Bremen as at Amsterdam the architect seems to have striven to obliterate by his screen of eclectic masonry the potential exterior majesty of the engineer's glass and metal. A decade later Marius Toudoire, *architecte du gouvernement,* and Denis, the engineer, began the St-Jean Station at Bordeaux. There, too, a fine shed was hidden behind a long mansarded building, a stiff version of the Milan Station of 1873.

In the same year that Eggert finished his Frankfurt am Main station, Georg Frentzen (1854–99) began one of his notable stations at Cologne. It was completed by J. E. Jacobsthal, the builder of the Berlin Stadtbahn stations. The site at Cologne, between elevated tracks and the cathedral square, required a raised shed and a station at the lower level. Towered and domed vestibules were erected, and the main clock tower was placed near the corner to compose with both of the adjoining elevations. The selected style, Romanesque, comformed somewhat uncomfortably to the prevailing picturesque canons. The external effectiveness of the main shed, 210 feet wide, was increased by its raised position. Its extreme length gave it the effect of having been stretched out, recalling the baroque delight in apparently infinite perspectives. Stairs and elevators brought passengers up to a central platform 160 feet wide, flanked by through lines, invaded by spur ones. Standing on this ample base and sheltered by the dimly hovering roof stood a fanciful pavilion, a building within a building, containing convenient restaurant and waiting rooms.[7] After its destruction during World War II, the ruins of the

7. This feature had been anticipated in a ruder form thirty years before by the one which stood on the platform of the Cincinnati, Hamilton, and Dayton Depot in Cincinnati and before that by the long vanished "Gothick" Court House which William Kent had set up on the dais of Westminster Hall. It was to reappear at Snow Hill, Birmingham, in 1913 and again in modern dress at a 1939 Amsterdam station.

shed resembled the wreck of a zeppelin. In its later years this Cologne station was not much appreciated, but its astounding vigor must have once commanded great respect.

Its architect, Frentzen, was called to Bucharest to build a great station there (Fig. 150). The scheme is close to that of Frankfurt am Main. The ends of the triple sheds were visible over the head-house in spite of several domed pavilions and bulky towers. Round-arched details and curved mansards added to the profusely displayed wares of the picturesque architect.

The Hauptbahnhof at Dresden (Figs. 151, 152), the best of the relatively new island type, was the main feature of an extensive relocation and consolidation of railroad facilities. On the ground floor the *salle des pas perdus* was accessible both from a vehicle court formed by widening the Prager Strasse and from the other adjoining streets. The site was so ample that most of the usual station facilities could be accommodated on the street level, leaving the viaduct level free for fifteen lines, some spur and some through, covered by a complex of four sheds (Fig. 149c). The main shed, 193 feet wide and 100 feet high, was almost perfectly semicircular. It was flanked by two longer ones, each 100 feet wide, which extended far beyond the ends of the main one; the fourth, only thirty feet wide and covering the freight lines, lay at the extreme east side. The masonry station house, tucked in between the arms of the two long sheds, raised its domes and towers from the vehicle court before the main shed. This intricate combination of materials and masses reflects the spirit of the age which created the Zwinger Palace nearby.

Other members of this spirited family in Dresden included the Wettiner Strasse and Neustadt Stations. The shed of the former spanned 145 feet; that of the latter was a complex of three spans of which the chief was 117 feet wide (Figs. 149a, b). The Dammthor Station at Hamburg, with a modest span, continued the Berlin Stadtbahn tradition. All three made the areas in which they stood sparkle. Lofty symbols of the dignity and importance then ascribed even to local transit, they were easily recognized by their glass cages.

We may now linger over a transitional example, the station at Antwerp, on our way to the colossi at Hamburg and Leipzig. Louis de la Censerie (1835–1909) completed the imposing Central Station at Antwerp about 1900. A terminal station served entirely by stub tracks, the shed extends back from a high-shouldered, pyramidal head-building on the plaza. A glass and iron dome not unlike the one at the Paris Exposition of 1889 rises above and behind domed towers which frame an arched and traceried window. The domes and the window proclaim the Crystal Palace lying behind, 212 feet in width. The iron work, seen from the side streets, is characterized by a delicacy and intricacy related to the Art Nouveau. This shed is still in use. Its glass has been replaced since World War II, as it was found that the iron, in spite of forty years of service, was in sound condition. This disproves the contention that iron and steel decay rapidly under train-shed conditions; durability and longevity seem to depend rather on the quality of the original metal.

Heinrich Reinhardt (*b.* 1868) and Georg Sössenguth built their great Hamburg station, 1903–06 (Figs. 149i, 153, 154), as a bridge over through lines. They took the Frankfurt am Main scheme and lifted it up, turned it around, and set it down across the cut containing the tracks. This meant that the axial Frankfurt am Main entrance vestibule could not be used as an entrance here; the ends of the cross-platform could, however, be made to serve for entrance and exit. Departing passengers drive up the Glockengiesserwall to a marquee from which they enter a concourse flanked by ticket windows on one hand and baggage room on the other. Then they pass on to the cross-platform, at the left of which are the waiting rooms and buffets. On the right hand, stairs descend to the platforms. A great shed, 239 feet wide, covers the cross-platform and extends over the depressed train platforms. Duplicate facilities are provided at the Kirchen Allee end of the cross-platform for arriving passengers, who can seek local transportation there. The main shed, rising 114 feet above the platforms, was buttressed by a series of smaller vaults perpendicular to it, one to each bay of the main shed. All the vaults were supported by bents [8] of the same shape, pointed at the apex, sloping on the sides and overhead. The glass cage stole the show; it had received a new lease on life from a new form resulting from a new structural system. Masonry was used only for the waiting room, vestibules, and towers. The rhythmical manipulation of flattened curves complemented by towers produces a harmonious and unified effect. Even in its partially ruined state, as seen in 1948, the shed with its change of levels and cross-gallery had an air of masterful assurance. From the opening day, this station has been recognized as combining elegance and practicality to an exemplary degree and as one of the supremely beautiful manifestations of the modern spirit.

The last two stations to be mentioned here, one modest and one surpassing grand, bring the series of great train-sheds almost to an end. The Wiesbaden Bahnhof is a transitional stage on the road that ends at Leipzig. Its domes and towers resemble those of Hamburg, but the five small sheds have been dropped down out of sight behind the panoplied head-house. At Leipzig the most enormous range of sheds in Europe was walled in, as if they were something to be ashamed of, behind a forbidding fortress of head-house 1,000 feet long.

These sheds, though concealed, are climactic (Figs. 155–7). Six parallel

---

8. A bent is a combination of columns and beams constructed as one unit. It is entirely rigid, exerting no diagonal thrust.

train-sheds, each 147 feet in width, were attached to a superb transept 80 feet wide and nearly 900 feet in length, approached by two mighty vestibules. Less classical than King's Cross, less dynamic than St. Pancras, the surging beat of these spaces is nevertheless irresistibly powerful. They were begun in 1907 to combine the scattered services ineffectively handled at outmoded stations; then military necessity carried the work to completion a year after the commencement of the war. Numerous old lines were reclassed into two groups, Saxony and Prussia, and each was allotted half the new station marked by identical vestibules. The head-building is of a rarely equaled ponderosity. Its roofs are carried up in three tiers to equal the height of the supporting walls. So extravagant a cult of the colossal is characteristic of a late style phase.[9] Devised in 1907 and executed as planned, it was the joint product of William Lossow (1852–1914) and Max Hans Kühne (*b.* 1874). A large element of civic pride was involved, and the city contributed nearly one-third of the cost. The left-hand part of the site had been the location of the earlier Thüringer Bahnhöfe which had inaugurated the tradition of notable Leipzig stations.[10]

The subordination of sheds in favor of the forebuildings which we see in Leipzig had also occurred in the United States in the 1890's. As we turn back to see the final examples of American shed building, we must also turn the calendar back to the early 1890's, when the citizens of St. Louis were being amazed by the romantic scenery that Theodore C. Link was building in front of George H. Pegram's train-shed (Fig. 158). The Romanesque head-building has been described in the preceding chapter.[11] The shed, however, is related to those of the third and final period. Although 600 feet wide and covering thirty-two lines, it rose only seventy-four feet. It was subdivided into five parts by rows of columns, with the widest span only 142 feet. A special truss was invented for the occasion. The upper chord continued in an unbroken curve from one side to the other, but the lower one was broken into five parts, each one convex to the platforms. The engineer hoped the continuous upper chord would lead the eye from side to side and so cancel out the distracting framework below it, but he was unduly optimistic; his economical invention was inert and grotesque.

The proven grandeur of the two arched Pennsylvania Railroad sheds at Jersey City and Philadelphia seems to have discouraged competition. After a few more attempts like the one at St. Louis with other types of sheds, the

9. "Leviathan among termini . . . the stupendous waiting room recalls the vast bare temples of the Nile." Briggs, the *Architect,* pp. 172 ff.

10. See above, pp. 46, 68.

11. See above, p. 107.

struggle ended. Two years after the St. Louis experiment a second very wide shed was undertaken in Boston (Fig. 149, n). Like the St. Louis one, it was more remarkable for its extent than for its beauty. The South Station was built to combine the services of several older lines scattered about that part of the city, including two depots less than twenty-five years old. The total span, thirty feet narrower than St. Louis, was managed in three jumps, any one of which would once have been considered enormous. The St. Louis idea of handling several spans as a unit was invoked with somewhat better results. There were three instead of five parts, and the lower chords were concave to the tracks, thus preserving the idea of three naves. The central span, like that of the Firth of Forth Bridge, was a combination of cantilevered arms and a floating middle truss 150 feet long.[12]

These two sheds, of which the utility far surpassed the beauty, covered the most gigantic areas at that time roofed over in this country. Only the St. Louis one now remains to testify to the greater convenience of even a poor train-shed over the individually roofed platforms of today. A shed protects passengers, baggage, and mails from sun and snow, but the modern platform cover in bad weather makes only a protective gesture; the rain can still spot one's luggage and the sleet get down one's neck.

The last of the great series of single-span arched train-sheds to be built in this country was the third built by the Pennsylvania Railroad; in 1947 it was demolished. It was part of their station in Pittsburgh (Fig. 159) completed in 1901 and was 240 feet wide, steeply curved and nobly proportioned. An innovation in train-shed construction was incorporated: one end of each rib was free to move. It was never more than partly visible from the main approach since there was a twelve-story office building in front of it. The constricted site did not permit the architect, Daniel Burnham, to indulge in the bombastic show he liked. The office building was hardly different from the semiskyscrapers he designed for banks and department stores. There was one feature, however, where he could let his imagination run riot: the carriage concourse in front of the head-house. It was built a little later than the two more essential parts. The design was revised from an earlier scheme, which had timid arcades, to the more daring scheme of a single dome resting on wide four-centered arches. It is a fantastic conception reminiscent of a Beaux-Arts *Esquisse-Esquisse,* an imaginary exercise in which "buildability" is unimportant; in spirit it is like Binet's audacious main entrance

12. When only thirty years old, it had been so affected by the combination of coal gas, sulphur, and sea air that there was no recourse but to take it down. This proved to be very difficult and protracted, partly because the station continued in active use under the wreckers and partly because the metal of the shed was too feeble to support the cranes that would normally be used.

to the Paris Exposition of 1900. Here again we see an impressive glass cage subordinated to the forebuilding. Only the carriage concourse tells us that this is a station and not just another office building.

In the same year, 1901, a shed by Frost and Granger was begun in Chicago at the new La Salle Street Station. The drive to build fine sheds was weakening rapidly, and a comparatively insipid crescent truss was used, very low for its width. It lasted only until 1934, when conditions for repair proved too difficult and two smaller spans of lighter construction replaced it.

The practicality of enormous single spans had been in question since 1861, and in 1898 W. H. Mills, reviewing the arguments for and against the large-span shed, came to the inevitable conclusion that only small ones could be justified economically. At the same time he recognized, in restrained engineer's language, what was often the first consideration: "Doubtless there is something very attractive about a large span roof, its bold outline stretching from side to side of a wide covered area imparts an imposing effect which cannot be claimed for smaller or more moderate spans." [13] The search for economical solutions led to Lincoln Bush's invention, the Bush shed, which he patented in 1904. The first installation at the Hoboken station of the Delaware, Lackawanna, and Western Railroad (Fig. 160) was ready for use in 1906. Each shed unit covers two lines of track and half of a platform on each side, in one low reinforced concrete span. The vault is only 16 feet above the rails, but the perishable steel is protected by concrete and copper, and the fumes escape through slots a few inches above the top of the smoke stacks on each track, whence it is discharged harmlessly above the roof. The deep sides of the slots reduce the penetration of snow and rain. Skylights parallel to the slots illuminate the platforms. Such a shed was cheaper to build and more economical to maintain, and gave nearly as much protection as the colossal ones. This was the deathblow of the great train-shed; by 1914 Bush sheds had been installed in twelve stations. The later ones eliminated metal columns and ribs and were made entirely of concrete. The rippling vaults, floating above the thin forest of columns, made a new kind of rhythmical interior space, not majestic but not lacking in dignity.

Having supplanted the glass cage, the Bush shed in its turn—and it was a much shorter turn—was abandoned. A still more economical solution, the butterfly shed (Figs. 149t, 197), was introduced. This covered only the platform and made no attempt to cover the lines or to exclude driving storms. The passenger be damned; the company saved money. It is surprising that no outcry was raised. Apparently the abandonment of both Bush and arched sheds went unlamented. Although $55,000,000 was spent on the construc-

13. *Railway Construction* (London, 1898), p. 271.

tion of the terminal facilities at Kansas City's third Union Station, a frugal platform canopy was used there too.

Just as the great glass cages were being condemned as impractical, a new method of locomotion appeared which might have saved them.[14] Electrification meant that the corrosive fumes of coal-burning engines would no longer weaken the structural frame. Its soaring curves would be kept free of soot; the glass could be restored to sparkling brilliance and the sublimity of their original appearance be revived. There was another potential savior in the noncorroding concrete used by Lincoln Bush in his low sheds, but it was not tried in vaster ones until 1930 at Reims. In its inexorable way taste had turned against the dramatic and favored the homely. The train-shed fell into eclipse; however, as we shall see, at the same time it was reborn.

The history of art records many instances in which a form is taken out of its original context and transferred to another, irrespective of its original meaning or medium. "Plastic forms are subjected to the principle of metamorphosis by which they are perpetually renewed . . . by which their relationship is, though by no means with any regularity of recurrence, first tested, then made fast and finally disrupted." [15] We can see metamorphosis at work in several ways relative to the train-shed. Let us first consider the whole family of structures incorporating glass, in which changes can be followed in two directions: the importance of glazed areas and of the use the structure has been put to. In stone-built Gothic churches decorative areas of glass hung in the interstices of the skeleton occupying a small part of the total wall area. In the wood-framed greenhouses of the 18th century, glass was allowed to fill all the walls and occupy part of the ceiling too. In the 19th century the greenhouse grew larger and iron was substituted for wood, thus increasing still further the glass areas and creating such tropical fairylands as the Palm House at Kew. In less poetic guise, glass and iron were applied to markets, exhibition buildings, and train-sheds. By this time glass had entirely devoured the wall and ceiling and had shifted from being an exclusively religious appurtenance to more prosaic commercial applications. This position did not prevail very long before it was disrupted. The designers of buildings for commercial and transportational functions began to shun glass and turn back toward more lithic effects. Masonry resumed its preponderant role over glass. Walls and ceiling no longer received homogeneous treatment but reverted to their former differentiated status. Glazed areas became vestigial; at the Gare d'Orsay, for example (Fig. 143), some feeling for the continuity

14. See above, p. 112.

15. Henri Focillon, *The Life of Forms in Art,* p. 6.

of wall and roof lingered on, but the glass was reduced to a decorative incident in a dense enclosure.

The form of the train-shed with its long, narrow vault was so particularly appropriate as a shelter for trains and platforms that at the close of its original career it was diverted to other uses and so renewed. The first steps in this process occurred in railway stations themselves: in the 1890's at St. Louis and Chicago the architects built richly decorated grand halls in the shape of train-sheds (Figs. 139, 141), while the actual train-sheds of the same stations (Figs. 106, 158), as described above,[16] were considerably less magnificent. In the Washington, D.C., Union Station (Fig. 161), which has no train-shed, there is a midway or train concourse 760 feet long and 130 feet wide, roofed by a gracefully arched vault, as though a train-shed had been lifted by some genie from its traditional position and set down again crosswise at the ends of the platforms. There is a second permutation here. The passenger concourse, or waiting room (Fig. 162), is a vast barrel-vaulted hall shaped like those at St. Louis and Chicago. Here for the first time this feature is allowed to dominate the exterior. Its roof rises above the entrance and is the most conspicuous external mass (Fig. 163). Changed in function and construction, the form again plays the compositional role it once played while serving its original function.

The train-shed form appears twice at the fabulous Pennsylvania Station in New York (Figs. 164–6), neither time in its original form or function and both times nearly invisible from the surrounding streets. Both halls are nearly as big as train-sheds. The first is the main waiting room, which has no seats on which to wait, and the second is the train concourse. The former is a lofty vaulted hall with masonry derived from the *thermae* of Rome (Fig. 165). Considered apart from its questionable utility, it is an awe-inspiring space—a train-shed raised to unparalleled monumentality. The functionalist critic's attack on such halls is typified by Dean Hudnut's comment: "Architecture at the time existed 'for its own sake' or at the most as an ornament applied to civilization . . . so judicious a creature as the Pennsylvania Railroad could heavily increase its corporate debt in order to hide the steel roofs of its stations under the vaults of Caracalla." [17] The train concourse serves mixed functions. It is not quite a train-shed, although trains and platforms two levels below are partly visible from it, somewhat as in the Gare d'Orsay; nor is it wholly a concourse, since the adjoining hall shares that function. Structurally it is equally ambiguous. The walls

16. Pages 89, 120.

17. Joseph Hudnut, introduction to Walter Gropius, *The New Architecture and the Bauhaus* (New York, 1938?), p. 8. (He has modified this view in more recent publications.) See also below, p. 133.

are masonry but the roof is glass supported by an independent steel skeleton (Fig. 164). There is still another ambiguity: the metal is shaped to suggest the piers, ribs, and domes of the masonry-built Basilica of Constantine. How is this to be understood? Which is intended to dominate—the traditional form or the assertive modern construction? Great size and agreeable luminosity make it more appealing and less overwhelming than the adjoining waiting room, hence it has come in for more admiration than its ambiguity entirely merits. Talbot Hamlin, for instance, once called it a "superlatively good example" of the frank treatment of steel-framed roofs when combined with glass.[18] Such vast halls deservedly command attention and praise, in spite of their questionable logic.[19]

The train-shed form recurs in yet another context. Freyssinet's hangars at Orly were the best known application of the old form to serve the purposes of a new type of transportation, the dirigible. In the 1920's it seemed likely that the dirigible might be creating a new need which would be met by a new series of wide-span structures. Instead, the airplane triumphed, and enormous sheds are built to house the planes but not for the convenience of passengers. Sheds may return to this function some day since the problem of completely covered access to planes is still unsolved. The use of a wide-span vault to cover the passenger concourse in the new airport at St. Louis leads to the speculation that the train-shed in its association with the airplane may develop from the point where it left off in railroad stations: as a cover for the concourse. In many of its current manifestations the vault is built not in iron and glass but in reinforced or shell concrete, so that it has lost its transparency and become dense and opaque; but as we shall see,[20] it has made a comeback in a recent railway terminal. However, several chapters of its history were to intervene.

Imperial Splendor

The conceptual image of a station was changing during the 1890's from the easily recognized one of the previous period toward that of an ordinary monumental public building. The old interest in sheds had yielded to the mania for grandiose head-buildings. Some of the reasons for this decline

18. *Architecture, an Art for All Men* (New York, 1947), p. 130.

19. For further information see C. H. Reilly, *A Monograph of the Work of McKim, Mead, and White* (New York, 1924), Pt. IV, pls. 300–10; and *Architectural Record, 27* (June 1910), 519–21.

20. Below, p. 154.

have been touched on—the approaching exhaustion of the picturesque aesthetic and the prevailing material prosperity.

It was noted that toward the close of the second period the High Victorian fancy dress had been lifted off to reveal the solid underbody. In the third period, the outmoded Victorian robes were firmly relegated to the attic, while from moldering trunks conservatively cut garments were taken out, looked over, and found to be quite pleasant to see. But as these classic costumes proved to be too small, rubber copies were made. When stretched to the limit they did well enough, except that they did not fit smoothly; there were too many bulges and bumps in the bodies underneath. It would take some decades more to get rid of the picturesque contours.

The tailors who would do the job were gathering in Chicago in the early 1890's. It has been generally recognized that the World's Columbian Exposition in Chicago in 1893 marked a turning point in American architecture; this has been interpreted in several ways, not all of them of equal accuracy. Sometimes it is hailed as America's aesthetic coming of age as compared to the "barbarism" of the Philadelphia Centennial Exposition of 1876. Sometimes it is regarded as the final defeat of the native tradition which turned the healthy face of John Bunyan's country into a ghostly "City Beautiful." Sometimes the Chicago school of architects, with its interest in structural invention, its love of the picturesque Richardsonian Romanesque, its original Prairie Houses and "Tall Buildings," and its new Sullivanian ornament is considered to have cravenly capitulated to the prestige of foreign-trained New York architects who autocratically imposed a classical style. All these views seem distorted.

We know that the architect John Root, Burnham's partner until his death in 1891, had intended the Fair to be romantic in spirit, Romanesque in style, rich and warm in color. These three aims were considerably modified but not entirely forgotten. The committee of architects was coping with the largest group of buildings that American architects had ever been called upon to design, and they may quite understandably have hesitated to depend entirely on their own inventiveness to see them through so incredible a labor in so short a time. It was agreed that the buildings around the Court of Honor should have a uniform cornice line at 60 feet and be executed generally in Renaissance styles but no one style in particular; Italian, French, Spanish were all foreseen. There was no pretence at building Roman or Greek, as a later critic, George H. Edgell, implied in 1928 when he called the style "a classicism which today seems a little archaeological. The debts to definite monuments of classical antiquity are perhaps a little too outspoken." [21] At the time, Henry B. Fuller more accurately described it as "one historical

21. *The American Architecture of Today* (New York, Charles Scribner's Sons, 1928), p. 44.

style, safe, stable, serviceable and universally adaptable, the style of the Romans as adapted for modern uses by the Italian, French and Spanish of the Renaissance." [22] Equally explicit was Mrs. Van Rensselaer's comment: "No other style could so well serve the purpose as the allied but not identical Renaissance because it resulted in agreement and yet permitted the expression of individual tastes and encouraged aesthetic plasticity." [23] As one looks through the photographs of the palaces which grew out of this program, he realizes that the councils of the board of design were not presided over by the shades of Iktinos or Vitruvius but by those of the baroque masters: Le Nôtre and Fontana for the Court of Honor, Michelangelo, Bernini, and Juvara for the individual buildings. Neither detail nor general plan was strictly classical. We do not find the closed courts of the Roman forums or the confined piazzas of the early Renaissance, but rather the great, loosely delimited avenues and vistas of the 17th century. There were only two important pseudoclassical buildings, the Festival Hall by Francis M. Whitehouse and Atwood's Fine Arts Palace—the latter delicate in detail, grandiose in plan. Even S. S. Beman's Merchant Tailors' Pavilion, using the Greek Ionic order, had a dome and curved wings.

The principle of contrast was invoked by Frederick Law Olmsted, who laid out an informal park adjoining the extremely formal Court of Honor. He placed Japanese tea houses on wooden islands. Cobb and Sullivan's Romanesque buildings looked at home in this traditional picturesque setting. Turning again to the critical examples of the great palaces around the main court, we are reminded of John Nash's stage scenery at Regent's Park. The piled-up towers and domes and the plastic variety of the outlines are remarkably picturesque and would have been more so had the original plans for coloring them externally been carried out (variety of tint was given up at the last minute to save time). The break with the High Victorian style was not as deliberate, extensive, or violent as has been assumed.[24]

Furthermore, what changes there were did not come about as the result of a sudden inspiration on the part of American architects; they stemmed from recent European buildings. Atwood's Fine Arts Palace was copied from Bénard's 1867 Prix de Rome project. The French Expositions of 1878 and 1889 and the railroad stations of Frankfurt am Main, Bucharest, Genoa, and Milan had used Renaissance idioms, as had many of our own public

22. *History of the World's Fair* (Chicago, 1893), pp. 85, 101.

23. Marianna Van Rensselaer, "The Artistic Triumph of the Fair Builders," *Forum* (Dec. 1892), pp. 527 ff.

24. See above, p. 11. The scenic attitude toward architectural composition survived well into the 20th century, notably in college campuses: for example, the Memorial Quadrangle at Yale by James Gamble Rogers, designed in 1917, is a masterly expression of 19th-century aesthetics.

buildings in the 1880's. State capitols after 1867 had kept close to the Renaissance-baroque tradition at Springfield, Illinois; Albany, New York; Austin, Texas; and Denver, Colorado. The architect of the Library of Congress, John L. Smithmeyer, went to Europe in the 1880's to study such new buildings as Calderini's Palazzo di Giustizia in Rome, the Palais de Justice in Brussels, and Wallot's Reichstagsgebäude in Berlin.

So there was in fact no violent break, merely a dramatization of the already changed form-feeling. This was reflected in the temporary station built on the fair ground directly behind the domed Administration Building (Fig. 168), which had first been intended to serve partly as a station. Although the interior of the latter was carefully finished, it was not actually used for anything in particular; instead, a separate station was built facing on the entrance court. This building had three deeply recessed arched portals, with engaged Corinthian columns framing the arches; towers surmounted by obelisks rose at the corners. The interior was derived from Roman baths. Its vaults showed as gables above the cornice. The motives come from ancient and Renaissance Rome and from Michelangelo and Serlio, and in addition they owed something to Paris. We have already seen many of these motives in 19th-century stations, but here at the Fair they were combined in a temporary building which was to have an influence wholly out of proportion to its length of life; this temporary station engendered a whole family of permanent stations which includes Washington, Kansas City, New York, New Orleans, Chattanooga, Detroit, and Toronto.

Who designed it? The committee had not assigned it to any of the famous firms because it was an afterthought. It must be counted among the sixty-odd buildings designed by the office of D. H. Burnham, the chief architect. He was too busy during these months to do any drafting himself; such work was done by his brilliant new partner Charles B. Atwood (1849–95). If Atwood was the architect of this influential station, as seems probable, it is important to recall that he had had a dazzling career, having been represented in one important competition after another, sometimes with two submissions. He was expert, superficial, sensitive, quick to adopt new fashions, an ideal partner for a steady, tactful administrator like Burnham, who had turned to him after Root's death.

Atwood did not invent ideas so much as he adapted them, with consummate finesse; this is what he did with the Fine Arts Palace and with the temporary station. The design has been attributed to the engineer J. F. Wallace, but his work must have been confined to the layout and track work. Regarded as a beautiful and costly building, "a model in its way," [25] it was

25. Harlow N. Higinbotham, *Report of the President to the Board of Directors of the World's Columbian Exposition, Chicago, 1892–1893* (Chicago, 1898), p. 140.

used by 100,000 persons daily and fixed itself in their minds as the archetype for future stations. After it the completely romantic station, such as Gilbert's Illinois Central one nearby, seemed old-fashioned. Burnham himself, after Atwood's death, followed its example; so did most of the great firms employed at the Fair. H. H. Richardson's successors, Shepley, Rutan, and Coolidge, who had been content to follow in his footsteps in the picturesque, rough-textured, asymmetrical twin station in Springfield in 1889, built two stations in Boston in 1893 and 1896, as classical and formal as Atwood's in Chicago. To Atwood's designs for the colonnade and triumphal arch across the end of the Court of Honor, the Fine Arts Palace, and especially the temporary station, we can trace the ancestry of many of the ensuing monumental American stations.

Since the triumphal arch was standard in any classical repertory, its appearance in a featured position at the Fair was not the only possible explanation for its use almost immediately after in the entrance screen of Boston's North Station, but the coincidence is unquestionably suggestive in view of the architects' preceding work.[26] Shepley, Rutan, and Coolidge used arches together with a colonnade three years later on the hybrid exterior of South Station at Boston (Fig. 167), of which the gigantic shed has been described. Three large arches marked the main entrance, which was wrapped around a blunted corner; above, Ionic columns extended through three floors. It was a poor design, echoing only feebly the grandeur of the sources.

D. H. Burnham and Company were the achitects for the Union Station in Washington, 1903–07 (Fig. 163), also derived from Atwood's at the Fair; what had been staff and plaster there was immortalized here in marble. The motive reappeared in 1908 at their comparatively minute Union Station in New Orleans. There was space for only one arch, but it is imperial in scale. Jarvis Hunt used three arches at Kansas City in 1910. In 1912 in Burnham's project for the Union Station in Chicago, arches appear above a colonnade. Apart from the numerous other monumental buildings Burnham designed, his application of this new style to his stations alone justifies the appellation "Burnham Baroque"; for even though the style emanated from Atwood's pencil, it received Burnham's blessing and became a hallmark of his work and the characteristic architecture of its time.

A long-lived firm first called Reed and Stem acquired a great and lasting reputation as station architects. They made deep bows to Atwood and Burnham in their New York Central station at Troy (1901–04), using five arches; one can also sense the hand of Hunt and the clamor of the Paris ateliers. Their masterpiece, Grand Central in New York (1903–12), is closer to Burnham

26. Burnham used a triumphal arch at the same time for his Columbus Union Station (1896).

Baroque. The scale—nearly that of Michelangelo at St. Peter's—was considered normal for public buildings in the early part of this century, although it has been said of Grand Central that "the attempted heroic scale becomes the vulgar grandiose." [27] The details of the evolution of this brilliant design are somewhat obscure. A limited competition was held in the exceedingly short time of two months; Reed and Stem were declared the winners and were undoubtedly responsible for the main outline of the final building, although the firm of Warren and Wetmore was associated with them in the execution. The reasons for this, like the competition drawings themselves, are currently inaccessible in the files of the New York Central Railroad. The clarity, directness, and simplicity of the final building has always been recognized. No better station of its size has ever been built; its only rival is the recently completed Stazione Termini in Rome. As real estate values rose in the surrounding area, Grand Central Station proved to be a successful investment as well. After fifty years, however, the situation has changed, and today operating costs are proving a heavy burden. As a result, the great concourse may soon be torn down to make way for more profitable office buildings, thus destroying one of the finest interior spaces ever erected (Fig. 170).[28]

At the time Grand Central was being built, other Burnham Baroque stations with domes and towers were rising. The Wabash Station in Pittsburgh (1902–04) has a dome perched uneasily above an office building supported by colossal arches. The dome of the Union Station at Tacoma (1909–11), by Reed and Stem, rests on the intersection of four barrel vaults each of which ends in a huge French arch. The Birmingham, Alabama, Terminal Station (1905–09), by P. Thornton Mayre, is an amazingly complicated composition of pavilions, domes, and towers. The second Union Station at Worcester, Massachusetts (1909–11), by Watson and Huckel, omitted the dome but raised a pair of white marble towers 175 feet, which however eventually had to be truncated because the foundations proved insecure.

The baroque spirit on our shores showed itself most uninhibitedly in the fairs which followed that at Chicago. The extravagant fair at St. Louis in 1904 was the climax. The Transportation Building by E. L. Masqueray (Fig. 171) was important. To judge by its appearance Masqueray attempted to design an ideal station. There were three enormous arches on the long front and another at each end of the simulated head-house. Curved roofs rose high above the stucco work. A pair of tower-like forms flanked the

27. Talbot Hamlin, *Architecture, an Art for All Men*, p. 90.

28. Reed and Stem's successors, Fellheimer and Wagner, still under the shadow of the masterpiece, built the Cincinnati terminal twenty years later, with a single colossal arch as its central motive. See below, pp. 157 ff.

triple main entrance. Stretched out behind was a long, low building housing exhibits—a narrow train-shed. The flowing curves of the "head-house" clearly reflect the period of its erection, a time when Art Nouveau and Beaux-Arts influences were intermingled. Masqueray's lush design stemmed from Atwood's earlier temporary station and was a successful expression of the conception of a station as a vast vestibule.

The three arched entrances at St. Louis were echoed nine years later in the new Michigan Central station in Detroit (Fig. 172), by Reed and Stem, and Warren and Wetmore, the arch-prone architects of the New York Grand Central Station. Arches, gables, columns, and roofs again composed a great vestibule; this vestibule was clearly separated from the connecting office building which towered above it, thus marking an advance in functional expression over the combined station and office buildings of Pittsburgh and Boston. In the same year an arched vestibule was added to the Union Station at Denver. The motive appeared as late as 1923 in Cass Gilbert's design for the third New Haven station. His original design was as Burnhamesque as any of the earlier ones, but in execution most of the richly wrought stone decoration was omitted, leaving only a bare brick core, thus reflecting another current which had begun in Claude Bragdon's Rochester station for the New York Central (1912–14). Although Bragdon's design was symmetrical, classical, rusticated, arched, and "atticked," it had no columns, and other ornament was almost eliminated as well. Within, particularly, there is an effect of bare simplicity and carefully molded space which relates it to the stations of the prewar German group.

Great as Atwood and Burnham's influence had been on the use of arches, both triumphal and portal, they had also sponsored a third major motive, the colonnade. Bernini's colonnades on the Piazza San Pietro in Rome remain the supreme example of what can be done with the colonnade in city design, but the humbler column-lined streets of Palmyra were a more useful prototype for the modern city. Atwood had brought these ancient ones back to mind at the Fair of 1893. Frost and Granger's North Western station in Chicago (1906–11) boasted six enormous Doric columns. The Pennsylvania Station in New York began to line Seventh and Eighth Avenues and two side streets with an almost uncountable number of columns and pilasters (Fig. 173). Burnham, who after all had a special claim to the idea, used still more of them on his project for the Union Station in Chicago (completed in 1925). After Burnham's death, his successors, Graham, Anderson, Probst, and White, carried out a revised scheme (Fig. 174). The plan centers on a concourse 320 by 200 feet, abutted by 20 stub tracks supplemented by three through lines, all below street level and reached by staircases and cab drives. Waiting rooms, offices, and other facilities are housed in a second block connected to the concourse by a tunnel. Both masses received a generous accouterment of the columns and other classical features which were still exercising their weighty influence.[29]

This confidently monumental mood was diffused widely over the continent, touching Minneapolis, St. Paul, and, most emphatically, Toronto (Fig. 175). The Toronto Union Station, designed by Ross and McDonald, Hugh G. Jones, and John M. Lyle and begun in 1914, was only partially completed when it was officially opened by the Prince of Wales in 1927. A fire in 1905 had cleared the necessary site on the lake front and extensive track relocation was undertaken between 1906 and 1913. During the war years the plans received further study and active work on the main building commenced in 1921 on a generous scheme intended to provide for the needs of both the Grand Trunk and the Canadian National Railways for many years to come, since the original six tracks could be doubled. The ticket lobby, 260 feet in length, is slightly wider than the vast Basilica of Constantine. The main façade stretches out for 720 feet, part of its length made more majestic by the inevitable classic columns, twenty-two unfluted Doric ones in Indiana limestone. The train concourse was placed under the elevated tracks. Pains were taken to keep in- and out-traffic separated; the lower level, reached by depressed driveways, was reserved for exits.[30]

Graham, Anderson, Probst, and White, having completed the Union Station at Chicago in 1925, carried on the Cleveland Union Terminal from 1925 to 1929 and built the Thirtieth Street Station at Philadelphia from 1927 to 1934. These were among the most important American station commissions of the time, and this firm of architects had the accumulated experience to solve the intricate problems each presented. In both of them, since the tracks were depressed, the concourse might have been the element to monumentalize. In Cleveland, however, the superimposed office building limited external expression of the submerged station to a few large entrance arches such as any skyscraper might bear; only at Philadelphia was there a real opportunity for display (Figs. 176–8). Doubly bolstered by their own Burnham Baroque tradition and the Pennsylvania Railroad's tendency to hugeness, they unhesitatingly built grandly in a wholly prewar spirit. The concourse encloses more cubic feet than that of the Pennsylvania Station in New York; the columns are exceptionally huge, the use of marble remark-

29. The following accounts are the most useful: A. B. Olsen, "Chicago Union Station Company," *Railway and Locomotive Historical Society Bulletin,* No. 49; and *Architectural Forum, 44* (1926), 85 ff.

30. The station was extensively reported in the railroad and engineering press. See particularly *Canadian Railway and Marine World, 30* (Oct. 1927), 568 ff.; *Architectural Forum, 40* (1924), 101 ff.; and *Railway Age, 83* (1927), 1243 ff.

ably lavish. All that was lacking was a fresh touch to change it from the chilly graveyard it is. As in many other stations, the functionally excellent plan and the direct and simple circulation are interred in an uninspired mausoleum.

Although colonnades are amenable to many different expressions, they are symbolically less appropriate to stations than to courthouses or libraries; rather, the arch and its portal associations more adequately express the daily flow of multitudes. This distinction between symbols, however, was often ignored in the prewar decades; the triple arches of the main entrance to the New York Public Library, for instance, would be appropriate for a station.[31]

It is easy to mock at this group of stations. It has been customary to condemn them on a variety of counts: the derivative forms and detail, the extravagant dimensions, the colossal scale, the wasteful use of land, the prolonged distances, and the sacrifice of convenience for ostentation. But these criticisms form the reverse side of the coin. A fair judgment requires a look at the obverse side also.

The form and detail are no more derivative than the vocabularies used in the Victorian Gothic and Romanesque revival buildings. To those to whom all columns look alike, there may seem to be more monotony; to them too the real inventiveness of the design may be hidden. As a matter of fact, however, the vocabulary, though classic, was varied and infused with the spirit of creative eclecticism.

The colossal scale, ample sites, and vast interiors resulted from deliberate choices. Architects and corporations, influenced by the ideal of the City Beautiful, wished to contribute splendid, monumental structures to the urban scene. They were perfectly aware that they were subordinating economy and convenience to other values; but they held these other values to be of more lasting significance. The designers accepted as valid the classic conception that public buildings should be supremely impressive. They adopted the classic means: fine materials, uniform color, colossal scale, and a comparatively narrow range of form. They gave long and careful thought to the refinement and perfection of the design and eschewed self-expression.

Subsequently these values came to be heavily discounted and even denied. In 1954, however, a striking vindication of their point of view occurred. When demolition threatened two of the most celebrated examples—Grand Central and Pennsylvania Station in New York City—the *Architectural Forum* interrogated the leading contemporary architects,[32] and an overwhelm-

31. Its architects, Carrère and Hastings, did use arches for their stations at Pocatello, Idaho, 1909, and Grand Island, Nebraska, 1916–18.

32. *Architectural Forum, 101* (1954), 134 ff.

ing majority held that both stations had architectural and symbolic values which merited preservation. Contemporary architects endorse the choices and sacrifices made by the original designers.

The wide use of arches and columns on European stations has already been noted. Their increased use here in the United States after the Fair of 1893 may have reinforced the existing trend in Europe, which had been greatly influenced by our lavish new stations. It will suffice to mention those at Aberdeen, Scotland, and at Waterloo, London, rebuilding from 1907 to 1922. Two French ones have been described, Tours and the Gare d'Orsay in Paris, and there was a third French one—a vestibule added to the station at Troyes.

It should be pointed out in conclusion that these arched and colonnaded stations represent a reaction against engineering. The potentialities of the train-shed had been rejected in favor of monumental head-houses. This reaction was not confined to buildings of classical derivation; there were romantic examples also.

Romantic Survivals: a New Family

The principles of the picturesque were only diluted by the introduction of classical motives, not extinguished. Movement and intricacy survived. Some colossal stations which had followed the Fair of 1893 clung to both principles. The picturesque was still strong enough in this period, its last, to engender a new family of stations on the continent as well as to leave its stamp on many new American stations. Down to the beginning of World War II asymmetrical and towered compositions persisted.

Meanwhile station architecture was separated from its glass cages and became predominantly lithic. The Hamburg station was the last in the great succession of frankly expressed glass cages. In 1948 the skeleton, minus its glass, stood powerfully proclaiming the superb modernity of its conception. Why did it have no significant followers? The glazed areas shrank in exposition buildings but the train-shed shape survived, though metamorphosed in material and function. What had occurred to revive the idea that engineer's architecture was inferior to masonry buildings? Lithic architecture was after all the strongest architectural tradition of the western world. To be sure, departures from it had occurred in Byzantium, in the Middle Ages, in some baroque buildings, and in the 19th century when dynamic concepts had temporarily erupted; but after such moments there was always a return to inert masses and the quiet sense of permanence they afforded, the unequivocal sense of enclosure. Engineer's architecture, like the Gothic revivals, in the long view had been but momentary deviations. Late romantic architecture became predominantly massive and solid everywhere.

In America these late romantic stations seem to be survivals rather than revivals. They include the Mount Royal Station at Baltimore (Fig. 179), begun the year after the Chicago Fair. Its Romanesque tower shoots up from a low porte-cochere between symmetrical but broken-up wings. Reed and Stem in 1901 temporarily reverted to the more colorful mode and composed their Seattle station around a lofty clock tower. Bruce Price (1846–1903) and his daughter, Emily Post, in their respective ways did much to keep alive some of the standards of the last century. Price, though not so original as Richardson, displayed the full gamut of picturesque devices in settings of exceptional appropriateness. Price built two picturesque stations at Montreal: Windsor, begun in 1888 (Fig. 180), and the one at the Place Viger a little later. Windsor is in the developed Romanesque manner, with diverse towers, including an ingenious double one. The second station is smooth and symmetrical but retains towers and gables.

The limited competition held in 1907 for the Delaware, Lackawanna, and Western Station in Scranton, Pennsylvania, and won by Kenneth M. Murchison, demonstrated the variety of currents prevailing in American architecture at that time.[33] Paragraph 27 of the program says: "A tower, dome, or other distinguishing feature, as needed, may be incorporated in the design, but should serve a useful purpose, such, for instance as providing office space required or prospective, and the display of a clock. But such feature must not be materially costly." [34] Murchison's mansarded Beaux-Arts scheme had an arched feature on axis (Fig. 181). In execution the scheme was considerably revised: the roofs and arches were omitted and the exuberant foreign look replaced by an inert boxy classicism (Fig. 182). Trowbridge and Ackerman's project was equally French, with five arched portals between a pair of pavilions and with a huge clock tower at the left end, thus making the composition violently asymmetrical. Benjamin Wistar Morris' design was closer to the one executed than any of the others, but like Murchison's it featured a single-arched portal. The French note visible in it was stronger in Rankin and Kellogg's design. Hale and Rogers (James Gamble Rogers), with a wasteful

33. The program and designs were published by the T Square Club of Philadelphia: *American Competitions, 1907*, pp. v–viii, pls. 25–42. The first prize went to Kenneth M. Murchison. The other competitors included: Trowbridge and Ackerman with H. W. Wilkinson; Benjamin Wistar Morris, III; Rankin, Kellogg, and Crane; Hale and Rogers; and Price and McLanahan. The competition was supervised by Lincoln Bush, whose sheds were required to be used. The areas allocated to each function were prescribed.

34. *American Competitions*, p. vi.

"T" plan and forced symmetry, proposed a lofty domed tower. Price and McLanahan of Philadelphia proposed an exceedingly picturesque building with wings, pointed towers, domes, and arches (Fig. 183), a design in which the chateau model was liberally salted with Art Nouveau. These competitive designs indicate that in 1907 American taste was heavily influenced by Burnham Baroque freshened by a strong breeze from the recent Gare d'Orsay and the Gare de Lyon.

A few years later (1909) McKim, Mead, and White built at Waterbury, Connecticut, a station (Fig. 184) with a three-arched central block, flanked by lower wings, which suddenly erupts with a campanile. This has generally been accounted for as a requirement imposed by the president of the company, who was freshly returned from Europe. If so, the architects followed their instructions with poor grace; the tower is so awkwardly superimposed that one wonders if the architects intended to demonstrate the folly of amateur interference. Except for this tower—the last to appear on an important American station for a quarter of a century—the design is so simple, horizontal, and boxy that it might well have been the first of a new series.

In Europe the story is different: the trend amounted to a picturesque revival. The continent had been far less dominated by the British concept of picturesqueness than America, yet in the 1890's we see the picturesque bursting out in public buildings and stations, clothed in various nationalistic garbs or in the clinging draperies of the Art Nouveau. It is hard to know how much of this was due to a belated recognition of the English High Victorian achievements and how much to American examples. Interest continued to be shown by Europeans in Richardsonian Romanesque down to 1910. The lavishly illustrated *American Architect and Building News,* which began publication in 1876, and numerous monographs (Mrs. Van Rensselaer's, for example) might have found their way across the Atlantic. American buildings were illustrated in foreign publications. European railroad experts crossed to study our technical practices. The weary eyes of Europe focused on our buildings. There may therefore have been a backwash from the tide which hitherto had been sweeping so steadily westward. Whatever the reasons, a renewed trend toward asymmetrical romantic composition was under way in Europe. We can see it in such conspicuous buildings as Nyrop's Copenhagen City Hall (1892–1903), Berlage's Bourse at Amsterdam (1898–1903), Olbrich's Hochzeitsturm (1907–08) at Darmstadt, the Peace Palace at the Hague (1907–13), Östberg's City Hall at Stockholm (1911–23), and throughout the clear plates of the trilingual *Architecture des XX Jahrhunderts,* Berlin (1901–14), which included American examples. One of the earliest stations of this group was the Hauptbahnhof at Cologne (1889–94), described above.[35] Far more startling because of its Parisian setting was Marius

35. Page 117.

Toudoire's new forebuilding at the Gare de Lyon, 1897–1900 (Fig. 185).[36]
Seven monumental arched portals extend along the front; over them lies a
modest second story and above that rise overpowering roofs punctuated by
two rows of dormers finished with cresting. A number of pavilions, bays, and
other devices give plasticity. At the right-hand corner the prevailing symmetry is destroyed by a gigantic clock tower echoing those of Scott and Burges
in shape though not in detail. The taste for a theatrical type of picturesqueness which had showed itself in Charles Garnier's work from Paris to Monte
Carlo was strengthening.

Towers were rising from buildings all over Europe as they had formerly
done in Britain. The station at Bucharest, 1893–95 (Fig. 150) had symmetrical ones. At Hamburg (1903–06) there were two towers which were composed asymmetrically with the entrance vestibules. At Wiesbaden a single
tower was balanced by a domed pavilion. Dervaux's Art Nouveau station at
Rouen has an asymmetrically placed tower. These are a few of the conspicuous examples. There were many others, some belonging to a new lithic family.

A *fin de siècle* family of picturesque stations was created by architects in
central Europe and Finland, reflecting the revolutionary movements of the
Viennese Sécession and the Belgian Art Nouveau; the common denominator
is an anticlassic, antitraditional attitude. The Art Nouveau influence shows
in the decorative treatment, the soft outlines, the use of naturalistic curves,
the delicate working of surfaces, and the exquisitely scored pylon faces. The
Austrians Olbrich, Hoffmann, and Wagner established the ideals of simplicity:
flat, plain surfaces and a predominantly horizontal emphasis; they also supplied one of the favorite entrance motives, an arch flanked by pylons surmounted by spheres, urns, or figures. Another portal motive, the wide arch
resting on stubby columns, may have come from H. H. Richardson's American buildings either directly or by the intermediary of C. Harrison Town-
send's similar designs in England. The Richardsonian vocabulary was well
known and popular in Germany. His style was imitated in houses, banks,
public buildings, and churches for two decades after his death. Notable examples by Curjel and Moser were to be found at Mannheim, Karlsruhe, and
Wik.

A contributing factor was the persistent current of nationalism, which increased in strength as the ominous year 1914 drew near. The architectural
journals reflected this tendency: whether they were published in Germany,

36. Toudoire was also architect of the contemporary Gare St-Jean at Bordeaux. The
Paris station is described in *L'Illustration,* April 20, 1901: "It is an imposing structure in
a composite style flanked on the right hand by a tower 64 meters in height." The clock
was second in size only to that of the Philadelphia City Hall. The interior was planned as
a single lofty hall, but it became necessary to divide it into two levels to gain more floor
area. The upper level with its "oversumptuous" decoration became a restaurant supplied
from kitchens in the attics.

England, or the United States, the volume of foreign material included in them dwindled from a generous proportion in 1900 to a mere trickle in 1911. As a consequence of this chauvinism Bavarian curvilinear roofs, which at the same time corresponded to the new interest in supple forms, abound— sometimes confined to the towers, at other times covering the whole edifice. They had been absent at the Hauptbahnhof in Dresden in 1898 but appeared on the towers of the Hamburg Hauptbahnhof five years later and increasingly frequently thereafter. Another often used feature is a large window subdivided by numerous thin mullions. Two other motives repeat this interest in delicate vertical decoration: the organization of the surfaces as a series of vertical planes and the use of thin pilaster strips supporting nothing.

From the point of view of planning there was much less novelty. Official engineers were largely responsible for the layouts and in Germany they were required to follow the revised code of 1901. As had happened so often, architects were permitted to design only the head-house.

No station of this group gained its station character by means of revealed sheds; instead the arch and tower were the persistently employed symbols, and all but two have both an arch and a tower. The two which lack towers, Mulheim and Lausanne, indulged instead in complex, articulated, and gigantic roofs.[37]

The best known station of the family is Eliel Saarinen's at Helsinki (Figs. 186–7), for which the competition was held the year after the Hamburg station competition. The administration wing was built first and the whole finished by 1914, though not put into use as a station until after the war.[38] From 1905 to 1907 Saarinen traveled in England, Scotland, and Germany and restudied his design. Previously—in 1904—with Herman Gesellius he

37. The following list includes some important members of the new family: Copenhagen, Central Station, competition 1900, begun 1906, H. E. C. Wenck (Fig. 145); Basle, Bundes Bahnhof, competition 1903 (Olbrich placed third); Antwerp, Central Station, 1899, Louis de la Censerie (1835–1909); Helsinki, Central Station, competition 1904, won by Eliel Saarinen, begun 1910, completed 1914 (Figs. 186, 187); Leipzig, Hauptbahnhof, competition 1907, won by William Lossow and Max Kühne, completed 1915 (Figs. 155, 156); Darmstadt, Central Station, competition 1907, won by Friedrich Pützer (Olbrich placed second), completed 1912; Basle, Badischer Bahnhof, 1910–15, Karl Moser; Oldenburg station, 1911–15; Viipuri Station, Herman Gesellius, competition won by Saarinen and Gesellius, completed 1914; Stuttgart, Hauptbahnhof, competition 1911, won by Paul Bonatz and F. E. Scholer, begun 1914, interrupted 1916–22, completed 1928 (Fig. 190); Lausanne, Main Station, *ca.* 1912; Rouen, Gare de l'Ouest, A. Dervaux, planned 1913, opened 1928 (Fig. 191); Königsberg Hauptbahnhof, Ernest Richter, completed 1929; Flensburg, Neubahnhof, opened 1927; Travemünde, Bahnhof, completed 1929.

38. A. Christ-Janer, *Eliel Saarinen,* Chicago, 1948; and Eva Gatling, *Eliel Saarinen Memorial Exhibition,* Bloomfield Hills, 1951.

had won another competition, for a new station at Viipuri. This station, completed by Gesellius in 1914, was far more graceful. Both men were engaged, like many others, in attempting to create a new style for the new century. They started not from new materials, new structure, or even new function, but by developing new forms. The results seemed fresh to their contemporaries and were hailed as the beginning of a new "functional style." As we look backward, we can see that the new style was just another eclectic one drawing upon relatively recent sources: Wagner and Hoffmann's emphasis on squares and verticals and Mackintosh and Olbrich's systems of ornament. Since a more radically "new" style with glass-cage affinities was being created at the same time, notably by Behrens and Gropius, we are struck by the ponderous weight of Saarinen's solidity, his unbroken enclosures, and his static space. These qualities are emphasized at Helsinki by the unfinished condition of the interiors and the miserable wooden sheds over the platforms. But judged as a late example of the 19th-century style, its features make spendidly pictorial compositions. It is conceived in three dimensions and is set in an ample piazza, and it abounds in towers, pavilions, arches, and vaults.

In some ways August Stürzenacker's Karlsruhe station (Figs. 188, 189) was both more typical and more exquisite. Both within and without it displays an admirable simplicity. The use of ornament on the façade and the willfully original shapes show a highly developed sensitivity. The interior of the concourse is serene and majestic; the vault rises from a low side wall, its surface broken only by coffering. Few stations of any period have shown more distinction. A similar spirit was evident in Karl Moser's Badischer Bahnhof at Basle, begun in 1910. Its arched entrance portal is recessed into a projecting pavilion balanced by a blunt clock tower. The simplified classic detail, handled more lightly than Saarinen's, emphasizes the unbroken slopes of the roof.

The important station at Stuttgart (Fig. 190) conceived in 1911 but not completed until 1928, has been classed by Werner Hegemann as a transitional building coming midway between romantic modern and postwar modern. He called it a combination of a castle and a cathedral "pre-Raphaelite playing" and blamed it all on Theodor Fischer.[39] It was begun at the east end and finished at the west end fourteen years later, turning simpler and harder as it grew. Bonatz' own account of its building shows how deeply the 19th century had marked these architects working in the new century. It was decided to rebuild the old station in a central location; a traffic count had revealed that 95 per cent of its frequenters used it as a terminal, and it therefore had to be both permanent and massive. After further study of the city

39. *Monatshefte für Baukunst und Städtebau, 12* (1928), 145–66.

plan it was resolved to maintain the square in front as a square and not turn it into a traffic center. New streets were devised which allowed the tower to be built on the axis of the Königstrasse and permitted "a freely arranged mass with strong movement, with more tension and more possibility for expression. . . . The detail was subordinated to the outline." [40]

The plan is a "U" like that used for many European stations, as in Rome, equipped with elevated stub tracks. The entrances are marked by arches at the right and left extremities of the main front, and the exits lie behind a long connecting colonnade; in this way the departing traveler's path is marked by arches and the arriving passenger waits for local transportation behind the colonnade, thus making use of two familiar station symbols. The mail department occupies the left wing and the express department the bulk of the right wing, and each is provided with its own independent tunnels to the platforms. The sheds, units of which cover two lines and one wide platform, are built of wood and iron, an ingeniously contrived postwar economy.

Stuttgart's station bulks no less ponderously than Helsinki's, though it totally lacks the painstaking attention to ornament of the latter. It seems now to be Nazi design *avant la lettre*. The battered walls and rough surfaced stone reveal that Sir Uvedale Price's voice was still audible; it would be heard again long after the guns along the western front had fallen quiet.

A. Dervaux's Rouen station (Fig. 191) overthrows the traditions of conventional masonry and classical form in favor of reinforced concrete and Art Nouveau detail. The site conditions were challenging, since the lines ran in a deep cut between tunnels. Dervaux's conception was to make a station entirely of bridges. The concourse itself—154 feet long, 75 feet wide, and 72 feet high and at the time the largest hall in reinforced concrete—led to a bridge concourse 164 feet long and 55 feet wide, connected by six covered staircases to the three principal platforms below, carefully separating in- and out-passengers. The platforms were covered by novel sheds in concrete and glass, not as light as Hector Guimard's delicate fantasies for the Paris Métro nor yet as severely functional as Lincoln Bush's sheds. As in the Kansas City Union Station (1910–13), the bridge concourse included waiting space. The mail and baggage services were on the opposite bank from the passenger building and connected with the platforms by elevators linked to an independent system of bridges. The tower rising 104 feet above the street is clearly visible from the platforms. In 1936 it was still hailed as the first modern station in France and as one which had anticipated many modern practices.[41]

40. *Ibid.*, pp. 145–66.

41. The station is described and illustrated in *L'Architecture d'Aujourd'hui, 7* (1936), 4; and *Génie Civil, 92* (1928), 601–7.

The Art Nouveau detail at Rouen reflects reinforced concrete handled both as a frame with infillings in the Perret manner and in the fluid form which Henri Van de Velde adopted for his theater at Cologne. Who can say whether the shapes suggested by concrete in its fluid or in its congealed state are truer to the material? The asymmetrically placed tower shows elements of fantasy and recalls de Baudot more than Olbrich but, strangely, still more Waterhouse and Burges. The degree of modernity shown by Dervaux is in sharp contrast with the contemporary American giants or the uninspired Snow Hill Station at Birmingham, completed in 1913 under similar site conditions. His Gare de l'Ouest at Rouen was more boldly inventive than the more romantic Karlsruhe station.

Excellent and fresh as many of these stations were, they do not tell the complete story of the period. Contemporary with them there were other conceptions and other projects, some of which pointed further toward the future while maintaining their relationship with their own day. An early project was Tony Garnier's, a part of his scheme for the "Cité industrielle." [42] The traditional elements include a colossal tower with open galleries supporting a bulbous clock, rather Art Nouveau in feeling. The prophetic elements were the reinforced concrete structure and the glass curtain walls. Eric Mendelsohn's sketches of 1914 (Fig. 192) begin where the Hamburg station left off. The glass cage is given a freer, more dramatic expression, as is the arched portal, and the tower has been eliminated. Antonio Sant'Elia, the young Italian representative of the new spirit, exhibited a sketch in 1913 (Fig. 193) which also dramatized the glass cage. He substituted detached pylons for the traditional towers, but made the scale of the shed enormous and its forms powerful.

It was these latter tendencies rather than the new spirit that were realized to an unfortunate extent by his compatriot Ulisse Stacchini at Milan, in a station (Figs. 194–6) which began as a fresh Art Nouveau conception and in execution sank to the depths of bombastic, retrogressive monumentality. Stacchini had won the competition held in 1913; the head-building, however, was not under construction until 1920 and was not in use until 1930. The early designs were modified, but the fact that the general scheme was adhered to partly accounts for its remarkably old-fashioned look.[43] It is a head station served exclusively by spur tracks which wind into it on seemingly endless viaducts. A bank of five sheds, among the most beautiful ever built, is entirely concealed from the piazza by a grotesque brontosaurus of a fore-

42. Work on this project began in 1901 and continued for some years. The station design has been reproduced in Sigfried Giedion, *Space, Time, and Architecture* (3d ed. Cambridge, 1954), p. 201 (1st ed. 1940).

43. These designs were published in the *Annuario di Architettura* (Milan, 1914), pp. 23–5.

building. For no station since Leipzig had so much pomp been attempted; for no later station would it even be tried. It eclipsed the prewar American ones in grandeur as well as ugliness, as befitted the last member of a nearly extinct species. It is not an example of Fascist monumentality, since it was designed before Mussolini came to power. It belongs to the group of over-weening 19th-century public buildings begun at Brussels and continued by Calderini in the Roman Palazzo di Giustizia. The façade stretches for 700 feet along the Piazza Andrea Doria. The most prominent external feature is a porte-cochere nearly 600 feet long, surely the most pretentious one in the world. Behind this, ticket windows and other services are contained in a second still larger mass, from which the traveler mounts to the concourse by palatial staircases. Only then does he approach the trains housed in the quintuple steel shed beyond. Every consideration of utility has been sacri-ficed to preserve an obsolete aesthetic conception of grandeur: time is wasted in walking through vast halls; abundant ornamentation camouflages the neces-sary signs and directions. With so much space and so ample a budget, all vehicles could have been brought up to the viaduct level to eliminate the tedious stairs. Within and without, the detail is made up of blocks piled together as though giants had been turned loose in a quarry, recalling the work of the early modern Italian architects Giuseppe Sommaruga and Gino Coppedé. The love of gigantism seems to be an attribute of the Milanese character, to judge by the cathedral and the Galleria as well as the station. The engineers, on the other hand, also working in an almost obsolete tradi-tion, nevertheless produced admirable sheds. The central arch spans 236 feet and all five together more than 600 feet. In 1948 it seemed that this glass cage was fated to disappear, so bady had it been blasted, but by 1952 the glass had been lovingly put back.[44]

This account of the stations of the last years of the 19th and early years of the 20th century also concludes the main story of the picturesque eclectic movement. After the hiatus of World War I, as we have seen, additional stations belonging to each of these families continued to appear; however, they were comparatively unimportant, since a new aesthetic movement was rising to generate new families of stations.

44. The bibliography for this station is long and international. Some useful accounts are: *La Technique des Travaux, 8* (1932), 283–4; *Modern Transport, 19* (1928), 3–5; and *Rassegna di Architettura, 3*, Nos. 10–11, Oct.–Nov. 1931.

6. THE TWENTIETH

CENTURY STYLE

(1914-1956)

Trials and Tribulations: the End of an Era

The decades following World War I are so close to us that they are difficult to interpret in their true perspective; but evaluation must be attempted. Most architectural critics agree that the significant phenomenon of those years was the emergence of a wholly new, noneclectic style called "functionalism" or the "international style" or merely "modern architecture," although it is still possible that the more conservative lithic work of Auguste Perret may in the long run turn out to have more lasting influence than the more obviously novel work of Walter Gropius or Le Corbusier. In either event it will be seen that picturesque eclecticism had run its course and had been succeeded by another aesthetic movement, whatever it may be called.

This new style has already passed through three phases. In the first phase the elimination of eclectic ornament was accomplished; this is the period in which buildings became bare, apparently solid cubes. In the second phase the absolutism of the cube was modified in two ways: the cubical block became rectangular and the enclosing planes were perforated so that they could be clearly understood to enclose space. Some of the planes became transparent, giving in a few cases the effect of a prismatic glass cage—unlike the cages of the last century, however, in that there were no curves. In the third stage, the one we are now in, the structural frame is fully revealed. Structural means are exploited to heighten expressiveness: the box is now an open glass container emancipated from the tyrannies of the rectangle and the prism, and the dome and other curved forms have reappeared.

During the second of these stages a manner of design which we may call the "carton style" flourished briefly. Carton-style buildings look as though their designers had proceeded by standing assorted up-ended containers in front of one another until the agglomeration met their standards of balance and massiveness. The results were usually executed in stone, though any material would have done, since the scale which might have resulted from more regard for material or human use was not observed. The most notorious collection of buildings designed in this manner were the happily temporary ones erected for the Chicago Fair of 1933. The carton style was quickly abandoned; functionalist doctrines which emphasized utility and truth led to a reappreciation of structure which made such lithic architecture unacceptable. The skeleton of metal or concrete was exposed. The architect recognized the potential sources for new form and new effects inherent in the great works of modern engineering, and engineer's architecture came into its own again.

These, then, are the formal characteristics of three phases of the new movement. The propagandists of modern architecture stressed its rationalism more than its aesthetic, which nevertheless also played an important role. We can list the qualities sought after as we did for the older movement: planarity, space-time, transparency, interpenetration, and simplicity (see Table 2, p. 5). These are the characteristic values of modern architecture to be seen in new buildings on every hand. It is indifference to these objectives which makes the new Toledo station (Fig. 227) so inept. The use of thin, light planes, either transparent or opaque, is to be seen in many stations.[1] The new Stazione Termini at Rome (Figs. 216, 217) is a particularly fine example. The indoor and outdoor portions, covered by a single floating roof, are lightly separated by transparent screen walls. Two additional signs of current trends appear in this great station. The first is its free use of curved trusses, giving it an organic quality which has led to its nickname "the dinosaur."[2] The second is a sculptured facia known as "the shirt-tail" along the front edge of the canopy; this sculpture, by Amerigo Tot, marks the return of a higher degree of collaboration among artists.

While the new architecture movement was developing, the railroad industry was taking some hard blows. There was a collapse of the 19th-century optimistic belief that progress would continue irreversibly. The new mood of diffidence had sent architects in search of more secure bases than mere individual preferences, such as dynamic symmetry and functionalism, and

1. For examples see Amsterdam (Figs. 212, 213), Burlington (Fig. 226), and the projects (Figs. 228–31).

2. This is remarked on by Milton Gendel in the *Art News, 53* (1954), 65.

forced railroad companies to economize. The extravagant era of station building came almost to a stop in 1914; never since have so many huge stations been built all at once, partly because with minor modifications old ones could still be made to serve, partly because the unchallenged supremacy of the railroad as the only possible transportation for long trips was being overthrown. The challengers came thick and fast: the family flivver, the airplane, the Greyhound bus. They beat the train at every point. The door-to-door flivver gave travel a new convenience, the bus cut fares, the plane was many times speedier; in fact, it is astonishing that the passenger train has survived at all. It did so only by cutting costs and providing more comfort and safety. Colossal terminals proved to be liabilities; in some cases terminal charges absorbed 80 per cent of the revenue from commuters' tickets. One result was the abandonment of separate stations for each company and consolidation of their services. Sometimes one of the old buildings could handle the combined traffic, sometimes new union stations were built. Other between-war methods of reducing the crushing overhead included the blight of garish advertisements, the minor nuisance of pay toilets, and the diversion of as much space as possible to concessions. In the spirit of economic determinism there were exaggerated efforts to analyze stations statistically. Data such as these were accumulated: "Rate of discharge from platforms; 15 per foot of width per minute, 50 passengers per minute can be passed through turnstiles," etc.

Some psychologically satisfying devices were introduced. The public address system, borrowed from airports, permits the passenger to relax while waiting for his train; he can pursue whatever activity occurs to him without keeping his eyes glued to the train board. In some small stations such as Sudbury Town, near London, the waiting room was opened up so that one could see the approaching train for himself and judge when to move out to the platform; or, as at Muiderpoort, small waiting rooms and buffets were placed directly on the platform itself. These palliatives are as close as modern design has come to bringing back the convenient station with completely covered platforms and tracks.

A new trend toward comfort began in the late 1920's. Formerly, the ladies' rooms had been luxuriously furnished: in the Mount Royal Station at Baltimore, for example, rocking chairs were provided. Later, wooden benches became the rule. But to meet competition, this trend had to be reversed and there was a striving for the atmosphere of the lobby of a big hotel. A reading room for men, equipped with leather chairs and current magazines, was provided at the Michigan Central station in Detroit. It is said that the sumptuously appointed lounge of the new Burlington, Iowa, station (1944), the pleasantest public room in the community, was sought by ladies' clubs as a meeting room. This recalls the heyday of the village depot with its pot-bellied stove, spittoons, and benches—a community center, rivaled only by the general store, where the whole town gathered to greet the afternoon train. At that time, too, the railroads had to lure passengers. In the modern stations, as upholstered furniture was reintroduced, color schemes were brightened to get rid of the depressing institutional atmosphere. Instead of building new stations, valiant—if tasteless—efforts to rejuvenate them were resorted to.

There were other changes. Telephone booths were increased, air conditioning introduced, escalators and electric-eye door-openers installed. The accelerated tempo of life had made the buffet and lunch counter more profitable than the once popular restaurants. An example is the size of the areas allotted to various functions in the Fort Street Union Depot in Detroit before and after its recent remodeling. The areas for the restaurant, kitchen, and men's and women's toilets were reduced, and increases were made in the waiting room (25 per cent), concourse (nearly 200 per cent), auxiliary restaurant facilities (nearly 400 per cent), and telephone and telegraph space (300 per cent). As the era of the Saratoga trunk waned and that of light hand baggage came in, baggage departments had to be altered and larger, more accessible parcel rooms were improvised—though rarely on the scale of the one at Leipzig, which required 35 attendants.

More because of the increase in population than popularity, operating conditions became congested. Fewer terminal tracks could be spared for standing trains, which therefore had to be kept far away from the passenger station. Space could no longer be found for separate luggage platforms. Costly land at the terminal had to be shared with the expanding post office and express services whose huge buildings with their vehicle courts, ramps, tunnels, and elevators added to the complexity and further compressed the passenger services. Under such conditions less and less money was available for the imperial display that had been symbolized by vast concourses and wide-span train-sheds, and in the United States even the Bush shed was abandoned after 1918 in favor of the still more economical platform canopy (Figs. 197–8).

Only in Europe were new sheds occasionally built. There, where the railway continued to be the leading system of transportation for the masses, the train-shed had a more deeply rooted tradition and had taken on symbolic value: a city's status was reflected in its grandeur. The story of the new sheds at Reims (Fig. 201) illustrates this. The railway officials had not wished to rebuild the sheds after their destruction in World War I, but the citizens vociferously demanded their restoration; it was felt that the city would be reduced in status if its station lacked sheds. This insistence on new sheds gave the engineers an opportunity to devise a different type, and low conoid vaults in reinforced concrete with slight ties were designed; MM. Limousin, the designers, used concrete because of its resistance to corrosion. The spans of about 100 feet are not astounding, though they remain the widest train-sheds to be built in concrete. The ribs formed deep troughs. Slots were provided in their sides which at one time ingeniously solved two of the drawbacks of older sheds: the tendency for fouled air to collect under the roof and the difficulties of keeping the glass clean. Here the glass could be reached through the slots by men standing in the trough. The people of Reims forced the train-shed to be brought up to date.

With the exception of the stations at Milan and São Paolo, the chief builders of train-sheds after World War I were the French.[3] One was built at Reims, two at Le Havre, and one at Cherbourg. The latter three were part of an intensified program to attract tourists. They provided French engineers with a chance to demonstrate their leadership in the application of reinforced concrete. In Germany a few stations, built after the war such as the one at Düsseldorf, had platforms completely protected by low sheds.[4]

At the risk of removing the last remnant of hide from a much-flayed horse, contrast the lack of adequate protection while getting passengers in and out of the trains with the elaborate modern provisions for getting them in and out of other vehicles under cover. When the traveler sets out today to cross the continent by train, starting and ending the trip in hotels, the only place during the entire journey where he might be exposed to bad weather is while boarding and leaving the train! At the entrance to the hotel, if the marquee is inadequate the porter will proffer an umbrella. Getting in or out of a taxi at the station, one is protected if not by an ample porte-cochere then by the roof of the tunneled driveway. But where the tradition of adequate shelter was most gloriously emphasized, in the traditional train-shed, the modern station has failed.

With the good and bad features described above, the history of the train-shed comes to a close. As we have suggested, the future of the form lies in one of its metamorphosed states: market halls which have surpassed the size of the parent; modern churches, a dwarfed variant; and hangars, most promising as well as most appropriate, since they too are connected with transportation. The latter appear to be initiating a cycle of their own, having passed through a period of experimentation with laminated wood just as

3. The São Paolo shed, by E. F. Sorocabana, was begun in 1926. It was of the familiar three-hinged arched type, 143 feet in span.

4. At Malmö, in 1925, four new sheds of 60-foot span were installed. The construction, otherwise agreeable, introduced no innovations and the shape of the ribs is marred by cambered tie rods.

train-sheds did a century ago. The second stage in this cycle is being reached at the St. Louis airport, where a graceful shell-concrete shed designed by Hellmuth, Yamasaki, and Leinweber covers the passenger concourse, just as fifty years earlier the iron and glass train-shed had been moved from its place over the tracks to the cross-platform.

European Stations Meet the Challenge

New conceptions of the planning and architectural design of stations were at first embodied in projects. Richard Neutra's station for Rush City Reformed, designed in 1925, is an instance.[5] A multilevel labyrinth was devised within a vast flat box, with the top deck intended for aircraft use. The forms were clean and free from derivative detail and at the same time large and monumental. This project was followed a few years later by one for Moscow.[6] The main hall was to be a pure block constructed in concrete and glass, and the various services were to be handled on three levels. Both projects have a boldness and simplicity characteristic of the best architectural thinking of the period; but these principles were only later to be realized in an actual station.

After World War I Britain had a minor renaissance of station building. In modest stations on limited budgets she showed that she was still capable of distinguished designs. These reflected the functional approach as well as her great 19th-century terminals reflected the picturesque approach. The architects, led by Charles Holden of Adams, Holden, and Pearson, were encouraged by the brilliant Frank Pick.[7] From 1925 to 1949 these ingenious, economical buildings restored England's lapsed standing as a contributor to the development of the depot. All of them reflected the pure geometry of the first phase of the modern movement: Mondrian patterns and hovering planes, cylinders (Arnos Grove, 1932, Fig. 199), cubes, and upright rectangular prisms. Novel train-sheds of modest size were created; a blocky and angular one was built at Uxbridge in 1938 (Fig. 200).

As a group these English stations have a sober, matter-of-fact air because they lack strongly individual touches and emphatic proportions.[8] An exception

5. Illustrated with inadequate description in W. Boesiger, *Richard Neutra, Buildings and Projects* (Zurich, 1951), p. 199.

6. Illustrated in *L'Architecture d'Aujourd'hui, 7* (1936), 15.

7. Other architects included S. A. Heaps, J. R. Scott, J. L. Martin, W. H. Hamlyn, and Frederick Curtis.

8. Other notable examples of this group include Queen's Park (1925), Osterly (1934),

—the new station for Plymouth by H. E. B. Cavanagh—begun before World War II and modified to meet conditions resulting from bomb damage, is a large one-sided station connected to several lines by a subway. The fore-building, accompanied by a multistory office block, makes an asymmetrical towered composition. The exterior with its light, clear treatment is enhanced by an imaginative, decorative grid which gives it suitable importance. The plan is uncomplicated and easy to follow.[9]

Across the channel in France new stations also arose, two of them at Le Havre and one at Cherbourg. Urbain Cassan designed the maritime stations at Le Havre (Fig. 202) and Cherbourg. Their sheds are, like the one at Reims, an excellent application of reinforced concrete, given distinction by clean lines and agreeable proportions. The concourse at Le Havre is a clearer expression of thinned-down structure. Henri Pacon was the architect of the city station at Le Havre (Fig. 203). Numerous specialized functions and an awkward site which demanded long passages prevented a simple plan. The masses are cubic and flat-roofed, but the inclusion of a tower at one extremity makes a composition as picturesque as many a station built a generation earlier. These three stations were government financed and conservatively modern in character. Good as they are, it is clear that officialdom did not care to follow Le Corbusier's architectural lead; as the interiors of the de luxe French transatlantic liners have always shown, official France preferred the more obvious and sybaritic high-style look of the fashionable decorators.

André Ventre's Gare du Chantier at Versailles, 1931–33 (Fig. 204) is an exceptionally interesting station of this period. The gracefully curved entrance pavilion makes a bow toward the famous palace nearby without echoing any detail of it, as does the simple interior. In 1933 this building struck the young visitor as an unusually distinguished contemporary building, and although it still seems more sensitively conceived than its fellow stations, it has not been a particularly prophetic design. Miës van der Rohe's Barcelona Pavilion and Le Corbusier's Swiss Pavilion have been more influential. A year or two later Urbain Cassan's project for a new station at Brest showed that the French railways were resolutely opposed to anything more daring than simplified classicism and were clinging determinedly to the favorite asymmetrically placed tower, however stark the detail.[10]

France had the honor of commissioning one major station—the Gare du

---

Surbiton and Leeds City (1937), Rayner's Lane and Malden Manor (1938), Gant's Hill (1947), and Hangar Lane (1949). These are illustrated in Barman, *An Introduction to Railway Architecture.*

9. Described and illustrated in the *Journal of the Royal Institute of British Architects,* ser. 3, *58* (1951), 218–21.

10. *L'Architecture d'Aujourd'hui, 7* (1936), 33.

Nord for Amiens—from Auguste Perret, an architect of international reputation. The designs, published in 1946 (Fig. 205), show a plan which was
handicapped by two contradictory conditions: the regularity demanded by
the *place* in front, and the curve of the depressed tracks in back. These tracks
run under a corner of the site and force an awkward platform arrangement.
The resulting project introduces a unique chapter to our story, an example
of Perret's highly personal classical style. The elevation on the *place* stresses
the waiting room, which rises higher than the short, four-storied wings. The
cantilevered marquee is perforated by low domes. Perret's attenuated,
downward-tapered, Cretan columns support the entablature and the roof
and form a separate outer pavilion under which stands a second pavilion
framed by tapered piers. This is the envelope of the main hall. Both pavilions
and the wings are of reinforced concrete manipulated with exceptional
subtlety of cross section and linear pattern.[11] Original in construction, conception, and detail, this design is nevertheless haunted by the ghosts of post-
and-lintel styles as well as by those of the domed Pantheon, of porticoed
temples, of the Grand Hall at Euston, and of 20th-century office buildings.
Only two shades once normal to stations are absent: the arch and the tower.

Both of these, however, continued in use in postwar Germany. As a group,
the postwar German stations made considerable advances in adapting new
architectural forms to station buildings; at the same time the designers did
not turn their backs abruptly upon the prewar stations with their traditional
towers and arches. The Hauptbahnhof at Düsseldorf by Kruger and Behnes
in association with the engineer L. A. Dormer [12] (Fig. 206), begun in 1931,
may be taken as representative. Unlike the slightly earlier station at Königsberg, it has eliminated the hipped roofs and pointed arches derived from
prewar examples; rather, like the contemporary station at Beuthen, it treats
the main masses as a few rather stiffly arranged blocks. As in Königsberg, the
entrance to the narrow end of the concourse forms the axis of an otherwise
symmetrical composition to which a stout clock tower has been affixed near
the right end—a device also found at Beuthen. In none of these, however,
was there any suggestion of transparency. A fourth station of this group, at
Duisberg, closely related in other respects to the three preceding ones, signals
the transition from the first to the second phase of modern architecture by
having windows rather than walls as the greater part of its exterior surfaces.[13]

This station was completed just before a more famous and striking one

11. *L'Architecture d'Aujourd'hui, 17* (1946), 16.

12. *Bautechnik, 9* (1931), 279.

13. The station at Beuthen is illustrated in R. Campanini, *Edifici dei Trasporti* (Milan,
1945), p. 23E. The station at Duisberg is illustrated in *Bautechnik, 13* (1935), 447–50.

at Florence (Figs. 209, 210), built 1934–36 by Michelucci. Around the corner from Alberti's façade at Santa Maria Novella, in sight of Giotto's campanile, it occupied as historical a setting as one can imagine. The Rockefellers poring over plans for Williamsburg could hardly have been more shocked by the sight of a modern design than the Florentines were at their first sight of this sensational station. If followed the spirit rather than the forms of Renaissance Florence when she had been a center of innovation. The station front is marked not by an arcade but by a cantilevered marquee, making its whole length available for unloading cars. The glass cage tradition is recalled in the roof of the porte-cochere, which starts at the far side of the driveway and runs across it, then climbs the wall of the entrance hall and continues over it as the roof—powerfully suggesting the direction in which traffic is to move. Another indication of this flow is contained in the canopy of the cross-platform, which slopes upward toward the spur lines. The only trace of monumentality, in the pejorative sense of the term, is the marble royal entrance at the right side.[14]

Also in Italy, Angiolo Mazzoni built a series of small stations in the 1930's during this brief period when Mussolini smiled upon the international style.[15] One of these, at Spoleto (Fig. 208), illustrates the general character of the group; a later one at Verona (Fig. 207) in attempting more accomplishes less. These stations are stylistically united by combining angular planimetric modern forms of extreme simplicity with the traditional Italian monumentality and richness of material.

Mazzoni's cubes and cantilevers have a magnificent positiveness quite unlike the lighter Scandinavian station. It is as though the former were weighted down with the dignity of the Caesars and the latter were buoyed up by Gothic aspiration.[16] In Finland several new stations were built; typical is the one at Tampere, 1933–38 (Fig. 211), by O. Flodin and E. Sepälä.[17] During the five-year period between the winning of the competition in 1933 and the time the station was put into use, several modifications were made by

14. This station was widely published. See particularly Campanini, *Edifici dei Trasporti;* and *Architectural Forum, 55* (1936), 210. The following architects, in addition to Michelucci, were associated in its design: N. Baroni, P. N. Berardi, I. Camberini, S. Guarnieri, and L. Lusanna.

15. Siena and Via Reggio (1936) and Reggio Emilia and Trento (1937). In 1939 there was begun in Rome the supreme station of the mid-20th century.

16. Compare, for example, the modest bleached station at Falköping, 1934–35, with those of Siena and Trento.

17. See Campanini, *Edifici dei Trasporti,* p. 27; and *Architectural Record, 83* (March 1938), 63.

direction of the state railways, one of which was an alteration in the most unusual feature—the pylon. This takes the place of the conventional tower, of which it is a slenderized version; a flanged shaft with cantilevered flat roof at the summit gave it the not inappropriate air of an enlarged signal tower. It bears the usual clock face and, more remarkably, serves as a standard for advertisements. Two levels are used; the tracks are on a viaduct, and the further platforms are connected to the concourse by a tunnel. The long wall of the restaurant and service wings passes behind the relatively lofty hall of the concourse (the equivalent of four stories), expressed as a box punctured by a rectangular window. The patterns of planes and masses and the careful study of proportions are related to the De Stijl movement with its patterns built of "L's." This station, though small, is one of the three or four outstanding station designs of the 1930's—clear, direct, free of associations with past styles, suitably but not excessively monumental. The only jarring note is a reinforced concrete cantilevered platform shelter running along the inner platform, its roof tilted up toward the track: the forceful angle disturbs the serenity of the general scheme.

Holland in the 1930's showed a tremendous advance, progressing from the inept carton style station of the late 1920's, exemplified by H. G. J. Schelling's Bussom Station, to his two small stations on the outskirts of Amsterdam, completed in 1939.[18] The Amstel and Muiderpoort stations (Figs. 212–13) serve growing suburban areas with heavy commuter traffic. The raising of tracks on viaducts in this region gave the opportunity for building new stations. Schelling solved the circulation problems with great finesse, keeping incoming and outgoing traffic well separated and using independent ramps and subways to handle baggage. The concourses, flooded with light, are glass boxes of exceptional elegance, considerably more refined than those in the English suburban series. Consistent with Dutch tradition, the buildings unpretentiously combine economy and dignity. Buff brick, glass, and metal sufficed, without recourse to marble, limestone, or bronze. The detail is clean, the scale delicate, and the ceilings lofty; no echo is heard of Burnham Baroque or other antique vocabularies of ornament. At Amstel the lines together with the platforms are covered by compact glass cages, repeating the larger cage, framed by bents, in the main hall. A restaurant and waiting room stand conveniently on the platform. The plainer ceilings and end walls contrast with the delicate trellis which supports the glazing. At Muiderpoort the almost symmetrical towered building is set between converging viaducts. These utilitarian build-

18. The Bussom station was published in Sheldon Cheney, *The New World Architecture* (New York, 1930), with rather extravagant praise. The two later ones were widely published in 1939 and 1940: see particularly *Ingénieur, 54* (1939), B209–20; and, more recently, *Architectural Review, 103* (1948), 210–14.

ings, with materials frankly and sensitively handled, are raised to the level of the best contemporary architecture, a level more familiar to us in our schools and churches than in our depots. These stations make effective use of metal and glass so rarely reinterpreted after 1900.

The influence of these excellent buildings is clearly shown in postwar stations at Vienna, Innsbruck, and Heidelberg; here also buff brick, glass, and metal are combined to enclose lightly rectangular sun-flooded concourses. Their architects struck an admirable balance between expressiveness and monumentality, economy and dignity.

Further evidence of the possibility of a revival of the railroad station as a building of major architectural importance can be seen in the terminals designed since World War II for Gothenberg, Oslo, and—most significantly —Rome. These also continue the current which carried the Amsterdam stations to their high level, and the Rome station reaches a new summit.

The new terminal for Gothenberg (Fig. 214) was designed by staff architects to combine the services of three scattered stations and a hotel. The site is that of the former Central Station considerably enlarged. A two-storied portico connects the hotel to the station and is continued across the lower floors of the station, tying the two blocks even more firmly together than the arcades of Bologna unify that city. This sophisticated urban convenience is no less appropriate for northern climates. The main entrance to the station is a glass wall inserted between two boxy four-storied buildings. Directly behind lies the concourse at ground level, and beyond this, stairs lead upward to a cross-platform serving nineteen spur tracks flanked by separate passenger and freight platforms, with both track and platforms covered by a low shed permitting loading of passengers and objects under weatherproof conditions. The freight and baggage station lies at a lower level, communicating with the platforms by ramps. Arriving passengers may exit from the end of the cross-platform to the plaza. Numerous interior courts and wings are masked, like the concourse, behind a uniform façade. One defect is that the passenger is forced to climb up a half-level from the concourse and then descend to the platform, to allow head room for freight handling under the cross-platform. It is not possible to evaluate the project further on the basis of the preliminary drawings at hand. In execution, the exaggerated regularity may be modified, and the materials and detailing enliven it.[19]

A new central station for Oslo (Fig. 215) was designed at about the same time. The competition, held in 1946, was won by John Engh and Peer Quam. Their project incorporated several features which appeared in the Gothenberg design; perhaps similar conditions called forth similar solutions. It was again necessary to combine in one central station services formerly handled

19. A set of preliminary drawings was kindly supplied by the Swedish State Railways.

by several separate ones. An adequate site is to be obtained by filling in part of the harbor. The main concourse will be entered at the center of one of its long sides and also through one of its short ends. Stairs will lead upward to the cross-platform, below which there will be a second concourse, reached from each of the platforms by more stairs. Both within and without, the forms are expressive and interesting. Instead of the inert concrete frame of Gothenberg with its monotonous exterior fenestration of the two main blocks, the masses advance and recede according to necessity—sometimes low and sometimes lofty. Both the main concourse and the train concourse have roofs which curve up and over toward the tracks, a refinement of the earlier example at Florence. A tower has been made at the salient corner by carrying the office block up an extra story. The exterior effect is light; extensive use had been made of glazing. Both Scandinavian designs express in varying degrees a contemporary approach to the century-old station problem, and particularly at Oslo success is attained without recourse to old formulas.[20]

The finest modern station to date is that completed in Rome in 1951 (Figs. 216, 217) after more than a decade of starts and stops. As in some other large European terminals, in spite of the fact that it was possible to provide separate freight and passenger platforms of ample width, no wide-span shed was contemplated. In 1931 Mussolini had felt that the old station of the 1870's not only was too small but was unworthy of its role as the entrance to his capital—the building which welcomed tourists and pilgrims to the most monumental city of Europe. Accordingly, a competition was held, and the winner was Angiolo Mazzoni, whose earlier station building experience qualified him for this supreme task. The old site, with the tracks at grade, had once been a baroque pleasure garden and was still extensive enough to contain the projected new ranges. Work began in 1931 on the lateral wings but ceased during the war, so that in 1948 the old head-house still stood casting a melancholy backward glance at its advancing supplanter. Mazzoni found the motives and materials of the Rome of the Popes inadequate to convey the character he aspired to and went back to the Rome of the Caesars for his arches and travertine. The right-hand wing, which ends in signal towers, has superimposed arcades, almost on the site of the Aqua Claudia which it echoes. Within, sumptuous marbles and brilliant mosaics recall the public buildings of Imperial Rome. Enormous, cold, monotonous, these lifeless arms lay awaiting a head and a heart. After Mussolini's degrading end at the close of the war a new spirit triumphed in Italy, one which could not brook the dictator's style; consequently a new competition was held for the completion of the

20. *Byggekunst*, Nos. 1 and 2, Stockholm, 1947. A set of drawings was very kindly supplied by the architects.

station. A major obstacle to a smooth, easy solution lay in the fragment of the Agger Serviano which ran diagonally into the proposed site and which for historical reasons could not be removed. Eugenio Montuori, architect, and Leo Calini, engineer, proposed a brilliant, organic solution which was put into execution and was essentially completed in 1951.

The finished station is a "U" building wrapped around 22 spur tracks at grade. The right-hand wing is used for suburban services, the left for mails and express. The central block, more than 2,000 feet long, faces the Baths of Diocletian. The ponderous vaults occupied by the Thermae Museum and Michelangelo's Santa Maria degli Angeli established an intimidatingly high standard. Montuori wisely avoided the banal lithic colonnaded conceptions of some competitors and made as striking a use of the materials of our day as Michelangelo had of his. The whole front on the Piazza dei Cinquecento as far as the old wall was opened up as a glass and metal screen protected by a floating, cantilevered roof. Not for forty years had these materials been so successfully wrought into monumentality; the station is unburdened by tradition yet worthy of its famous neighbors. The head-building brought the whole complex to life. It is expressive of its function, welcoming, directing, awe-inspiring, utterly different from the depressing midway at Washington or the vast derivative concourses at New York. Here the recent cycle of form development reached the third stage—that of the open glass container emancipated from the twin tyrannies of the rectangle and the prism.

Behind the great vestibule is the midway, a handsome covered street opening at both ends to busy avenues, and beyond that is a system of exceptionally generous platforms. Secluded by the ancient wall, the elegant restaurant with its garden lies to the left of the entrance. This new terminal in Rome is entitled to double honors: not only is it the finest modern station, it is also one of the finest modern buildings.[21]

American Stations Join the Battle

In the United States the years after World War I witnessed the building of several large stations entirely lacking in a constructive architectural approach. Some of these have been described in the previous chapter. Graham, Anderson, Probst, and White—D. H. Burnham's successors—and Fellheimer and

21. See Campanini, *Edifici dei Trasporti,* 13–14E, for Mazzoni's scheme. The second competition is illustrated in *Metron,* No. 21, 1947. The completed building is illustrated in the *Architectural Review, 107* (1950), 420, and *109* (1951), 208–15; and in *Das Werk, 39* (1952), 206–10. The full list of those responsible for the design is: L. Calini, M. Castellazzi, V. Fadigati, E. Montuori, A. Pintonello, and A. Vitellozzi.

Wagner were responsible for several of them. The most prominent American architect of the period, Bertram G. Goodhue, recognized the modern movement only to the extent of sloughing off ornament, treating his masses as boxes, and making deep bows to the classicism he was degrading; what then was to be expected of lesser men? They either cleaved to the Burnham tradition or forsook it for the Goodhue manner, which they reduced to the carton style.[22]

Frank Lloyd Wright, Walter Gropius, and Ludwig Miës van der Rohe —the architects who might have been able to give station architecture a new and positive direction—were not entrusted with the spending of corporation monies; in the opinions of conservatively managed railway companies they were far too radical. On the same grounds they were not commissioned to build city halls or post offices. This prejudice forced them to make their experiments and contributions under private sponsorship and deferred their careers as institutional architects. Far more courage had been shown by Continental governments in the prewar days when Saarinen, Otto Wagner, Hector Guimard, and Paul Bonatz were given their opportunities.

The Burnham Baroque stations had had movement to save them from complete lethargy, but one can detect no effort to animate such stations as the Omaha Union Station of 1929 by Gilbert S. Underwood (Fig. 218). From the outside, it is as impossible to imagine that these buildings have interiors as it is to visualize the internal chambers of the pyramids. They are the antithesis of the glass cage. McKim, Mead, and White's Pennsylvania Station at Newark (1932–35), also a member of this family, had fully covered tracks and platforms. The narrow-span sheds, lacking the grace of lighter cage-type sheds, suggest that a confused engineer was thinking of bomb shelters.

Fellheimer and Wagner, authors of numerous secondary stations throughout the country, received three large station commissions in the 1920's: Boston, Buffalo, and Cincinnati. Both the Boston and the Buffalo ones, begun in 1927, required extensive readjustments of the city plan.[23]

At Buffalo a heroic decision to move the whole terminal complex two

22. See above, p. 144.

23. The second North Station in Boston was combined with a colosseum to seat 14,000. An office building and hotel were contemplated but omitted; the presence of the colosseum was a serious enough complication, since its supports pierced the station areas below. There was little opportunity for external architectural effect since the head-house backed up on a train-yard and faced elevated railway tracks. A still greater obstacle was that a different firm—Funk and Wilcox—was employed to design the colosseum portion. An extensive use of ramps helped cope with the intricate circulation. The main concourse was forced into corridor proportions, 40 feet wide and 275 feet long, with an insignificant height of 22 feet. A description with illustration may be found in *Railway Age, 85* (1928), 337 ff.

miles east of the old station permitted adequate room for a well planned station (Fig. 219), and the work of clearing the site began in 1926. Connecting highways to the central part of the city with separate routes for trolleys, buses, trucks, and taxis were laid out. Passengers were thus subjected to the inconveniences connected with outlying airports; but ease of operation was the company's prime consideration. The plans were accepted in 1927 and the station was in use in 1929. The main external feature—the sixteen-story office tower—minimizes the station, large as it is. Seven long platforms are reached from a bridge concourse. The brick exterior does not mark any stylistic advance, nor does it show a finesse comparable to contemporary Dutch and German brick work. In short, the station is an efficient machine.[24]

Up to this time the standing of this competent firm had been high in official circles even though the architectural results had not been distinguished; then in 1929 they began their masterpiece at Cincinnati (Figs. 220–2). As in Buffalo, this station was a badly needed replacement for a clutch of decrepit stations scattered about in the lower parts of the city subject to flooding. Far out from the urban center, an ample site was secured on which to build as ideal a station as could be conceived. The tracks were made to swing past at the rear, and an enormous elevated plaza was raised in front. The conception was that of a half funnel laid on the ground, the wide mouth gathering in the streams of travelers and the narrow end ejecting them onto the platforms. Circulation was the fundamental consideration. From the plaza, passengers enter the semicircular concourse at grade level. Three curving ramps lead down to the lower level, where buses or taxis deposit departing passengers and pick up arriving ones, then loop around and continue back up the ramp to the plaza. This remains today the most elaborate provision for vehicular traffic in any modern station. Back of the concourse a combined waiting room and train concourse 450 feet long stretches out over eight platforms and is connected to them by ramps and stairs, so that passengers have to go from the tracks up to the concourse and then down again to the vehicle ramps. Though simple enough in theory, this up-over-and-down journey must be rather arduous in practice; nothing can be made too simple for the hurried traveler.[25]

Inside this Cincinnati station the era of sumptuous stations had left its traces. The prosperity and optimism of the years before the great Wall Street crash had stimulated a revival of mural decoration, and Winold Reiss was commissioned to decorate the interior in mosaics. Externally, the station

24. See *Canadian Railway and Marine World, 32* (May 1929), 297; *Architectural Forum, 53* (1930), 161–3; and *Railway Age, 86* (1929), 1147–53.

25. Louis Sullivan's comments on this type of public-be-damned design have been quoted above, p. 108.

is an example of the carton style. The entrance is a great arch 200 feet in diameter—the unchallenged giant of station portals. The plaster vault behind is hung from six arched trusses of which the largest weighs 380 tons. This ponderousness characterizes all the detail and led a German writer to observe smugly but correctly that from an architectural standpoint this station was inferior to German ones.[26] The stepped profiles and gross mouldings mirrored the dilemma of the architect who is forced to reject tradition but lacks positive conviction with which to fill the vacuum.[27]

Further evidence of the lack of a major architectural direction in the first postwar period is provided by the existence of still another stylistic current which swept the western and southern parts of the United States. From Texas to California the original ramshackle stations, and in a few cases the second more permanent but inadequate stations, were being replaced by larger and more pretentious ones in a style which sprang from the indigenous Spanish tradition. This group of mission-inspired depots with arcades, balconies, and belfries had counterparts in hotels and mansions. Together they reflected a conspicuous outbreak of regionalism, a mutation of the nationalist virus which had determined the stylistic garb of so many late 19th-century buildings in Europe. Like them they embodied the canons of the picturesque. The culminating station of this group was the one at Los Angeles, 1934–39 (Fig. 223), by Donald and John Parkinson—the last large terminal to be completed in the United States before World War II.[28] It was done in a freer version of the Santa Fe's ubiquitous mission style, with a bow to the modern in the simplicity of its forms. There is an echo of the lavishness of the Meadville, Pennsylvania, depot of the 1860's in its landscaped grounds. A union station, it provided fifteen spur tracks, with their platforms shaded by umbrellas and connected by tunnels to the picturesque forebuilding. Sensible use was made of the change in levels, and various kinds of traffic were kept distinct. The automobile was better provided for than at any previous station, with extensive parking lots which were immediately in front and not cut off by an intervening highway.

The most progressive station yet built on this continent is that of the Canadian National Railways at Montreal (Figs. 224, 225), involving twenty-seven acres. A by-product of an extensive redevelopment begun in 1928, it

26. *Monatshefte für Baukunst und Städtebau, 17* (1933), 472.

27. *Architectural Forum, 58* (1933), 453 ff.; *La Technique des Travaux, 9* (1933), 725–31; and Cincinnati Chamber of Commerce, *The Cincinnati Union Terminal, a Pictorial History,* Cincinnati, 1933. See also Alfred Fellheimer's contribution to *Forms and Functions of Twentieth Century Architecture,* ed. Talbot Hamlin (4 vols. New York, 1952), *4,* 433–74.

28. The most complete publication is to be found in *Railway Age, 106* (1939), 768–78.

was heralded as a combined Rockefeller Center, Grand Central, and multi-level highway system. From the north the tracks emerge from the Mount Royal tunnel, pass under the station, and continue south to the St. Lawrence bridge. The station astride them is surrounded by old and new streets. In 1931 work on the project was temporarily halted, to be resumed in 1938 under John Schofield, who was also the architect of Canadian stations at Hamilton and London. It was pushed to completion in spite of the war and opened in 1943. The plan combines a maximum of directness and a minimum of pyrotechnics. One large room functions as bridge-concourse, waiting room, cross-platform, and vestibule; ticket windows, restaurants, and newsstands surround it, and staircases and escalators connect it with the platforms below. Flanking the long sides of this hall are parking spaces and taxi stands, thus making the horizontal distance to be traveled from one mode of transportation to another very nearly as short as in the stations of a century before. Under the tracks are mail, express, and baggage rooms, communicating by elevators and ramps to the platforms above. This skillful use of levels has made possible a direct, comprehensible station, and the combination of functions in one large hall has brought simplicity back into the large terminal.

Ultimately, the air rights over the whole complex will be developed so that all the platforms and lines will be out of sight and under cover. Since the station will be overshadowed by skyscrapers, the simplicity which characterizes the plan has been extended to the enclosing building. The Montreal station design may be considered a wedding of functional principles and Beaux-Arts practice as seen at Laloux's Gare d'Orsay, with the picturesque aesthetic as a conspicuous bridesmaid. The elevator towers at either end of the hall recall both the traditional station clock tower and the towers of the modern city halls at Dagenham, Greenwich, and Hilversum: there is the same aesthetic of overlapping planes and interpenetrating blocks. Montreal exemplifies the skillful handling of a major terminal on a large scale, just as the Amsterdam stations exemplify the small; but unlike the latter, Montreal does not point toward an architecture of lightness and openness. Structure is not revealed or used as a source of heightened expression. The conception is that of the closed box.[29]

The buildings we have been looking at give on the whole a depressing picture of American architecture between the wars, but there are more hopeful signs among recent stations. To be sure, in this group—which consists largely of small way stations—many between-the-war tendencies continued; at the same time there has been a genuine effort to create fresh and rational solutions. These stations are characterized by thin, widely extended

29. The station is well described in the *Architectural Record, 94* (Dec. 1943), 91–101; and in the *Railway Gazette, 80* (1944), 571–3, 594–8, and *84* (1945), 15–18.

roofs—today's materials permit floating planes of astonishing thinness—reminiscent of a century before when the will to cover the platform by overhanging eaves was accomplished with lunging brackets.

The example of the closed boxes of the Tampere station (Fig. 211) was followed by Holabird and Root in the station at Burlington, Iowa, 1944 (Fig. 226),[30] one of the best recent American stations. It is less imposing but not less successful than the one at Tampere, to which it is obviously indebted.

The new station at Toledo (Fig. 227), opened in September 1950, is an example of a station designed by a staff architect; this means that architectural considerations have been subordinated to engineering and operating needs. It is unwise to entrust a major station to an architect who is controlled by technical associates, for his hands are tied. At Toledo a unique opportunity presented itself: the city is famed for its glass products. But what might have been a triumphant expression of the potentialities of this material sank to the level of a peddler displaying his wares. It was natural to make use of these products—thermopane, glass block, transparent doors, glass-tile walls, and fiberglass insulation. However, glass tile has not yet been successfully bent to monumental or acoustic uses; and the thermopane windows inset in panels of glass block look like afterthoughts. In spite of the glass, the box conception dominates and the desired transparency is more wished for than realized. As with most engineer's architecture, the effect is neat and clean; but it fails to transcend these qualities which are so appropriate for a laboratory.

The planning conception, on the other hand, represented an improvement over the architectural conception. Although the bridge-concourse, potentially a dramatic feature, is overheavy, the approach bridge over Emerald Avenue from the new high-level parking plaza is better. The circulation scheme is a satisfactory, well tried one, presenting no practical difficulties to the traveler. One admirable feature was revived: the waiting room seats are so placed that one can watch the movement of the trains.[31]

Toledo surely is not the last word that American architects will speak on the subject of the modern depot; two imaginative student projects, for example, propose better solutions to the conjoint problems of circulation and expres-

---

30. Holabird and Root also built the station at La Crosse, Wisconsin, 1940. Other architects who designed small stations in a similar spirit include L. P. Kimball and Taylor and Fisher at Akron, Ohio, 1950. Notable examples include several by Raymond Loewy and Lester Tichy, Garfield, Harris, Robinson and Schafer, and Edgar I. Williams, at Ridley Park, Pennsylvania; Aberdeen Proving Ground, Maryland; Prince, West Virginia; and Valley Stream, Long Island respectively. See Fellheimer in *Forms and Functions; Architectural Forum, 78* (1943), 86–8; and *Pencil Points, 26* (1945), 70.

31. There is a brief, appreciative account in *Interiors, 110* (1951), 110–12; and a more detailed description in *Railway Age, 129* (1950), 69–71.

sion. The first, planned for Columbus, Ohio (Fig. 228),[32] using conventional structure, arranges the circulation on three levels: freight at street level under the lines, then a passenger concourse level, and finally the platforms. The building is imposing but not extravagant, expressive of its character and function. The second project, for New Haven (Figs. 229, 230),[33] employs the newest type of wide-span construction: a space frame composed according to tetrahedron principles to cover the concourse. The dynamic effect of this concourse should be compared with the inert one at the Thirtieth Street Station in Philadelphia and the more recent one at Montreal. In all three the great hall lies immediately above the platforms and communicates directly with them. The project handles the *parti* more freshly and gives rise to hope for the future development of the American railway station.

A third station project, designed before the author's death in 1950, has recently been published (Fig. 231). Matthew Nowicki's sketch is for a station to be built in India at Chandigarh. The plan shows a one-sided station in a physical situation not unlike that at Cincinnati. A comparison of the two reveals the enormous difference in attitude toward station architecture which has come about during the last twenty years, reflecting the rapid development of modern architecture from its first to its third phase.

The Caboose

The character of more than twelve decades of architecture has been analyzed by means of a sampling of a particular type of building, the railroad station. There are two reasons for granting validity to this sample. In the first place, stations do not represent only the work of exceptionally able architects: either from indifference on the architects' part or through lack of confidence in them on the part of corporations, many outstanding architects never built a railway station. But because works of genius are infrequent, it does not follow that railway architecture was either mediocre or unimportant. Its value as a sample derives in part precisely from the fact that it reflects a solid core of taste and talent, one that was neither riddled by excessive conservatism nor tinged with the ephemeral fancies of the extremist. Stations are, therefore, representative. The second basis for accepting stations as typical of the building activity of the last century is their connection with one of the

32. Seymour Auerbach, "Transportation Center for Columbus, Ohio," Bachelor of Architecture thesis, Yale University, 1951.

33. Duncan W. Buell, "Railway Station for New Haven, Connecticut," Bachelor of Architecture thesis, Yale University, 1953.

tormenting problems of the period: the resolution of the relationship between architecture and engineering. Railway stations were in fact one of the chief scenes of this drama. The buildings of the 19th century rarely achieved ideal balance because in engineer's architecture (as represented for example by the Crystal Palace) structure predominated, whereas in architect's architecture—as exemplified by the Manchester City Hall—form-feeling predominated.

In the building of stations both were present but they were often separated, and an examination of the stations of this period affords a singularly revealing insight into their interactions. Attempts to combine the efforts of engineer and architect in the same building were rarely successful. To be sure, exceptions were noted in America in the train-barns and in Europe in the stations of the Stadtbahn and their progeny. In the great majority of cases the architect went his own way, paying little heed to the stunning accomplishments of the engineer and preferring to be creative on his own more limited terms. He was offended by the dematerialized effects of his rival's glass cages and clung instead to lithic modes of expression. The latent rationalism of the period, implicit in Pugin and effectively preached by Viollet-le-Duc, had more immediate meaning for the engineer; but not until the 20th century was in its second quarter did the message reach the architectural profession as a whole, and even then it was laggard, accepting a rationalism of form and function before it was ready to acknowledge the broader concept which included structure. The integration of all three factors showed itself in stations for the first time at Amsterdam just before the outbreak of World War II and recurred more brilliantly a decade later in the new station at Rome. This masterpiece demonstrates the harmonious fusion of form and structure at a level which recalls the accomplishments of Greek and medieval architects.

Recent observers have too often failed to realize that it was not structure alone which gave distinction to Gothic architecture or to the architecture of any other great building period; rather, it was the fusion between structural system and pervasive form-feeling. As John Ely Burchard recently pointed out, "Architecture has almost never applied to the hilt what was currently available in technology. . . . Roman architecture is more than an architecture of arches and domes; Gothic more than an architecture of buttresses and vaults; the architecture of the past hundred years is more than an architecture of structural steel and glass." [34]

The "more" to which Dean Burchard refers was embodied in two aesthetic systems during the past century, invented to fulfill the longings which occupied man's spirit. The earlier one—the cult of the picturesque—arose at a

34. "Architecture in the Atomic Age," *Architectural Record, 116* (Dec. 1954), 119, 126.

time when, as Goethe reveals, young spirits were wearying of exclusively intellectual philosophies.[35] In search of another standard, inquiring minds turned back to nature. The new concept, natural man, emphasized human emotions more than pure reason; nature ceased to be regarded as orderly and was viewed romantically as wild and uncontrolled.[36] The sublime and the picturesque were substituted for traditional concepts of beauty. Sources of delight discovered in the landscape were isolated and held up as the goals of artistic creation. The new aesthetic—picturesque eclecticism—accordingly regarded architecture primarily as a visual art, like painting, meaningless to the blind. The rules of this style demanded the rejection of classical principles and the achievement of striking effects to be obtained through variety, movement, irregularity, intricacy, and roughness. The emphasis on the relative importance of these qualities in addition to horizontality and verticality resulted in three principal phases. In its long life, the picturesque devoured not only Gothic and Renaissance detail but with equal voracity the soberer Italian villa, Second Empire, and baroque styles as the means to creating the new style. The borrowed eclectic adjuncts were given new vitality by juxtaposition. Unprecedented combinations created new content. The second aesthetic movement began like the first with blocky cubistic forms; and today, in the third phase, the solid blocks have yielded to powerful inner pressures which are opening them up and revealing their dynamic structural cores.

It would be an oversimplification to assume that because picturesque eclecticism was anticlassical, the succeeding style will be classical. The sequence through the course of time is not oscillating but spiral. It is not yet time to give a final name to our own aesthetic. To call it "atomic" is merely glib, as that word does not have aesthetic meaning. "Social" is another term which lacks specific applicability. Julian Huxley's "evolutionary humanism" is too new a label to have found an artistic referent. "Organic" is not only overworked but, like "firmness," "commodity," and "delight," is not discriminative; these terms apply to all styles. The handiest label now in circulation is Giedion's "space-time." [37] Not only is it derived from the science and art of our day, but it has been given currency through his widely studied books. In architecture it identifies two of the main characteristics of the modern style: simultaneity of effects made possible by transparency of the defining shell, and the relativity of three-dimensional composition which to be apprehended must be seen from a multiplicity of vantage points.

What observations of general application relative to the future of architec-

35. Johann Wolfgang von Goethe, *Poetry and Truth*, Bk. XI.

36. In the 20th century nature is alleged to follow scientific law.

37. Giedion, *Space, Time and Architecture*.

ture can be derived from the examination of railroad stations? There are signs of development in two directions: primeval and monumental.

The primeval type is a station reduced to its starkest fundamentals, as if to illustrate the words of Henri Pacon, the architect of the city station at Le Havre, to the effect that in its simplest form a station comprised three elements: vestibule, barrier, and platform-track area.[38] Economic conditions encourage the building of extremely basic stations. Such a station has recently been erected near Boston, called "Route 128." It occupies cheap land which is easily accessible to a large suburban population. The platforms are at grade level and the enormous parking lot can be expanded almost indefinitely at small expense. Advantages of this station include convenience for persons using automobiles, small investment, and low operating costs. But these results are not accomplished without sacrifice. Tunnels or footbridges for crossing safely from the platform to the parking lot are lacking. There is no shelter on the platforms and a minimum in the shack which serves as a waiting room. There are few conveniences, no amenities. These primitive station arrangements are exactly the kind that were given up a century ago; barely feasible under the conditions which prevail at Route 128, such stations are impossible in urban situations.

Does this one station imply a major architectural trend? Probably instead it is a current manifestation of an age-old situation: the coexistence of several levels of architecture, of which only the upper one or two are significant because of their scope and quality. Route 128 is purely mechanical expedient, not to be confused with puritanism or with the simplicity which results from sophistication. The quality of simplicity requires constant striving for, and is an attribute of, greatness. In stations it is achieved not by eliminating essential elements but by reorganizing them. The primeval type is not the only possible alternative to the type of monumentality in which efficiency was deliberately sacrificed. The simple, but not primeval, station of the future will accomplish the following objectives with distinction: short clear routes for arriving and departing passengers, mechanical transportation of hand luggage, waiting areas adjacent to the platforms, frequent exits from the platforms to local transportation, and an atmosphere of dignity and quiet.

The second major direction, monumentality, is also promising. During the last century the psychological value of monumental buildings in the urban landscape was taken as a matter of course; critics like Ruskin often excluded from the category of monumentality buildings which we have come to recognize as possessing it, but they never denied its validity. Sometimes this quality was justified in railway buildings on the grounds that railroad travel was a fearful experience requiring that the timid traveler be reassured by the

38. "Gares," *L'Architecture d'aujourd'hui,* 7 (Aug. 1936), 5.

sturdy grandeur of the stations; later, private companies lavished their resources on imperial display. But railroad corporations can no longer afford such magnificent gestures, nor would their public relations departments approve. Luxurious lounges like the one the Burlington Railroad built at Burlington, Iowa, a few years ago are now considered just as irrelevant to the character of a station as Corinthian columns. But there were and are other considerations. The stations projected for Gothenberg and Oslo and the one built at Rome perform functions which transcend utility: the expression of the dignity of government and of their role as a formal entrance to the city. It is entirely possible that the Oslo and Rome stations are initiating a contemporary monumental style.

The program of modern architecture did not at first recognize that emotional and symbolic functions have a validity equal to that of utility, and it will not be entirely mature until it succeeds in harmonizing the functional and the expressive components. Even the headquarters of the United Nations in New York City lacks this harmony. Some recent attempts at expression have turned out to be dead ends: the "new empiricism" and the "new cosiness" are not blazing new trails so much as meandering down familiar byways. But the struggle will go on. We may expect to see future stations increasingly invested with symbolic character, with their designers heeding Miës van der Rohe's warning to the effect that "the mechanistic principle of order overemphasizes the materialistic and functional factors in life, since it fails to satisfy our feeling that means must be subsidiary to ends and our desire for dignity and value." [39]

What about stations surviving from earlier periods? Have they any value judged by modern standards?

No age can be wholly isolated from its past no matter how valiantly the break is attempted. The decades just ended were conditioned to impermanence and to pragmatism in its narrower sense. The extreme left hysterically attacked tradition and privilege, and the preservation of the artifacts of the past ceased to enlist popular support. Only natural wonders received protection. The atmosphere is calmer now and a wiser view can be entertained. As time passes the indubitable merits of picturesque eclectic buildings will receive wider recognition and the ruthless destruction of them can be halted. Their legacy of inspiration for our own buildings will be safeguarded so that it may be readily available in many places for those who will certainly seek it out. In the days to come calculated use will be made of such 19th-century experiments and false starts as the room-street, and both train-sheds and shopping arcades may be studied as the starting points for new developments.

39. Philip Johnson, *Miës van der Rohe* (New York, 1947), p. 194.

Another consideration demands acknowledgment: picturesque eclecticism was primarily a creation of the English-speaking world. It has been demonstrated that its philosophy and works must be credited largely to Britain and her colonies and to the United States. Although the latter nation was long the debtor, she came to full participation in the movement with its world-wide impact. Americans, therefore, have a particular obligation to safeguard the disappearing manifestations, which offer two lessons much needed today.

The first lesson is that of unhesitating experimentation. The architects and engineers of the last century were bolder in this respect than our own, both technically and stylistically, as their bridges, tunnels, train-sheds, and skyscrapers bear witness. Picturesque eclecticism, with its capacity to mold all the forms and shapes of the past to its own ends, affords more evidence. Adventurous as many of our contemporaries seem to us, they do not exceed in depth and range the creativity of the 19th century, or its uninhibited audacity as has been demonstrated in the preceding pages. The manifestations include the somewhat obviously striking silhouettes, flamboyant constructive coloration, exaggeratedly well-like or tunnel-like spaces and the rugged heaped-up masses of Richardsonian Romanesque. One reason that these achievements do not meet with general admiration today is that our society unfortunately places a higher premium on conformity than on individuality.

The second lesson comes from the Burnham Baroque and Art Nouveau period, where the opposite point of view achieved memorable results. At that time some architects disciplined their ingenuity and strove for delicacy and refinement in an earnest, selfless manner. A few architects today are aiming at the same standards, but once again the general level of performance does not rise so high. The attitude prevails that such striving is rarely worth while.

Both lessons so deeply embodied in railroad stations deserve serious consideration in the mid-20th century. The quality of the architecture mirrors the integrity of the architect.

166

THE ILLUSTRATIONS

1. Liverpool, Crown Street Station. John Foster II, architect (?), and
George Stephenson, engineer, 1830. (See also Fig. 7.)

2. Baltimore, Mount Clare Station, 1830.

3. Bewdley, Worcestershire, tollhouse, 1801.

4. Cumberland National Highway, tollhouse with shed.

5. Lowell, Mass., Boston and Lowell Railroad "Car House," 1835. Drawing.

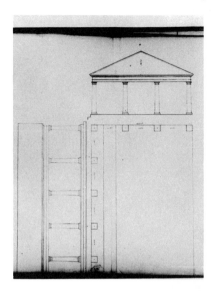

6. Lowell, Mass., Boston and Lowell Railroad "Car House," 1835. (below) General view. (See also Fig. 5.)

7. Liverpool, Crown Street Station. Conjectural plan, one-sided combination type. (See also Fig. 1.)

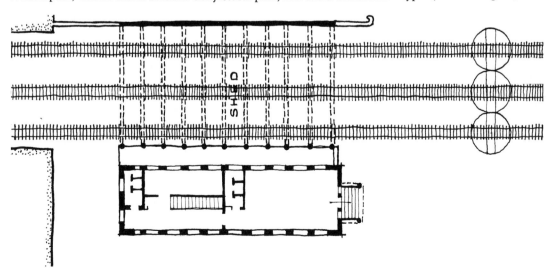

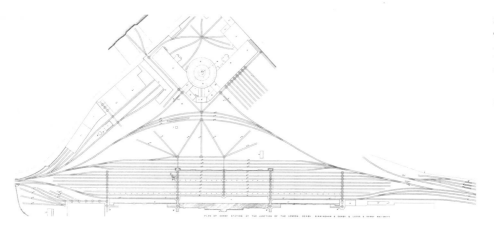

8. Derby, Derbyshire,
Trijunct Station. By
Francis Thompson, architect
and Robert Stephenson, engineer,
1839-41. Plan, one-sided
combination type.
(See also Figs. 16, 19, 40.)

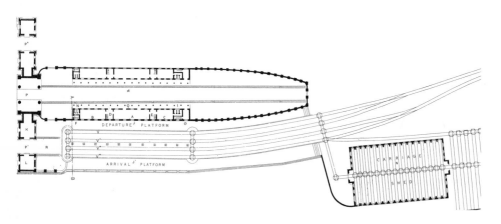

9. London, Euston Station.
Philip Hardwick, architect,
Robert Stephenson, engineer,
1835-39. A typical
early two-sided plan.
(See also Figs. 15, 17, 41.)

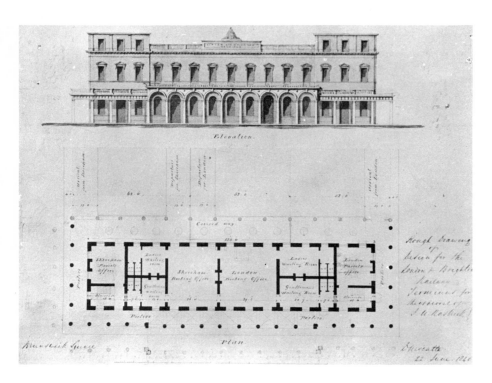

10. Brighton, Sussex,
early head-type station.
By David Mocatta, 1840-41.

11. York, The Railway Station. By G. T. Andrews, 1840-41. Plan.

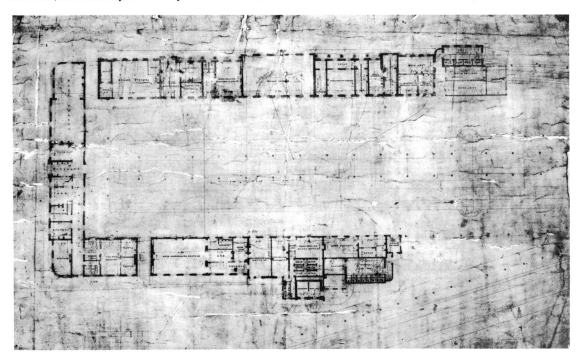

12. Kassel, Germany, train-shed, 1840's.

13. London, Nine Elms Station. By Sir William Tite, 1837-38. Detail of shed. (See also Fig. 20.)

14. Bristol, Great Western Station (Temple Mead I). By I. K. Brunel, 1839-40. Interior of train-shed.

15. London, Euston Station. Interior of train-shed. (See also Figs. 9, 17, 41.)

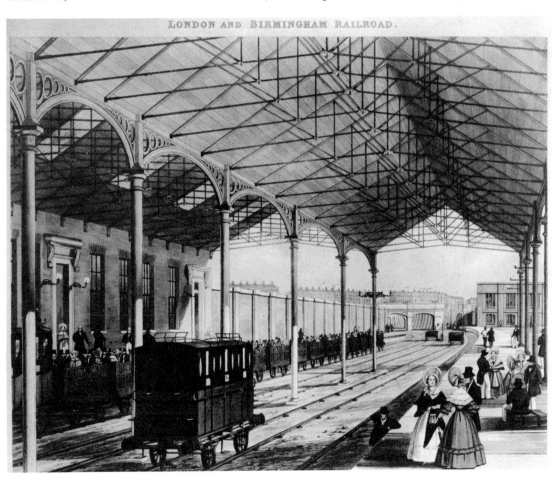

16. Derby, Derbyshire, Trijunct Station. Interior of train-shed. (See also Figs. 8, 19, 40.)

17. London, Euston Station. Façade. (See also Figs. 9, 15, 41.)

18. Belper, Derbyshire, station. By Francis Thompson, 1840's.

19. Derby, Derbyshire, Trijunct Station. Exterior. (See also Figs. 8, 16, 40.)

20. London, Nine Elms Station. General view. (See also Fig. 13.)

21. London, London Bridge Station. By Thomas Turner and Henry Roberts, 1844.

22. Leipzig, First Thüringer Bahnhof. By Eduard Pötsch, 1840-44.

23. Edward Lampson Henry, "The 9:45 A.M. Accommodation, Stratford, Connecticut," 1867.

24. Frederick, Md.,
Baltimore and Ohio
Station, 1831.

25. Syracuse, N.Y.,
Syracuse and Utica
Railroad Station.
Daniel Elliot, architect
and builder, 1838.

26. Exeter St. Thomas, Derbyshire, Great Western Station, 1846.

27. Schenectady, N.Y., "First Railroad Depot," Mohawk and Hudson Railroad, 1838 (?).

28. Hanover, Conn., New Haven Depot.

29. Boston, Mass., Boston and Lowell Station, 1835. Possibly by Richard Upjohn.

30. Boston, Mass., Haymarket Station. By George M. Dexter, 1844-45.

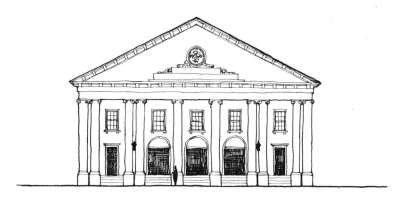

31. Boston, Mass., Kneeland Street Station. By Gridley J. F. Bryant, 1847.

32. New York, Hudson River Railroad Depot, Tenth Ave. and 30th St., 1860-61.

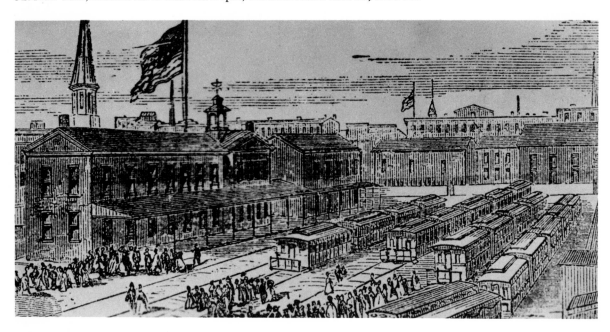

33. New Orleans, La., Illinois Central Station. Louis Sullivan and Frank Lloyd Wright, architects, and J. F. Wallace, engineer, 1892. General view. (See also Fig. 105.)

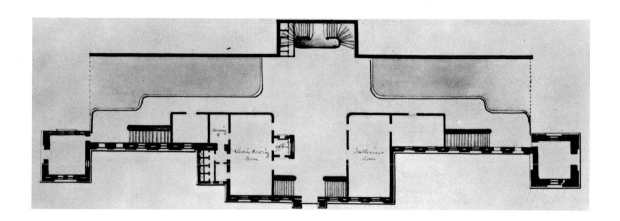

34, 35, 36. New Haven, Conn.
Union Station. By Henry Austin, 1848-49.
34 (above) Plan.
35. (at right) Sections.
36. (below) Perspective.

37. Norton, Mass., Depot.
By Richard Upjohn, 1852-5
Original drawing.

38. New Bedford, Mass.
Old Pearl Street Depot,
built before 1840.

39. Salem, Mass.,
Boston and Maine Depot.
By Gridley J. F. Bryant, 18

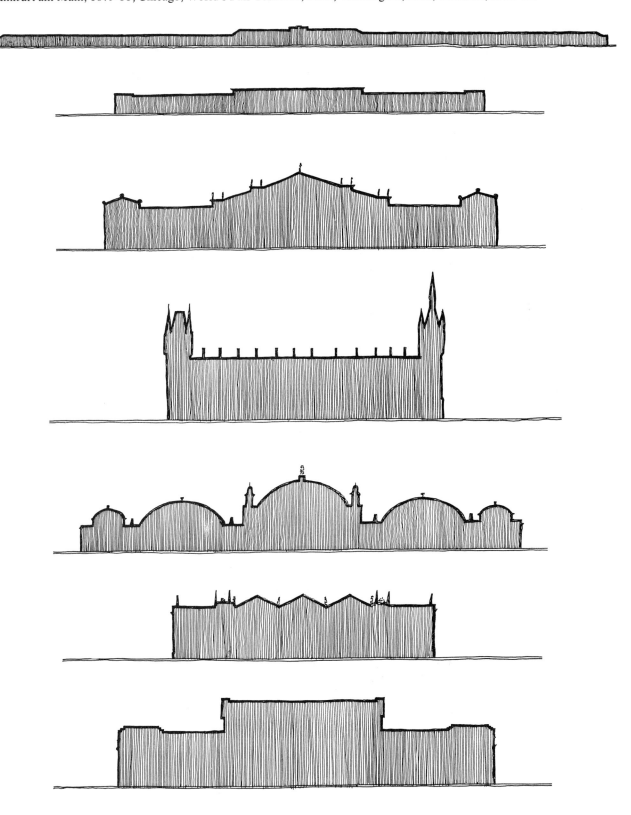

9. Silhouettes of a sequence of large railroad stations. Derby, Trijunct Station, 1839-41;
Newcastle Central Station, 1846-55; Paris, Gare de Nord II, 1861-65; London, St. Pancras Station, 1863-76;
Frankfurt am Main, 1879-88; Chicago, World's Fair Terminal, 1893; Washington, D.C., Terminal, 1903-07.

41. London, Euston Station, "Grand Hall." By Philip C. Hardwick, 1846-49. (See also Figs. 9, 15, 17.)

42. Liverpool, First Lime Street Station. By John Foster II, 1836.

43, 44. Newcastle, Northumberland, Central Station. By John Dobson and Thomas Prosser, 1846-55.
43. (below) Exterior sketch.   44. (bottom) Interior of train-shed.

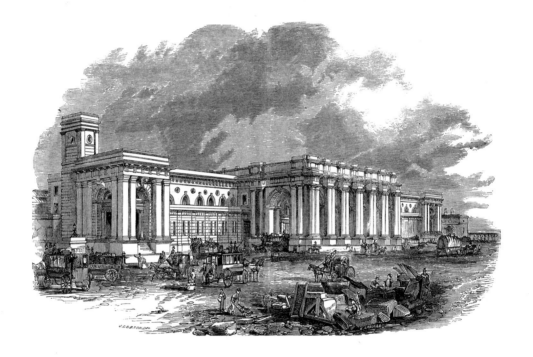

45. London, King's Cross Station. By Lewis Cubitt, 1851-52. Plan. (See also Figs. 52, 57.)

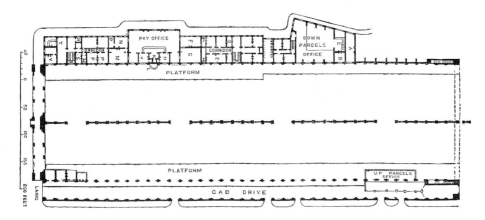

46. London, Paddington Station II. By I. K. Brunel and M. D. Wyatt, 1852-54. Plan. (See also Fig. 56.)

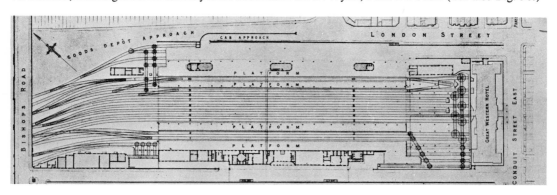

47. Paris, First Gare du Nord. By Léonce Reynaud, 1845-47. Plan.

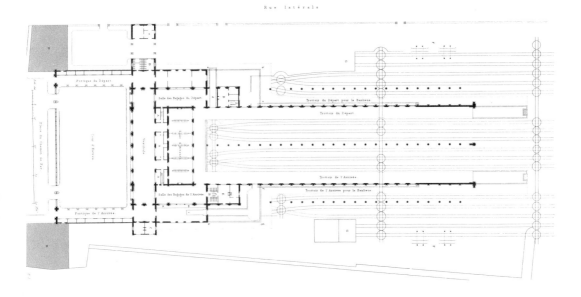

48. Paris, Gare de l'Est.
By François Duquesney, 1847-52. Plan. (See also Figs. 50, 51.)

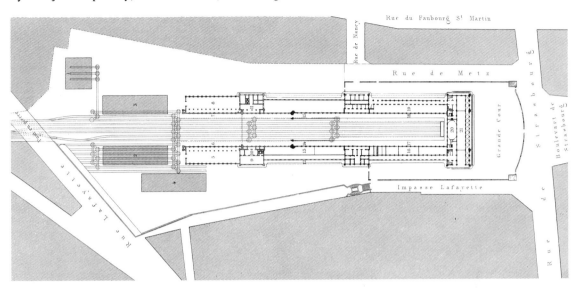

49. Paris, Second Gare du Nord.
J. I. Hittorf, architect, and Léonce Reynaud, engineer, 1861-65. Plan. (See also Figs. 40, 55, 61.)

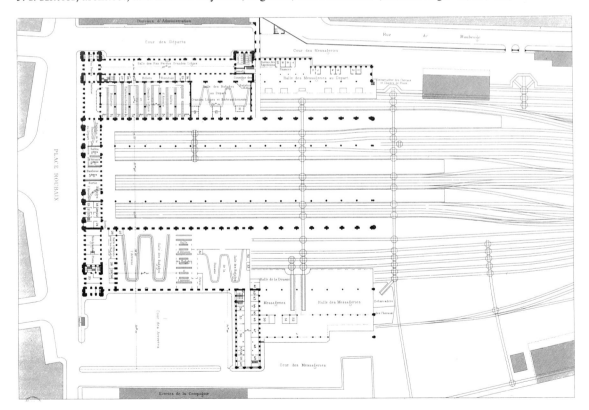

50. Paris, Gare de l'Est. Exterior. (See also Figs. 48, 51.)

51. Paris, Gare de l'Est. Section of train-shed, tied arch. (See also Figs. 48, 50.)

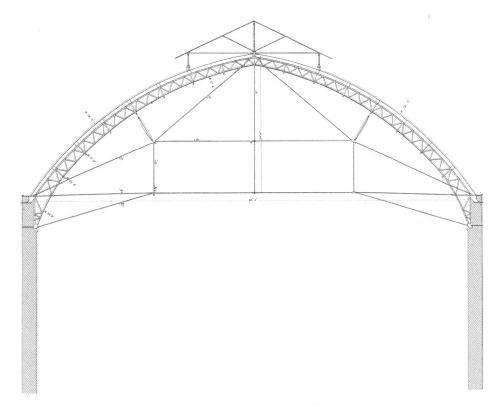

52. London, King's Cross Station. Interior of shed. (See also Figs. 45, 57.)

53. Munich, Hauptbahnhof. By Friedrich Bürklein, 1847-49. Interior of train-shed. (See also Fig. 58.)

54. Birmingham, Warwickshire, New Street Station. E. A. Cowper, engineer, 1854. Truss.

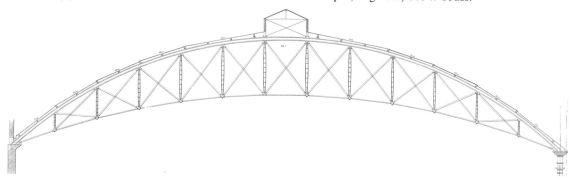

55. Paris, Second Gare du Nord. Half section of shed. (See also Figs. 40, 49, 61.)

56. London, Paddington Station II. Interior of train-sheds. (See also Fig. 46.)

57. London, King's Cross Station. Exterior. (See also Figs. 45, 52.)

58. Munich,
Hauptbahnhof.
Exterior.
(See also Fig. 53.)

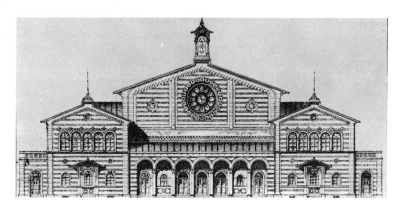

59, 60. Paris, Gare Montparnasse. Victor Lenoir, architect, and Eugène
Flachat, engineer, 1850-52.   59. (above) Section, showing original sheds.   60. (below) Elevation.

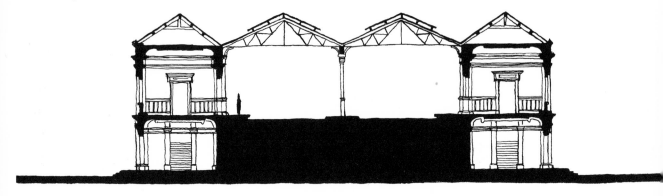

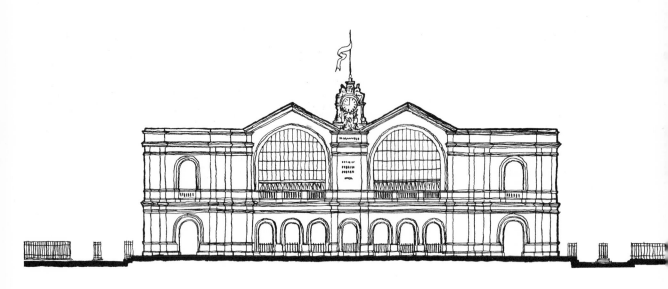

1. Paris, Second Gare du Nord. Exterior. (See also Figs. 40, 49, 55.)

62. Zurich, Hauptbahnhof. By J. F. Waner, 1865-73.

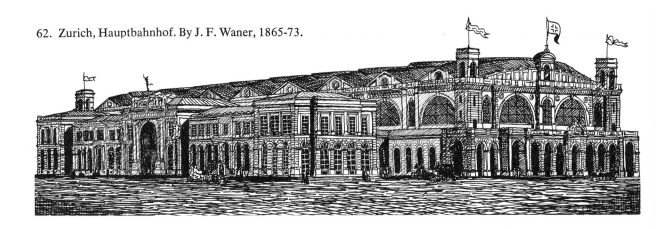

63. Chester, Cheshire, General Station. Francis Thompson, architect, and Robert Stephenson, engineer, 1847-48. Exterio

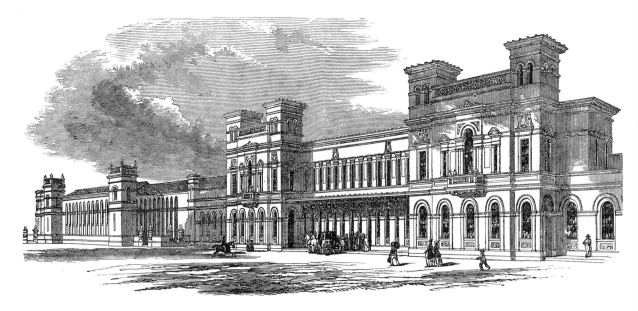

64. London,
Great Western Hotel,
at Paddington Station.
By Philip C. Hardwick,
1851-53.

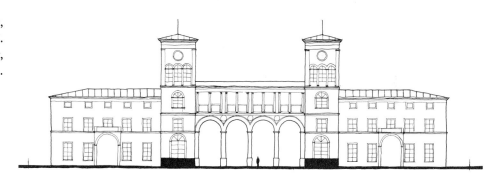

65. Leipzig,
Second Thüringer Bahnhof.
E. Brandt, engineer,
1855-56. Sketch.

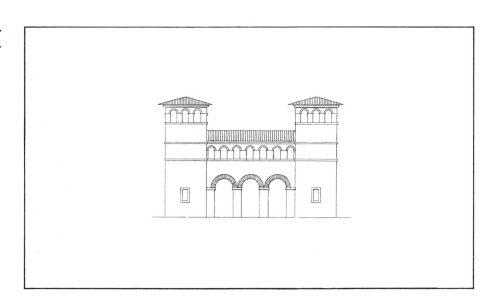

66. Design.
J. N. L. Durand, 1802.

67. Anonym
design for a
passenger sta
tion of the lat
1850's at St-
Germain-en-

68. Providen
R.I., Union S
tion. By Tho
Tefft, 1848.
Exterior.

69. Troy, N.
Union Railr
Depot, 1857.

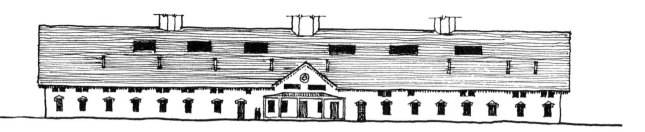

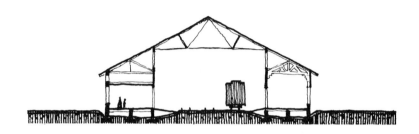

70, 71, 72. Meadville, Pa.,
Atlantic and Great
Western Depot, 1862.
70 and 71. (above)
Exterior and Section.
72. (at right)
Interior of dining hall.

73. Baltimore, Camden Station. By J. R. Niernsee and J. C. Nielson, 1852-56. Original design.

74. Harrisburg, Pa., Union Station, 1850's.

75. Chicago, Great Central Station. By Otto Matz, 1855-56. Rear.

76. New York, Harlem and New Haven Joint Station, 1857.

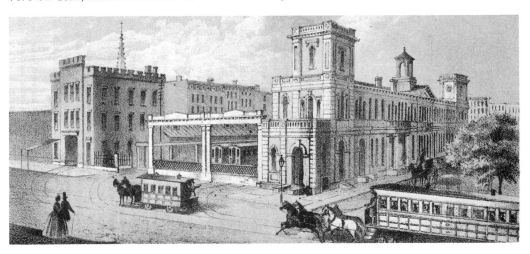

77. Cincinnati, Ohio, passenger station, 1854.

78. Columbus, Ohio, Union Depot, 1862.

79. Ithiel Town, architect, lattice truss, patented in 1826.

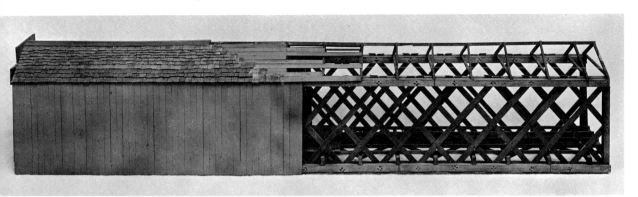

80. Philadelphia, Pa., Philadelphia, Wilmington, and Baltimore Depot, 1851-52. Interior of train-shed.

81. Henry Holly, "Design No. 34," 1861.

82. Taunton, Mass.,
Old Colony Station.
By Henry Holly (?),
1865. Exterior.

83. Berlin,
Stettiner Bahnhof.
By Theodore Stein,
1876. General view.

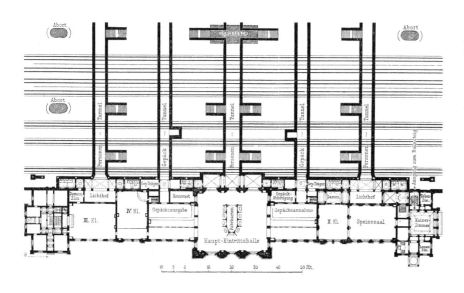

84. Hanover,
Hauptbahnhof.
By Hubert Stier,
1876-79. Plan.
(See also
fig. 149g.)

85. Stuttgart, Neuer Bahnhof. By Georg Morlok, 1863-68. An example of a "T" plan.

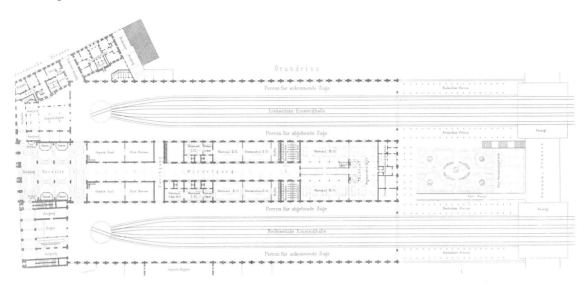

86. Berlin, Alexanderplatz Bahnhof. By J. E. Jacobstahl, 1880-85. Stadtbahn station, section.

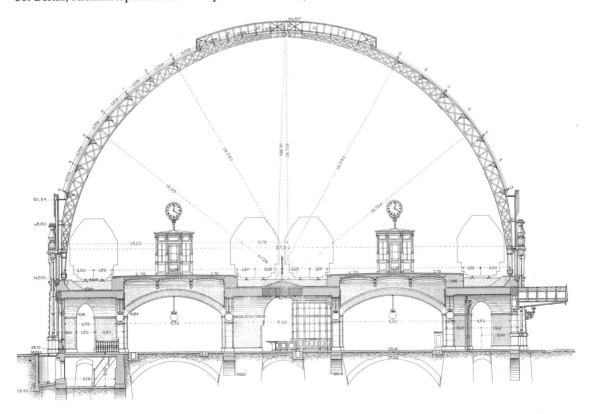

87. Berlin, Schlesischer Bahnhof.
Römer, architect, and L. Schwartzkopf, engineer, 1867-69. Section showing crescent-type truss.

88. Vienna. Nord-West Bahnhof.
By W. Bäumer, 1870-72. Section through train-shed showing modified Warren truss.

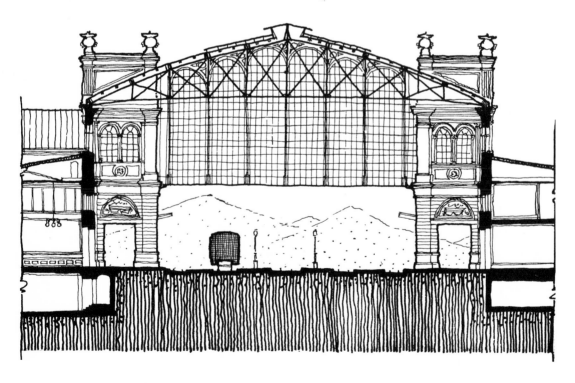

89. London, Liverpool Street Station. By Edward Wilson, 1874-75. Interior of train-shed.

90. Budapest, West Bahnhof, 1873-77. Section showing train-shed by Eiffel and Co.

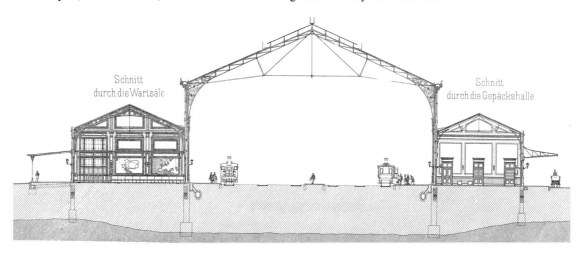

91. London, Victoria Station. Robert J. Hood, engineer, 1859-66. Sections through train-shed, tied arch.

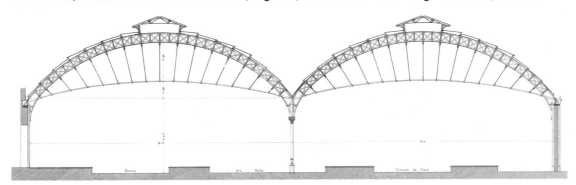

92. London, St. Pancras Station. By Sir George Gilbert Scott, architect,
W. H. Barlow, and R. M. Ordish, engineers, 1863-76. Interior of shed. (See also Figs. 40, 109, 110.)

93. London, Charing Cross Station. John Hawkshaw, engineer, 1862-64. Interior of train-shed.

94. Glasgow, Queen Street Station, 1875. Section through train-shed roof truss.

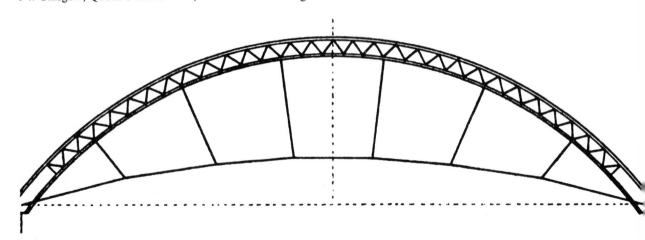

95. York, station. By Thomas Prosser, Benjamin Burley, and William Peachy, 1871-77. Interior of train-sheds.

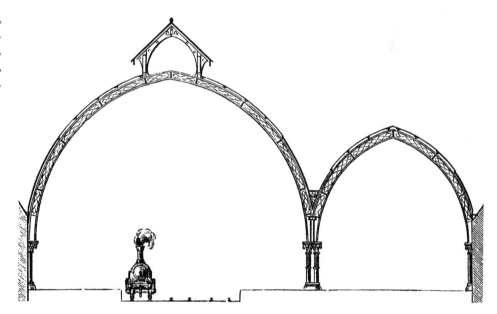

96. Middlesbrough, Yorkshire, station. William Peachy, architect, and Cudworth, engineer, 1875-77. Section.

97. Liverpool, Central Station. John Fowler, engineer, 1874. Exterior.

98. New York, First Grand Central Station.
By Isaac C. Buckhout and J. B. Snook, 1869-71. Interior of train-shed. (See also Figs. 119, 120, 121.)

99. Louisville, Ky., Union Depot. By H. Wolters, 1882-91. Section of train-shed, bent girder.

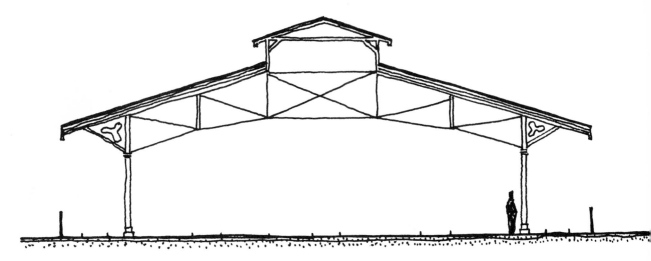

100. Boston, Mass., Park Square Station.
By Peabody and Stearns, 1872-74. Interior of train-shed. (See also Figs. 122, 123.)

101. Jersey City,
Central Railroad of New Jersey Station, typical maritime station plan. By Peabody and Stearns, 1887-88.

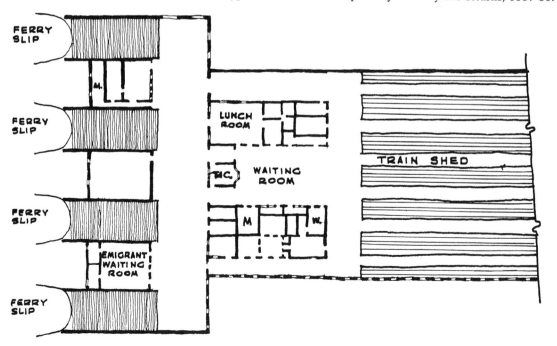

102. Jersey City, Pennsylvania Station. C. C. Schneider, engineer, 1888. Section through train-shed.

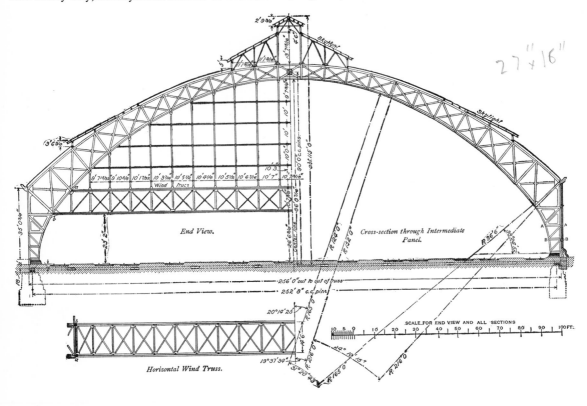

103. Philadelphia, Reading Station.
F. H. Kimball, architect, and Wilson Bros. and Co., engineers and architects, 1891-93.
View of rear of train-shed. (See also Fig. 128.)

104. Philadelphia, Broad Street Station. Wilson Bros. and Co., engineers and architects, 1892-93. Section through train-shed. (See also Figs. 126, 127.)

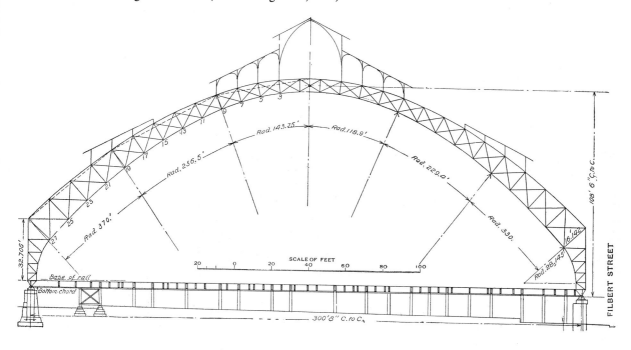

105. New Orleans, Illinois Central Station. Section through train-shed. (See also Fig. 33.)

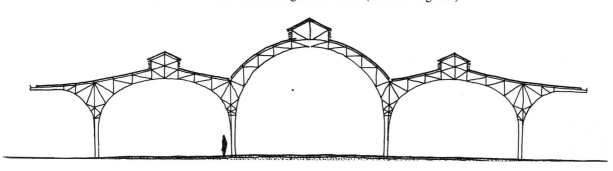

106. Chicago, Illinois Central Station. Bradford L. Gilbert, architect, and J. F. Wallace, engineer, 1892-93. Section through train-shed.

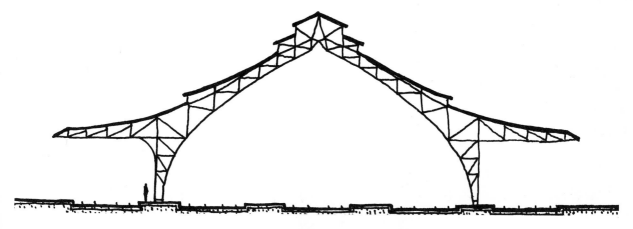

107. London, Cannon Street Station. By E. M. Barry, 1863-66. Exterior view.

108. Liverpool, Third Lime St. Station, Northwestern Hotel (at left). By Alfred Waterhouse, 1869. Exterior.

109, 110. London, St.
Pancras Station.
109. Section showing
profile of shed.

110. Plan.
(See also Figs. 40, 92.)

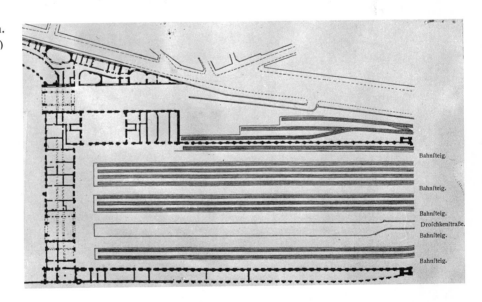

111. Emden, Germany,
station, 1856-63.
Exterior elevation.

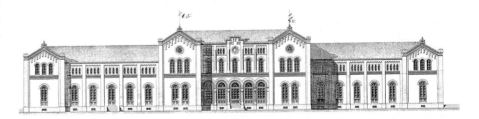

112, 113. Berlin, Anhalter Bahnhof. Franz Schwechten, architect, and Wiedenfeld, engineer, 1872-80.
112. (top) General view. 113. (bottom) Interior of train-shed.

114. Turin,
Stazione di Porta Nuova.
Carlo Ceppi, architect,
and A. Mazzucchetti,
engineer, 1866-68.
Exterior.

115. Genoa,
Stazione Piazza Principe.
Exterior.

116. Rome,
First Stazione Termini.
By Salvatore Bianchi,
1874. Exterior.

117. Naples, Stazione Centrale. By Nicolo Breglia, *ca.* 1880. Exterior view.

118. Budapest, Ost Bahnhof. By Julius Rochlitz, 1881. Exterior.

119, 120, 121. New York,
First Grand Central Station.
119. View from 42nd. St.

120. Plan.

121. Rear view.
(See also Fig. 98.)

122, 123. Boston, Mass., Park Square Station.
122. (top) Exterior.   123. (bottom) Plan adapted for use as a public library by Henry Van Brunt.
(See also Fig. 100.)

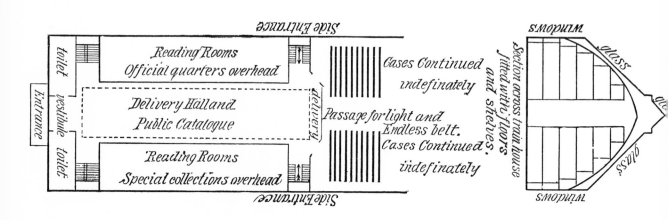

124. Worcester, Mass., Union Passenger Station.
By Ware and Van Brunt, 1875-77. General view.

125. Washington, D.C., Baltimore and Potomac Railroad Depot.
By Joseph M. Wilson, 1873-77. Exterior.

126, 127. Philadelphia, Broad Street Station.   126. (top) Exterior. 127. (bottom) Interior of lobby.
(See also Fig. 104a.)

128. Philadelphia,
Reading Station.
Exterior.
(See also Fig. 103.)

129. Chicago,
Dearborn Station
("Polk St. Station").
By C. L. W. Eidlitz,
1883-85.

130. Chicago,
Grand Central Station.
By Spencer Solon Beman,
1888-90. General view.

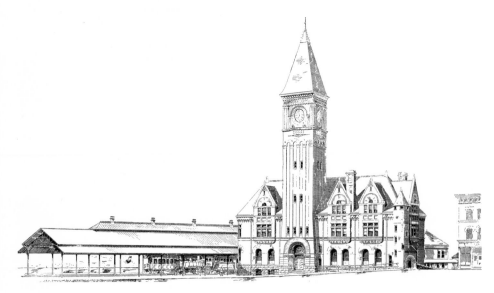

131. Milwaukee,
Chicago and North
Western Station.
By Charles S. Frost,
1889. Exterior.

132. Chicago,
Chicago and North
Western Station.
By W. W. Boyington,
1880's. Exterior.

133. Detroit,
Michigan Central Station.
By C. L. W. Eidlitz,
1882-83. General view.

134. Detroit,
Union Depot.
By Isaac S. Taylor,
1889. Exterior.

135. Indianapolis, Union Station.
By Thomas Rodd, 1886-89. General view.

136. North Easton, Mass., Station.
By H. H. Richardson, 1886. General view.

137. New London, Conn., Union Railroad Station. By H. H. Richardson, 1885-87. Exterior.

138, 139. St. Louis, Union Station. Theodore C. Link and Edward D. Cameron, architects, and George H. Pegram, engineer, 1891-94.   138. (top) Exterior.   139. (bottom) Grand Hall. (See also Fig. 158.)

140, 141. Chicago, Illinois Central Station, 1892-93.   140. (at left) Exterior.   141. (at right) Interior of "Rotunda."

142. New York, Second Grand Central Station.

By Reed and Stem, and Warren and Wetmore, 1903-13. Sectional view. (See also Figs. 169, 170.)

(1) Hotel Commodore; (2) Biltmore Hotel; (3) Hotel Roosevelt; (4) New York Central Bldg.; (5) Graybar Bldg.;
(6) Grand Central Terminal Office Bldg.; (A) Cab baggage service; (B) Travel information bureau; (C) Newsreel theatre;
(D) Lower level; (E) Stairways from Vanderbilt Avenue to upper and lower levels; (F) Ticket offices;
(G) Grand Central Art Galleries; (H) Office space; (J) Main waiting room; (K) Restaurants; (L) 42nd street entrance;
(M) Parcel rooms, shops, and stores.

143. Paris,
Gare d'Orsay.
Victor Laloux,
1897-1900. Interior.

144. Tours,
Gare.
Victor Laloux,
1895-98. Exterior.

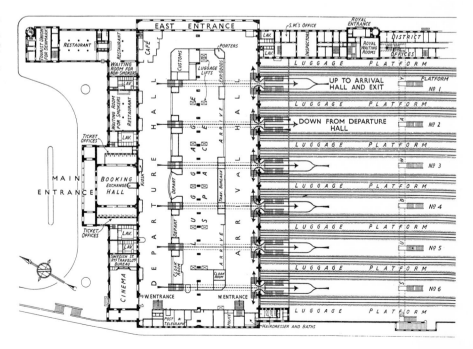

145. Copenhagen,
Central Station.
Plan after alterations of
1906-11 by H. E. C. Wenck.

146, 147, 148. Frankfurt am Main, Hauptbahnhof.
By Georg P. H. Eggert and Faust, 1879-88.
146. (above) Air view.   147. (at left) Plan.
148. (facing page) Interior of sheds.

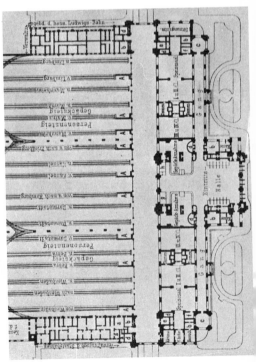

149. Sections of train-sheds.

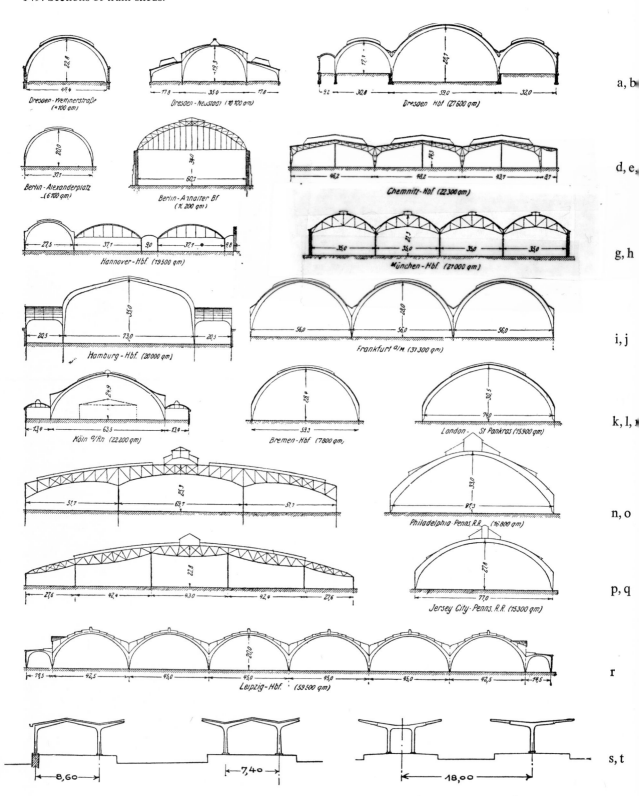

a, b

d, e,

g, h

i, j

k, l,

n, o

p, q

r

s, t

150. Bucharest, Bahnhof.
By Georg Frentzen,
1893-95. Exterior.

151, 152. Dresden,
Hauptbahnhof.
By C. F. Müller, 1892-98.
151. View of
interior of shed.

152. Exterior.

153, 154. Hamburg, Hauptbahnhof. By Heinrich Reinhardt and Georg Sössenguth, 1903-06.
153. (above) Exterior.   154. (below) Plan.

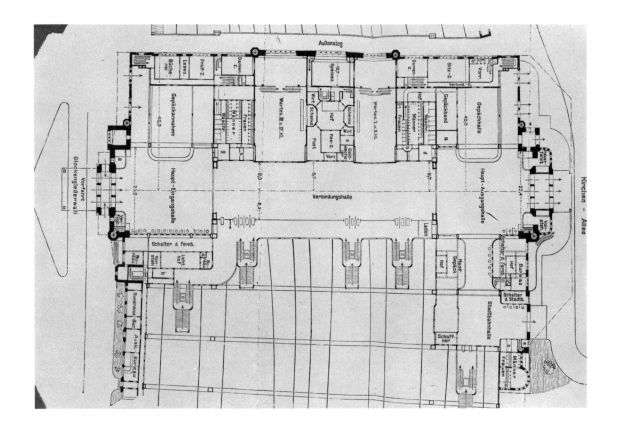

155, 156, 157. Leipzig,
Hauptbahnhof.
William Lossow and
Max Hans Kühne, architects,
and Louis Eilers, engineer,
1907-15.
155. General view.

156. Plan at track level.

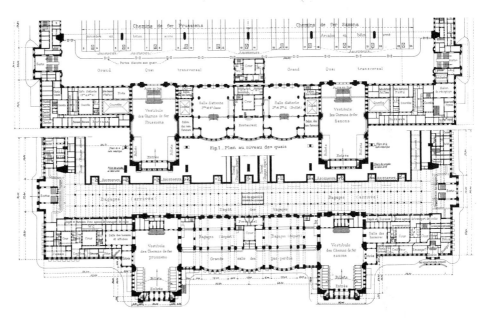

157. View of cross-platform.

158. St. Louis, Union Station. Train-shed. (See also Figs. 138, 139.)

159. Pittsburgh, Pennsylvania Station. By D. H. Burnham, 1898-1901. General view.

160. Hoboken, N.J., Delaware, Lackawanna, and Western Railroad Station.
Kenneth M. Murchison, architect, and Lincoln Bush, engineer, 1904-05. View of train-shed.

161, 162, 163.
Washington, D.C.,
Union Station,
1903-07.
161. Train concourse.

162. Concourse.

163. General view.

164, 165, 166. New York, Pennsylvania Station. By McKim, Meade, and White, 1906-10.
164. (top) Concourse.   165. (bottom left) General waiting room.   166. (bottom right) Plan. (See also Fig. 173.)

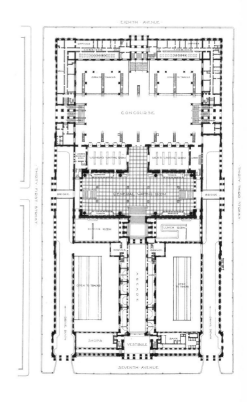

167. Boston, Mass., South Station. By Shepley, Rutan, and Coolidge, 1896-99. General view.

168. Chicago, World's Fair Terminal (left). By Charles B. Atwood, 1893. General view. (See also Fig. 40.)

169, 170. New York, Second Grand Central Station, 1903-13.
169. (above) Exterior.   170. (at left) Concourse.
(See also Fig. 142.)

171. St. Louis,
Exhibition of 1904,
Transportation Building.
By E. L. Masqueray.
General view.

172. Detroit,
Michigan Central Station.
By Reed and Stem,
and Warren and Wetmore,
completed 1913.
General view.

173. New York, Pennsylvania Station.
Exterior. (See also Figs. 164, 165, 166.)

174. Chicago, Union Station.
By D. H. Burnham and Co., 1916-25. General view.

175. Toronto, Union Station.
By Ross and MacDonald, Hugh G. Jones, and John M. Lyle, 1914-27. General view.

176. Philadelphia, Thirtieth Street Station.
By Graham, Anderson, Probst, and White, 1927-34. General view. (See also Figs. 177, 178.)

177, 178. Philadelphia,
Thirtieth Street Station.
177. Concourse.

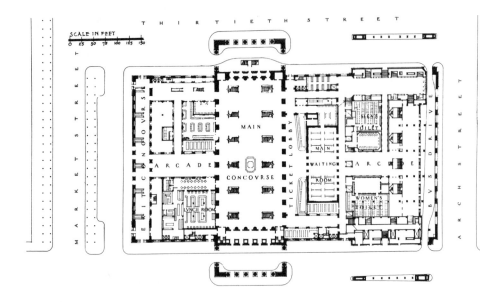

178. Plan.

179. Baltimore, Mount Royal Station.
By Francis Baldwin and Josias Pennington,
1894-95. General view.

180. Montreal, Windsor Station.
By Bruce Price, begun 1888. General view.

181, 182, 183. Scranton, Pa. Delaware, Lackawanna, and Western Railroad Station. By Kenneth M. Murchison, 1907.
181. (below left) Competition design.   182. (below right) General view.
183. (bottom left) Competition design. By Price and McLanahan, 1907.

184. (below right) Waterbury, Conn., Union Station. By McKim, Meade, and White, 1909. General view.

COMPETITION OF THE SCRANTON STATION
D·L·&·W·R·R·CO·

185. Paris, Gare de Lyon.
Marius Toudoire, architect,
and M. Denis, engineer,
1897-1900. General view.

186, 187.
Helsinki, Central Station.
By Eliel Saarinen,
1910-14.   186. General view.

187. Concourse.

188, 189.
Karlsruhe, Bahnhof.
By August Stürzenacker,
1908-13.
188. Exterior.

89. Interior of concourse.

190. Stuttgart,
Hauptbahnhof.
By Paul Bonatz
and F. E. Scholer,
1911-28. General view.

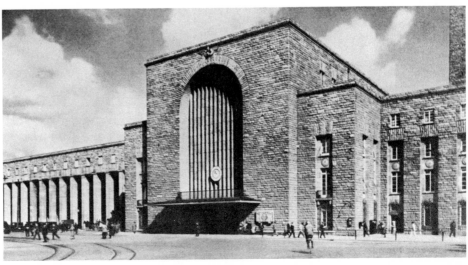

191. Rouen, Gare. By Adolphe Dervaux, 1913-28. General view.

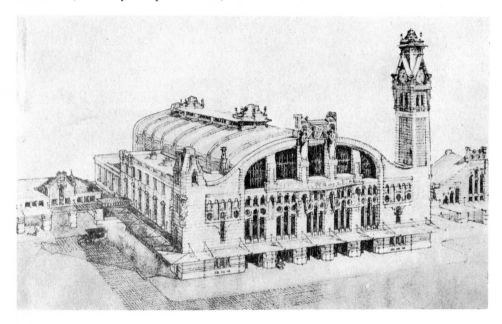

192. Sketch of a station. By Eric Mendelsohn, 1914.

193. Sketch of a station. By Antonio Sant'Elia, 1913.

194, 195, 196.
Milan, Stazione Centrale.
By Ulisse Stacchini, 1913-30.
194. Competition
design of 1913.

195. View of sheds.

196. General view.

197. Butterfly shed.
Designed by the
New Haven Railroad.

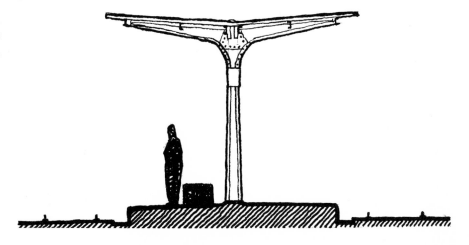

198. Loughton, Essex,
station platform.
General view.

199. London,
Arnos Grove Station.
By Charles Holden, 1932.
General view.

200. Uxbridge, Middlesex,
station. By Charles Holden,
1938. Train-shed
and concourse.

201. Reims, Gare Centrale. By M. LeMarec of MM. Limousin, 1930-34.
View of conoid sheds in reinforced concrete.

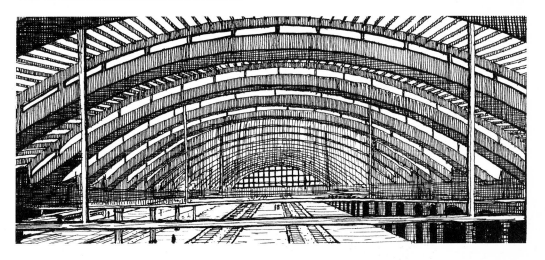

202. Le Havre, Gare Maritime. By Urbain Cassan, 1936. Interior of train-shed.

203. Le Havre, Gare de la Ville.
By Henry Pacon, 1930-33. General view.

204. Versailles, Gare du Chantier.
By André Ventre, 1931-33. Concourse.

205. Design for a station for Amiens. By Auguste Perret, 1944. Elevation.

206. Düsseldorf, Hauptbahnhof. Kruger and Behnes, architects, and L. A. Dormer, engineer, 1931. General view.

7. Verona, station, *ca.* 1950. General view.

8. Spoleto, station, *ca.* 1939. General view.

209, 210. Florence, Stazione Santa Maria Novella.
By G. Michelucci and others, 1934-36.   209. (top) General view.   210. (bottom) Interior.

211. Tampere, Finland,
station. By O. Flodin
and E. Seppälä, 1933-38.
General view.

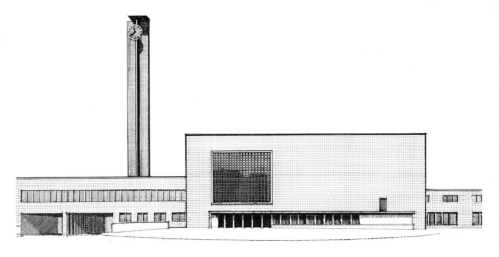

212. Amsterdam,
Amstel Station.
By H. G. J. Schelling, 1939.
General view.

213. Amsterdam,
Muiderpoort Station.
By H. G. J. Schelling, 1939.
General view.

214. Design for a central station for Gothenberg. By Swedish State Railways. Plan, platform level.

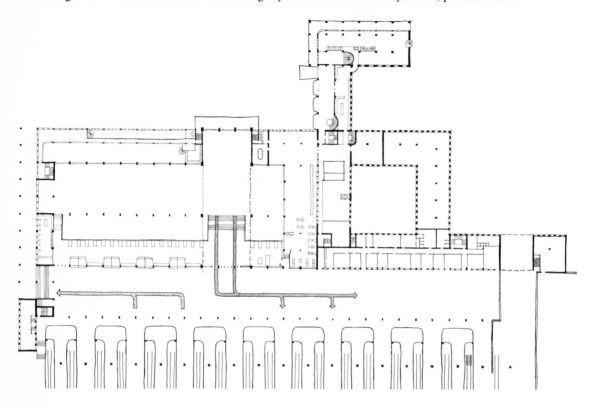

215. Design for a central station for Oslo. By John Engh and Peter Quam, 1946. Perspective.

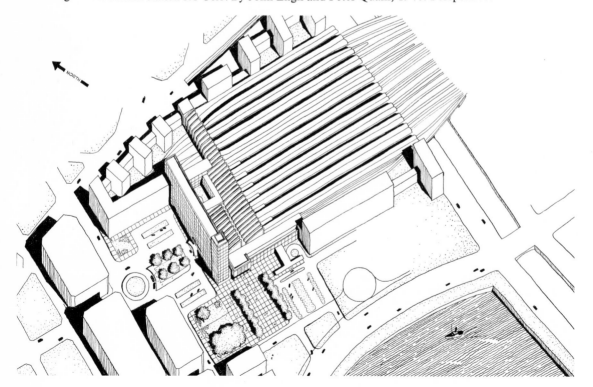

216, 217. Rome, Second Stazione Termini. Angiolo Mazzoni and E. Montuori, architects, and Leo Calini, engineer, 1931-51.　216. (top) General view.　217. (bottom) Concourse.

218. Omaha, Union Station. By Gilbert S. Underwood and Co., 1929-30. General view.

219. Buffalo, Central Station. By Fellheimer and Wagner, 1927-29. General view.

220, 221, 222. Cincinnati, Union Station. By Fellheimer and Wagner, 1929-33.
220. (below left) General view.　221. (below right) Interior of bridge concourse.　222. (bottom) Section.

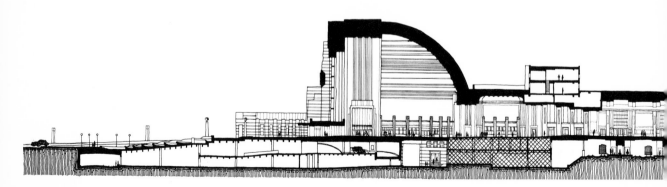

223. Los Angeles, Union Passenger Terminal. By Donald and John Parkinson, 1934-39. General view.

224, 225. Montreal, Canadian National Railways Station. By John Scofield, 1938-43.
224. (below) General view.   225. (bottom) Section.

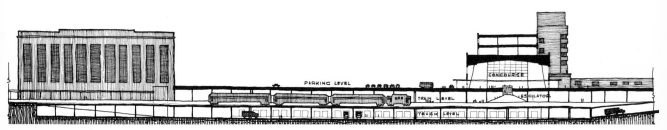

226. Burlington, Iowa, Chicago, Burlington, and Quincy Railroad Station. By Holabird and Root, 1944. General view.

227. Toledo, Union Central Terminal. R. L. Corsbie, architect, and E. A. Dougherty, engineer, 1950. General view.

228. Design for a station for Columbus, Ohio. By Seymour Auerbach, 1951. Perspective.

229, 230. Design for a station for New Haven, Conn. By Duncan W. Buell, 1953.
229. (below) Concourse.   230. (bottom) Diagrammatic sections of roof system.

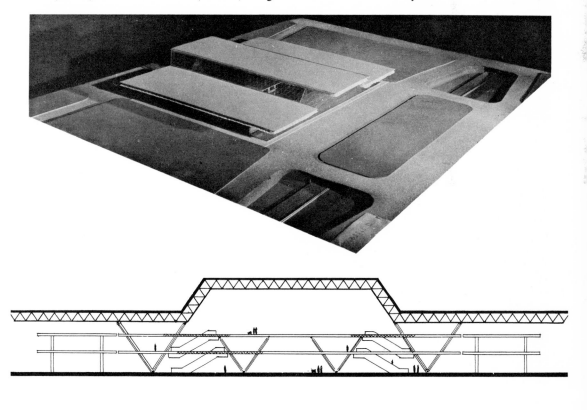

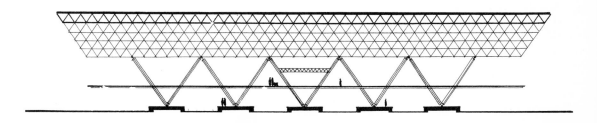

231. Project for a station to be built at Chandigarh, India. By Matthew Nowicki, 1950. General view.

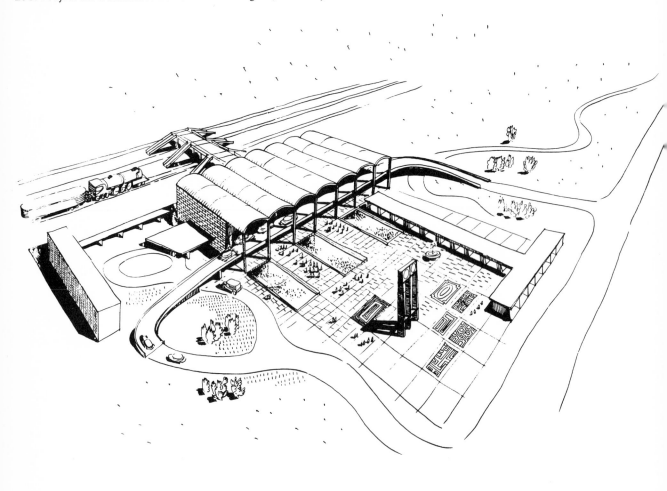

APPENDIX

APPENDIX

Comparative Table of Train-sheds *

Date	Place	Name	Total Span	Separate Spans	Maximum Height	Length	Type	Figure No.
1850's								
1845–47	Paris	Gare du Nord I	176	88, 88	—	345	truss	47
1846–51	Liverpool	Lime St. II	153	—	—	360	crescent truss	51
1847–52	Paris	Gare de l'Est	100	—	75	500	tied arch	54
1850–54	Birmingham	New St.	211	—	80	1100	crescent truss	52
1851–52	London	King's Cross	210	105, 105	72	800	laminated wood arch	—
1851–52	Philadelphia	S & W RR	150	—	—	—	arched Howe truss	—
1852	London	Fenchurch St.	106	—	—	—	crescent truss	56
1852–54	London	Paddington II	238	68, 102, 68	—	700	arched girders	77
1854	Cincinnati	Station	90	—	30	465	bowstring truss	—
1855	Chicago	La Salle St. I	116	—	—	335	Howe truss	75
1855–56	Chicago	Great Central	166	—	42	—	arched Howe truss	59
1850–52	Paris	Gare Montparnasse	118	59, 59	—	—	—	—
ca. 1858	"	" new shed	131	—	57	—	—	91
1859–66	London	Victoria	241	124, 117	63	740	tied lattice arch	55
1860's								
1861–65	Paris	Gare du Nord II	232	58, 116, 58	125	584	Polonceau truss	93
1862–64	London	Charing Cross	164	—	—	—	bowstring truss	—
1863	Amsterdam	Central	120	—	—	300	arched tubular trusses	107
1863–66	London	Cannon St.	190	—	—	680	bowstring truss	

* Unhappily, published dates, dimensions, and descriptions differ. "What is Truth?"

Comparative Table of Train-sheds (continued)

Date	Place	Name	Total Span	Separate Spans	Maximum Height	Length	Type	Figure No.
1863–76	London	St. Pancras	243	—	100	689	pointed arch lattice rib	109, 149, m
1863–68	Stuttgart	Neuer Bahnhof	202	101, 101	72	541	wooden crescent truss	85
1866–68	Turin	Porta Nuova	154	—	98	450	arched	114
1866–72	Berlin	Görlitzer	118	—	—	397	—	—
1867–69	Berlin	Ost	119	—	64	—	segmental arched truss	—
1867–69	Berlin	Schlesischer	120	—	62	600	bowstring truss	87
1868–72	Berlin	Potsdamer	118	—	60	561	bowstring truss	—
1868–72 (rebuilt 1872)	Chicago	La Salle St. II	186	—	—	400	iron and wood trusses	—
1869–71	Berlin	Lehrter	118	—	—	585	—	—
1869–71	New York	Grand Central I	200	—	100	600	arched lattice truss	98
1870's								
1870–72	Vienna	Nord-West	128	—	75	521	pseudo "Warren truss"	88
1871–77	York	Central II	234	81, 55, 55, 43	50	—	arched rib	95
1872–80	Berlin	Anhalter	205	—	92	571	arched lattice truss	113, 149, e
1872–74	Boston	Park Square	128	—	65	600	pointed arch, lattice truss	100
1873–77	Washington	B & P RR	130	—	—	510	arched truss	125
1873–77	Budapest	West	135	—	—	—	Polonceau truss	90

Date	City	Station					Type	Ref
1874	Liverpool	Central	169	—	—	—	bowstring truss	97
1874–75	London	Liverpool St.	278	109, 109, 30, 30	76	—	trusses	89
1875–77	Middlesbrough		133.5	73.5, 60, 43	60	—	arched lattice rib	96
1875	Glasgow	St. Enoch's	198	—	80	518	5-centered arch, lattice rib	—
1875	Glasgow	Queen St.	170	—	—	—	tied, arched lattice rib	94
1875	Glasgow	Central	213	—	—	—	tied, arched lattice rib	—
1875–77	Worcester, Mass.	Union	228	114, 114	67	—	arched, lattice rib	124
1876	Berlin	Stettiner	123	—	82	423	segmental arch	83
1876–80	Manchester	Joint Central	210	—	—	550	bowstring truss	—
1876–79	Hanover	Hauptbahnhof	282	120, 120, 30, 12	—	—	tied, arched lattice rib	84, 149, g
By 1879	Liverpool	Lime St. III	400	200, 200	—	—	segmental arch	—
1879–88	Frankfurt am Main	Hauptbahnhof	549	183, 183, 183	93	610	3 hinge, arched lattice rib	148, 149, j

1880's

Date	City	Station					Type	Ref
1880–85	Berlin	Alexanderplatz (Stadtbahn)	123	—	62	538	3 hinge, arched lattice rib	86, 149, d
1880–85	Berlin	Friedrich Str. (Stadtbahn)	121	—	60	482	ditto	—
1880–85	Berlin	Schlesischer (Stadtbahn)	178	—	62	680	ditto	—
1880's	Chicago	C & NW RR	125	16, 46, 46, 16	—	400	—	132
1881–82	Philadelphia	Broad St. I	160	80, 80	—	450	pointed, arched rib	—
1882–91	Louisville	Union	100	—	50	400	bent trusses	99
1883–85	Chicago	Dearborn	165	—	60	600	truss	129
1884–85	Concord	Union	105	—	—	770	truss	—

171

Comparative Table of Train-sheds (continued)

Date	Place	Name	Total Span	Separate Spans	Maximum Height	Length	Type	Figure No.
1885–89	Bremen	Hauptbahnhof	193	—	92	—	3 hinge arched lattice rib	149, k
1885–86	Milwaukee	C M & St. P.	100	—	—	600	truss	—
1886	Jersey City	Erie	140	37, 66, 37	56	600	truss	—
1887	Jersey City	CRR of N.J.	214	36, 142, 36	70	512	truss	101
1888	Jersey City	Penn. RR	252	—	86	652	3 hinged, arched lattice rib	149, q, 102
1888–90	Chicago	Grand Central	119	—	60	560	arched	130
1889–94	Cologne	Hauptbahnhof	298	44, 210, 44	79	834	3 hinge, arched lattice rib	149, k

1890's

Date	Place	Name	Total Span	Separate Spans	Maximum Height	Length	Type	Figure No.
1890–94	Edinburgh	Prince's St.	183	—	—	—	flat truss	—
1891–94	St. Louis	Union	600	90, 139, 142, 139, 90	74	630	inverted arched Pegram truss	149, p, 158
1891–93	Philadelphia	Reading	256	—	90	559	3 hinge pointed arch	103
1892–98	Dresden	Hauptbahnhof	429	101, 193, 105, 30	100	—	3 hinge pointed arch	149, c; 151
1892	New Orleans	Ill. C. RR	145	17, 35, 41, 35, 17	30	—	arched truss and cantilever	105
1892–93	Chicago	Ill. C. RR	180	36, 108, 36	—	—	3 hinge pointed arch and cantilever	106

Date	City	Station					Type	Ref.
1892–93	Philadelphia	Broad St. II	300	—	108.5	595	3 hinge, 5-centered arch	104, 149, o
1896	Boston	North Station	398	85, 228, 85	—	—	truss	—
1896–99	Boston	South Station	570	171, 228, 171	63	602	curved truss and cantilever	149, n
1897	Dresden	Neustadt	235	59, 117, 59	62	—	arched with lean-to	149, b
1897	Dresden	Wettiner Str.	145	—	92	350	arched	149, a
1897–1900	Paris	Gare de Lyon	386	143, 143, 100	—	—	flat trusses	185
1898–1902	Bordeaux	St-Jean	189	—	84	985	pointed arched truss	—
1898–1901	Pittsburgh	Penn. RR	240	—	110	550	pointed arched	—
1899	Antwerp	Central	212	—	106	574	lattice rib arched	159

1900's

Date	City	Station					Type	Ref.
1901–03	Chicago	La Salle St. III	207	—	60	578	crescent truss	—
1903–06	Hamburg	Hauptbahnhof	369	65, 239, 65	114	610	bents	149, i, 153
1904	St. Louis	Transp. Bldg.	105	—	52	—	flat truss	171
1907–15	Leipzig	Hauptbahnhof	984	6 at *ca.* 147, 2 at 49	69	—	arched truss	149, r, 157

1910's

Date	City	Station					Type	Ref.
1912–24	Cologne-Deutz	Bahnhof	213	62, 89, 62	—	584	arched	—

1920's

Date	City	Station					Type	Ref.
1920–33	Milan	Centrale	612	40, 148, 236, 148, 40	—	—	arched	195

Comparative Table of Train-sheds (continued)

Date	Place	Name	Total Span	Separate Spans	Maximum Height	Length	Type	Figure No.
1926	São Paulo	Station	141	—	65	656	3 hinge arch	—
1929	Königsberg	Hauptbahnhof	384	121, 142, 121	—	—	truss	—
1930's								
1930's	Chemnitz	Hauptbahnhof	482	widest, 158	46	—	bents	149, f
1930–34	Reims	Central	213	115, 98	52	345	conoid arch in reinforced concrete	201

174

Bibliographical Essay

Bibliographical sources for the architectural history of railroad stations embrace a wide variety of material, reflecting the range of influence of the railroad system from primarily pictorial records through articles in popular books and magazines to technical journals. The architectural historian is therefore required to winnow an extensive literature and comes to prize the grains that he eventually accumulates.

In the listing which follows, no attempt at exhaustiveness has been made; a catalogue of important stations with detailed bibliographical references to each would constitute a second volume and would be of value to a limited public.

Many of the general items mentioned will be familiar to the specialist. The comments are intended to assist those less familiar with the period, so that many books are mentioned whose titles promise more than the contents give.

In each section books are listed first, followed by periodicals.

A. *Works on Picturesque Eclecticism*

1. THEORY

The concepts which form the code of picturesque eclecticism were derived from the works of Sir Uvedale Price: *An Essay on the Picturesque,* London, 1794–98; *Essays on the Picturesque,* London, 1810; and *On the Picturesque,* Edinburgh, 1842, edited by Sir Thomas Dick Lauder. The latter was reviewed anonymously in the *Quarterly Review, 98* (1855), 206 ff., under the title "Landscaping Gardening." Edmund Burke's *A Philosophical Inquiry into the Origin of Our Ideas of the Sublime and the Beautiful* (London, 1757) provided a starting point. Related conceptions were expressed by Robert Adam in his *Works, 1,* London, 1773, and Sir Joshua Reynolds in his *Discourses on Art,* London, 1769–91. Richard Payne Knight in his *Analytical Inquiry into the Principles of Taste* (London, 1805) had advocated principles equally alien to academic ones.

The next generation carried these ideas further. It made them both more explicit and more confined by limiting their application to medieval styles. The primary spokesman was Augustus Welby Northmore Pugin in his *The True Principles of Pointed or Christian Architecture,* London, 1841, and *An Apology for the Revival of Christian Architecture in England,* London, 1843. John Ruskin in a far more discursive manner and with somewhat less pertinence reinforced the doctrines in *The Stones of Venice,* London, 1851, and *The Seven Lamps of Architecture,* London, 1849. The influence of both the above writers is reflected in the more prosaic statements of Robert Dale Owen in his *Hints on Public Architecture* (New York, 1849) apropos of the exceedingly picturesque Smithsonian Institution in Washington. The American architect and landscape architect, Andrew Jackson Downing, popularized the principles of the movement, which he knew from personal contacts in England, through his *Landscape Gardening and Rural Architecture,* New York, 1841, and *Rural Essays,* New York, 1853. The movement was further supported by books as well as edifices from the hands of such distinguished architects as Sir George Gilbert Scott and Sir Matthew Digby Wyatt. Scott's *Remarks on Secular and Domestic Architecture* (London, 1857) is both eloquent and specific in its support, though his *Personal and Professional Recollections* (London, 1879), while full of historical interest, is less cogent. Wyatt's *Fine Art* (London, 1870), the text of lectures given as Slade Professor at Oxford, is particularly illuminating on the eclectic point of view.

2. PATTERN BOOKS

The theoretical treatises listed above were followed by a series of pattern books giving examples of the application of picturesque principles to the design of specific buildings for a variety of purposes. Many of them are mentioned in my "Henry Austin and the Italian Villa" in the *Art Bulletin, 30* (1948), 145 ff. Sometimes the text is explicit on the fundamental principles invoked; sometimes the message is implicit in the illustrations. A few important ones spanning the century are listed here. Pierre Clochar published sketches made in Italy as a repertory of picturesque architectural compositions under the title *Palais, maisons et vues d'Italie,* Paris, 1809. An Englishman, G. L. Meason, fulfilled a similar objective in his *On the Landscape Architecture of the Great Painters of Italy,* London, 1828. Meason made a series of lithographs of architectural groups found as incidents in Italian paintings. John Claudius Loudon, one of the most active and practical cultural missionaries of his day, included considerable picturesque propaganda in his *Encyclopedia of Cottage, Farm and Villa Architecture,* London, 1833, and *Supplement,* London, 1842. Charles Parker, in a series of titles called collectively *Villa Rustica* and issued in London from 1832 on, combined Meason's and Loudon's approaches, showing how specific compositions could be adapted for specific purposes. In 1870 in London, C. J. Richardson published his *Picturesque Designs in Architecture.* His explicitly picturesque text is more significant than the accompanying designs, which are of mediocre merit. Toward the end of the century Henry Heathcote Statham, editor of the *Builder,* in *Modern Architecture* (London, 1897; New York, 1898), while discussing the various eclecticisms of his day, was employing picturesque values in his criticisms.

3. CRITICISM

Since the end of the 19th century a number of evaluations and interpretations of the architecture of that century have appeared. Geoffrey Scott's *The Architecture of Humanism* (London, 1914; later editions 1928, 1954), while primarily concerned with the architecture of the Renaissance, offers many penetrating comments on the architecture of the 19th century and its theorists in a language as remarkable for its beauty as for its conciseness. Christopher Hussey's *The Picturesque* (London, 1927) is the pioneer historical treatment of the subject; in spite of the reservations made above, Chap. 1, it is still the basic work. Sir Kenneth Clark's *The Gothic Revival* (London and New York, 1929; new edition 1950) is an indispensable supplement to Hussey, since it carries the story further through the century; and it does so with wit as well as wisdom. The most recent entry in this field is the urbane *English Architecture since the Regency* (London, 1953) by H. S. Goodhart-Rendel, the dedicated but not partial authority on 19th-century British architecture.

Each of the following books makes a contribution to the study of 19th-century theory. F. L. Chambers, *The History of Taste* (New York, 1932) organizes the characteristic qualities of the period effectively. Agnes Gilchrist's *Romanticism and the Gothic Revival* (New York, 1938) is a short and thoughtful study of the meaning of the early stages of eclecticism. Jacques Barzun's *Romanticism and the Modern Ego* (Boston, 1943), though not primarily concerned with architecture, is indispensable to an understanding of the romantic point of view. John P. Coolidge's *Mill and Mansion* (New York, 1942), which studies in detail the early development of Lowell, Massachusetts, contributes many acute observations applicable to the architecture of the period in its wider aspects. The most comprehensive treatment of 19th-century architecture in Europe and America is the work of the Swiss historian Sigfried Giedion in *Space, Time and Architecture,* Cambridge, Mass., 1941 (3d edition, revised and enlarged, 1954). His other important book in this area, *Mechanization Takes Command* (New York, 1948)—a pioneering work about some of the anonymous consequences of the Industrial Revolution—has a chapter on the railroad car.

B. *Miscellaneous Source Material for Stations*

Primary source material for the history of the railroad station is found in collections and in contemporary treatises and journals. The principal collections of railroadiana in the public domain are in the Railway Museum in York, England, and the Transport Museum in London. Primary in the United States are the J. P. Morgan scrapbooks and the collections of the Railway and Locomotive Historical Society, both at the Baker Library at Harvard University, Cambridge, Mass. The Boston Atheneum contains a series of folio records of the work of several railroad architects: Gridley J. F. Bryant, George Minot Dexter, and Nathaniel J. Bradlee. In New York the William Barclay Parsons Collection, belonging to Columbia University, includes many prints of stations and engines, both European and American. The Avery Library at Columbia owns the original designs for the Norton, Mass., station by Richard Upjohn.

The engineers' offices of railroads everywhere have working drawings of many of their stations and are generous in making them available. The public relations offices of these railroads are equally generous with their collections of photographs.

Printed source materials are included in the bibliographies by regions given below.

Picture postcards can be very helpful. Rare indeed is the depot—large or small, here or abroad—which did not find immortality in a plain or colored postcard with or without sparklettes.

C. *Bibliographies*

There is as yet no bibliography dealing with the architecture of the railroad station. Numerous bibliographies, however, exist on other aspects of railroading which can be of service to the architectural historian by bringing him in contact with material in which the station appears even though only incidentally. The Bureau of Railway Economics in Washington, D.C., has published the following: *Railway Economics, a Collective Catalogue of Books in Fourteen American Libraries,* 1912; *List of References on Railroad Terminals,* 1916; and *Railroad Bibliographies,* 1938.

The very early stages of railroad development can be traced with the aid of the following: Thomas Richard Thompson, "Check List of Publications on American Railroads before 1841," *Bulletin of the New York Public Library,* Pt. I, January 1941, pp. 3–68, 175–247, Pt. II, July 1941, pp. 533–84, Pt. III, October 1941, pp. 859–940; P. A. Peddie, *Railway Literature 1556–1830,* London, 1930; and the Baker Library, Harvard University, *The Pioneer Period of European Railroads,* a bibliography, 1946. A second and more extensive bibliography for this period is Max Möltzel, *Aus der Frühzeit der Eisenbahnen mit einer Bibliographie* (Berlin, 1935), which contains lists of early railroad periodicals in all languages.

Katherine McNamara's *Railroads in the City Plan, a Bibliography* (Cambridge, Mass., 1946) is the best guide to this aspect of the railroad.

Frank Pierce Donovan's *The Railroad in Literature* (Boston, n.d.) does not include architectural references.

The Engineering Index has often proved to be more helpful than any other series of this type in supplying references to descriptions of specific stations. It began publication in New York in 1891 with a volume covering the period 1884–91. The later volumes increase in thoroughness of coverage.

D. *Books Dealing with Railroad Stations in General*

Specialized books on railroad stations have not been numerous. J. A. Droege's *Passenger Terminals and Trains* (New York, 1916) is an engineer's account and analysis of station practice of the World War I period. Verner Owen Rees' *Plan Requirements of Modern Buildings* (London, 1931) has a chapter on the planning of the railway station. The most recent long discussion of the planning and practice of stations is a chapter called "Railroad Stations" by Alfred Fellheimer, himself a distinguished station architect, in Talbot Hamlin's *Forms and Functions of Twentieth Century Architecture, 4* (New York, 1952), with illustrations and brief bibliography. A monograph by R. Campanini, "Edifici dei Trasporti," *Documenti,* Series E, Fascicle 1, Number 3 (Milan, 1947), contains plans and photographs of modern stations, chiefly European, with brief notes. Three useful German compendia of station architecture containing plans, sections, and data include material for other countries as well as Germany. The most complete is Eduard Schmitt, *Empfangsgebäude der Bahnhöfe,* Handbuch der Architektur, Part IV, *2,* Number 4, Leipzig, 1911. The other two are Victor von Röll, "Empfangsgebäude," in *Encyklopädie des Gesamten Eisenbahnwesens, 3* (Vienna, 1890–95), 1419 ff.; and Paul von Röll, "Empfangsgebäude," in *Encyklopädie des Eisenbahnwesens, 4* (Berlin, 1912–23), 301 ff.

There is some material of a more general character in D. Joseph, *Geschichte der Baukunst des XIX Jahrhunderts,* Leipzig, 1902–09.

E. *Publications by Country*

1. BELGIUM

The development of the railway station in Beigium in its early stages is picturesquely treated in two books. J. P. Cluysenaar, an architect, describes his own station designs and illustrates them in colorful plates in his *Bâtiments des stations et maisons de garde du chemin de fer de Dendre et Waes, et de Bruxelles vers Gand par Alost,* Paris, 1862. A second book, in which the illustrations are tiny cuts, is Alphonse Wauters, *Atlas pittoresque des chemins de fer de la Belgique* (the third edition was published in Brussels in 1844).

2. FRANCE

French railways have received more extensive treatment, and French writers have contributed several books of comprehensive range. Pierre Chabat's *Bâtiments de chemins de fer* (2 vols. Paris, 1862–66), now rare, is a singularly valuable source of station plans of the time. The plates are large, clear, and beautifully engraved. The contents include British and German as well as French examples. Auguste Perdonnet's *Traité élémentaire des chemin de fer* (generally known only in the 3d edition, Paris, 1865), quoted extensively in this book, describes and criticizes the railway stations of France, Britain, and America. Léon Benouville wrote the article "Gare" in Planat's *Encyclopédie de l'architecture et de la construction, 4,* Part II (Paris, 1889–92), 785 ff. This was published in translation in the *American Architect and Building News, 40* (1893), 79 ff., 95 ff. This illustrated article is a sound summary of later 19th-century station theory in Europe.

Léonce Reynaud's *Traité d'architecture, contenant des notions générales sur les principes de la construction et sur l'histoire de l'art,* in two volumes with atlas (Paris, 1850 *et seq.*), from which I have quoted in Chapter 3, is the work of the distinguished engineer. Railway architecture occupies only a small part of his attention, but he does supply material on iron train-shed roofs. The once influential Julien Guadet provided a chapter on the design of railway stations, written from a theoretical and chauvinist point of view, in his *Éléments et théorie de l'architecture,* 4 vols. Paris, 1903–05. The best illustrated single volume on the railroad station, past and present, was the joint product of Charles Dollfus, Edgar de Geoffroy, and Louis Baudry de Saunier, *Histoire de la locomotion terrestre, les chemins de fer,* Paris, 1935. This reproduces rare prints and photographs of stations for the whole period in all Europe.

French periodicals dealing with the subject begin with *Revue Générale de l'Architecture et des Travaux Publiques,* Paris, 1840–90. This was edited by César Daly, who was deeply interested in everything connected with the railway and consequently published both critical and descriptive articles with engraved plates. *Génie Civil* (Paris, 1880 *et seq.*) gives to selected stations extremely detailed coverage including plans and photographs. The *Revue Générale des Chemins de Fer* (Paris, 1878–) does not emphasize station architecture. *Architecture d'Aujourd'hui* (Boulogne, 1930–) contains the most abundant material on more recent stations.

3. GERMANY AND AUSTRIA

The following list of histories and manuals, though far from complete, includes titles I have seen and found useful; there are others, less accessible in this country. Theodor Stein, *Erweiterungsbauten der Berlin-Stettiner Eisenbahn* (Berlin, 1864–69) is an example of these histories. G. Stürmer, *Geschichte der Eisenbahnen* (2 vols. Bromberg, 1872–76), contains lists of railroad lines and the dates of their openings. W. Flattich and F. Wilhelm Flattich, *Der Eisenbahn-Hochbau der Königlische privaten Südbahn-Gesellschaft* (Vienna, 1873–77) 1st and 2d series and atlas, is carefully illustrated and includes both important and rural stations. The first volume of Königlisch Preussischen Ministers der Öffentlich Arbeiten, *Berlin und Seine Eisenbahnen* (2 vols. Berlin, 1896) deals with the history of stations from the earliest to the current ones and is adequately illustrated. The principal source for Austrian railroad history is Königlisch Ministerium der Eisenbahnen der Österreichisch-Ungarischen Monarchie, *Geschichte der Eisenbahnen der Österreichisch-Ungarischen Monarchie,* in five parts, Vienna, 1898. This illustrates the whole sequence of station building during the 19th century. Alfred Gotthold Meyer, *Eisenbauten, ihre Geschichte und Aesthetik* (Esslingen, 1907) is helpful for a few spectacular train-sheds. Wilhelm Cauer, *Personen Bahnhöfe* (Berlin, 1913) is concerned with station planning and analyzes the plans of numerous stations, principally German; the second edition (1926) is enlarged. The 1914 volume of the *Jahrbuch des Deutschen Werkbundes, Der Verkehr* (Jena, 1914) is a well illustrated survey of the most advanced German stations of the day. Otto Blum, *Personen und Güterbahnhof* (Berlin, 1930) is an engineering manual in which station plans are incidental to track plans. H. Gescheit and K. Wittman, *Neuzeitlicher Verkehrsbau* (Potsdam, 1931) illustrates a few German and Belgian stations and projects. The Reichsverkehrsministerium für Eisenbahnwesen published a short but comprehensive history of the railways of Germany entitled *Hundert*

Jahre Deutsche Eisenbahnen (Berlin, 1938), with a chapter on stations. This is particularly valuable for old views of German stations and is a succinct history of German station design.

German periodicals during this period (not all of them accessible in complete runs to the American student) were often of high quality with respect to their coverage as well as the excellence of their meticulously detailed plates. Those which proved useful to me include the following: *Allgemeinen Bauzeitung,* Vienna, 1836–1918 (the atlases of this journal, which begin in the 1860's, are particularly good); *Organ für die fortschritte des Eisenbahnwesens,* Wiesbaden, 1845–63, and new series, 1864–1906 (more occupied with engineering than architecture); *Der Civilingenieur,* Freiberg and Leipzig, 1848–50, 1854–96 (which occasionally gives station data but rarely with architectural emphasis); *Zeitschrift des Architekten-und Ingenieur-Verein,* Hanover, 1851–95 (which includes well documented station material with plates in its earlier years, as does the *Zeitschrift für Bauwesen,* Berlin, 1851–1921, with atlas of large folding plates).

4. GREAT BRITAIN

The most complete single source for the plans and structure of early railway stations in all Europe is Samuel Charles Brees, *Railway Practice, a Collection of Working Plans and Practical Details of Construction in the Public Works of the Most Celebrated Engineers,* London, 1837, 2d edition 1838, second series 1840, third and fourth series 1847. The format is small and the text minor, but the completeness of the drawings is exemplary. Larger in format although concerned not with stations but with engineering is F. W. Simms, editor, *Public Works of Great Britain,* London, 1838, 2d edition 1846.

Francis Whishaw, *Analysis of Railways* (London, 1837, and 2d edition, 1838) compiled reports on railway lines under construction and projected without architectural material. His *The Railways of Great Britain and Ireland Practically Described and Illustrated* (London, 1840, and 2d edition 1842) includes only one station plan, but the lists of stations included in the description of each line are useful for dating.

G. Drysdale Dempsey, a civil engineer, wrote many books on railroads, including *The Practical Railway Engineer,* London, 1847 and 1855; *Working Drawings of Railway Stations,* London, 1856; *Iron Applied to Railway Structures,* London, 1850; and *Iron Roofs,* London, 1850. Unfortunately none of these emphasizes the architectural aspects. John Weale published two works: *Ensamples of Railway Making* (London, 1843) is a work on civil engineering, and *Iron Roofs of Recent Construction* (London, 1859) contains brief descriptive notes and plates illustrating significant train-shed roof construction, both French and English examples. William Humber's *Record of the Progress of Modern Engineering* (2 vols. London, 1863–65, 2d edition 1864) includes among engineering works in general the structural design of the stations at Victoria and Cannon Street, London, and at Amsterdam by the English engineer Ordish; these are thoroughly illustrated. J. W. Grover, a civil engineer, published, without text, *Estimates and Diagrams of Railway Bridges . . . and Station Buildings* (London, 1866, 2d edition 1870); the stations included are rather small, ranging in cost from £400 to £4000. Ewing Matheson's *Works in Iron (Bridge and Roof Structures)* (London, 1873, and 2d edition 1877) illustrates and describes the roofs of several British stations and public buildings. William H. Mills, *Railway Construction,* is one of Longman's Civil Engineering Series, London, 1898. Chapter LV is concerned with examples of station roofs—including English and other European examples, briefly described and illustrated in section—and station planning, with a discussion of the advantages and appropriate use of the various types of station.

There are three pre-eminent English authorities on the history of British railways. Their works are only incidentally concerned with station architecture but are primarily valuable for their interpretation of the early history of railroading in England, its trials and accomplishments, the personalities, the legal and financial experiments. H. G. Lewin is the most concise and authoritative: *The British Railway System . . . to 1844,* London, 1914, *Early British Railways . . . 1801–1844,* London, 1925, and *The Railway Mania and Its Aftermath, 1845–1852,* London, 1936. Charles E. Lee deals with more specialized aspects of the story in *The Centenary of Bradshaw,* London, 1940, *Early Railroads in Surrey,* London, 1944, and *The First Passenger Railway,* London, 1942. His *The Evolution of Railways* (London, 1937, and 2d edition 1943) is a short, well written historical account. C. F. Dendy Marshall has written both generally and specifically. His *Centenary History of the Liverpool and Manchester Railway* (London, 1930) is illustrated with color reproductions of the Ackermann prints of that line and of many items of railroad memorabilia. His *A History of the British Railways down to the Year 1830* (London, 1938) summarizes material otherwise scattered in the histories of individual railways. Marshall has also written a general history called *A Hundred Years of Railways,* London, 1930, and *A History of the Southern Railway,* London, 1936.

There are several books of a semipopular character which trace the highlights of railway history, with the author's attention divided about evenly among anecdote, engines and rolling stock, and stations. The best of these are J. Pendleton, *Our Railways,* London, 1894, and 2d edition 1896; Vernon Sommerfield, *English Railways,* London, 1937; Cyril B. Andrews, *The Railway Age,* London, 1937 (very well illustrated); and of the same order but more particularized are George A. Nokes, *Locomotion in Victorian London,* London, 1938, and Graham Royde Smith, *Old Euston, an Account of the Beginning of the London and Birmingham Railway and the Building of Euston Station,* London, 1938.

The histories of individual railroads are naturally of much more value since they are more detailed and better documented. Among these the following are particularly good: E. T. MacDermot, *History of the Great Western Railway* (2 vols. London, 1927–31), which describes Brunel's originality and achievement in detail; Wilfred L. Steel, *The History of the London and North Western Railway* (London, 1914), in which architecture and engineering play a small role; and William W. Tomlinson, *The North Eastern Railway, Its Rise and Development* (Newcastle-upon-Tyne, 1914), an exceptionally complete and well illustrated monograph.

Books of the sort mentioned above draw upon a number of earlier guides, as well as upon such pictorial accounts as the following, which amply testify to the enthusiasm engendered by the new mode of transportation at its inception: Henry Booth, *An Account of the Liverpool and Manchester Railway,* Liverpool, 1831; Thomas T. Bury, *Colored Views on the Liverpool and Manchester Railway,* London, 1832, and also his *Six Colored Views on the London and Birmingham Railway,* London, 1837 (these views include stations and are frequently to be found in reproduction); John Blackmore and J. W. Carmichael, *Views on the Newcastle and Carlisle Railway,* Newcastle, 1836; and Thomas Roscoe, *The Book of the Grand Junction Railway,* London, 1839. The most lavish volumes of this type are John C. Bourne, *Drawings of the London and Birmingham Railway* (London, 1839) and his *History and Description of the Great Western Railway* (London, 1846), both folios, with impressive lithographic plates.

Coming somewhere between these categories are early histories: for example, Robert Ritchie, *Railways, Their Rise, Progress and Construction* (2 vols. London, 1846), without architectural emphasis; and Frederick S. Williams, *Our Iron Roads, Their History, Construction and Social Influence* (London, 1852, and 2d edition, much enlarged, 1883), popular but usefully detailed. Williams' *The Midland Railway: Its Rise and Progress* (3d ed. London, 1877) is in the same vein, primarily useful for recording contemporary attitudes.

There are only two recent books on the architecture of British railway stations: Christian Barman, *Railway Architecture* (London, 1950), a short and thoughtful book with numerous illustrations; and Henry-Russell Hitchcock, *Early Victorian Architecture in Britain* (2 vols. New Haven, 1954), which covers far more thoroughly the architecture and engineering of early British stations down to the 1850's.

The most fruitful source of material on British stations is periodicals. The *Builder* (London, 1842–) is the primary source; its pages abound in both descriptive and critical articles. The *Illustrated London News* (London, 1842–) shows a comprehensive interest in the subject and its pages frequently contain illustrations to be found nowhere else, even though the stations are introduced only incidentally as the setting for royal receptions. The third British magazine—hardly inferior to the *Builder*—was the *Building News and Engineering Journal* (London, 1854–1926), in which a vigorous interest in railway architecture was reflected in lively editorials and illustration. The *Engineer,* which began publication in London in 1856, and *Engineering* (1866 *et seq.*) complemented the more specialized architectural magazines with occasional lengthy technical articles thoroughly illustrated. More recently *Modern Transport* (London, 1919–), the *Architects' Journal,* and the *Architectural Review* have from time to time included stories on recent continental as well as English stations. The *Journal of the Royal Institute of British Architects,* London (3d series beginning in 1893) published lengthy discussions of the problems and reviewed the accomplishments of railway architecture.

5. ITALY

The architecture of 19th-century Italy has been treated as a whole only once, by Nello Tarchiani, *L'Architettura Italiana dell'Ottocento,* Florence, 1937. Although this book deals only incidentally with railway stations, it is the handiest available source of names and dates. A similar purpose is served by Angelo de Gubernatis, *Dizionario degli Italiani viventi, pittori, scultori e architetti,* Florence, 1889 (a later edition was edited by Ugo Matini, 1906; both editions are rare). On the whole the most readily available and best detailed source for Italian stations is the superlative series of guide books, *Guida d'Italia,* in 22 volumes, published in Italy by Touring Club Italiano. The most comprehensive bibliography of Italian architecture during the 19th and 20th centuries is provided in Bruno Zevi, *Storia dell'architettura moderna,* Turin, 1950.

The period since 1900 is covered for one region in a recent volume: Francesco Sapori, *Architettura in Roma, 1901–1950,* Rome, 1953.

The determined historian will find the Italian periodicals his most helpful assistants; unfortunately he will also find that full runs are exceedingly rare in the United States. Some of the more likely ones are the following: *Il Politecnico,* Milan, 1839–1905; *Annuario Scientifico ed Industriale,* Milan, 1863–1927; and *Illustrazione Populare Italiano* (Milan, 1873 *et seq.*), which showed some interest in railroad affairs, as did the corresponding publications in other countries. The first Italian magazine to have large plates and wide coverage was the *Ricordi di Architettura,* published by the Società di Architetti Fiorentini, 1878–1900. Unfortunately, few examples are included, since railway architecture did not play an important role in Florentine practice. In 1889 *Architettura Pratica* was founded in Turin, approaching modern standards in format and coverage; *Edilizia Moderna,* initiated in Milan in 1892, comes even closer. Its finely printed plates set a very high standard. Two other magazines which are of great value even though architecture was not their primary concern are *Emporium,* founded in Bergamo in 1895, and *Rassegna d'Arte Antica e Moderna,* which began publication in 1914. Currently the well known magazines *Casabella, Domus, Spazio,* and *Metron* cover the Italian field brilliantly.

6. MEXICO

There are two items of particular interest dealing with the railways of Mexico: Gustavo A. Baz and E. L. Gallo, *Historia del ferrocarril mexicano,* Mexico, 1874, English translation by George F. Henderson, *History of the Mexican Railway,* Mexico, 1876; and Casimiro Castro, *Album of the Mexican Railway* (with texts in English, Spanish, and French), Mexico, 1877.

7. THE UNITED STATES

The need for manuals for early railroad construction in the United States, beyond what was included in civil engineering handbooks, was apparently met by the importation of European ones. As periodicals became more common, several appeared dealing exclusively with railroading, and these further reduced the need for local manuals.

The first books dealing with American railroads were discursive and include the following: William Prescott Smith, *The Book of the Great Railway Celebrations of 1857,* New York, 1858; H. Bartels, *Amerikanischen Eisenbahnen,* Berlin, 1879; and John Luther Ringwalt, *Development of Transportation Systems in the United States,* Philadelphia, 1888 (this is concerned only incidentally with stations). In the same decade a much more comprehensive treatise appeared in Paris: E. Lavoinne and E. Pontzen, *Les Chemins de fer en Amérique, 1,* 1880, and *2,* 1882. A few books contain valuable detailed information on station design; one of these is Walter Gilman Berg, *Buildings and Structures of American Railroads,* New York, 1904 (preface dated 1892), and another is Bradford L. Gilbert, *Sketch Portfolio of Railroad Stations* (New York, 1895), a compendium of his own designs. Of still more restricted scope were two publications by Clarke Dillenbeck, both published in Philadelphia in 1896: *Specifications for Stone and Brick Passenger Stations, Form A,* and *Specifications for Frame Passenger Stations, Form B.* Some material on American stations was included in Röll and Schmitt and in other German publications listed above.

A number of railroad guides appeared during the century which are remarkably evocative of bygone attitudes and enthusiasms but which offer little to the architectural historian other than occasional woodcuts, some of which show depots. Representative of this class of material are John B. Bachelder, *Bachelder's Popular Resorts and How to Reach Them,* Boston, 2d ed., 1874; D. W. Beslisle, *Hazard's Railroad Guides—Trenton Line to New York,* Philadelphia, 1853; and C. P. Dare, *Philadelphia, Wilmington and Baltimore Railroad Guide,* Philadelphia, 1856.

Detailed information concerning the date of erection and identity of architect, as well as other pertinent facts, can sometimes be found in one of the innumerable histories of railroad companies, mixed with other types of lore, statistics, anecdotes, and lurid accounts of competitive skullduggery.

The Pennsylvania Railroad has inspired more of these histories than any other line. They begin with William B. Sipes, *The Pennsylvania Railroad* (Philadelphia, 1875) and continue with James Dredge, *The Pennsylvania Railroad,* London, 1879; W. B. Wilson, *History of the Pennsylvania Railroad,* Philadelphia, 1899; and William Couper, *History of the Engineering, Construction, and Equipment of the Pennsylvania Railroad New York Terminal and Approaches,* New York, 1912. The most recent is Edwin P. Alexander, *The Pennsylvania Railroad: A Pictorial History,* New York, 1947.

Other railroads have been treated in recent histories, and several authors have made a specialty of the field. One of the best is Edward Hungerford, among whose works are *The Story of the Rome, Watertown and Ogdensburg Railroad,* New York, 1922, and *The Story of the Baltimore and Ohio Railroad, 1827–1927* (2 vols. New York, 1928), one of the best of all company histories; in 1938 he published *Men and Iron, the Story of the New York Central* (New York), followed by his *Men of Erie, a Story of Human Effort,* New York, 1946. A second specialist is Alvin F. Harlow: his *Steelways of New England* (New York, 1946) is stuffed with anecdotes as well as facts, and he also wrote of the New York Central in *The Road of the Century,* New York, 1947. One or two other histories particularly

185

worthy of mention are Kincaid A. Herr, *The Louisville and Nashville Railroad, 1850–1942,* Louisville, 1943; Walter A. Lucas, *From the Hills to the Hudson,* New York, 1944; and Sidney Withington, *The First Twenty Years of Railroads in Connecticut,* New Haven, 1935.

Considerable material of more localized character is to be found in the publications of historical societies. Notable among these are the contributions of Francis B. C. Bradlee to the *Historical Collections of the Essex Institute* from 1918 to 1922, some of them reprinted in separate covers. Thomas Hill published a long paper, "The Beginnings of the Boston and Worcester Railroad," in the *Proceedings of the Worcester Society of Antiquity, 17* (1900), 527–76. Others include Herbert C. Taft, "Early Days of Railroading," in *Contributions to the Lowell Historical Society, 1* (Pt. III, 1913), and Warren Jacobs' numerous papers in the *Railway and Locomotive Historical Society Bulletin* (Nos. 55, May 1941, and 65, Oct. 1944), dealing with old stations in New York City. This bulletin's occasional papers on railroad stations are helpful.

The oldest of the magazines devoted to railroading was the *Railway Review,* Chicago, 1868–1926. This and the *Railroad Gazette* (Chicago, 1881–1908) included station data in nearly every issue, as did the *Engineering News-Record* (Chicago and New York), which began publication in 1874. Good illustrations of stations appeared from time to time in *Ballou's Pictorial Drawing Room Companion,* Boston, 1851–59, the *New York Illustrated News,* New York, 1859–64, *Harper's Weekly,* New York, 1857–1916, and *Leslie's Illustrated Weekly Newspaper,* New York, 1855–1922. However, the more strictly architectural magazines which appeared in the 1870's and 1880's with greatly improved illustrative material proved more valuable for the later part of the century. One of the first of these was James Osgood and Company's *Architectural Sketch Book* (New York and Boston), which was published for a few years beginning in 1873, and the invaluable *American Architect and Building News,* which began publication in Boston in 1876. Other magazines of considerable usefulness followed: the *Brickbuilder* in 1892, the *Inland Architect and News Record,* Chicago, 1883, and the *Architectural Review,* Boston, 1891. The files of such current magazines as the *Architectural Forum* and the *Architectural Record* have been very helpful for the period they cover.

INDEX

Individual stations will be found under "Railroad stations," listed alphabetically according to locality.

Index

Index

Index

Index

Index

Index

Index

Index